Karen Brown's
NEW ENGL

Alyce's Dunscroft-By-The-Sea
Harwich Port, Massachusetts

Quebec

4

Greenville

Maine

Waterville

Sunset

Burlington

Lancaster

3

Vermont

Portland

ATLANTIC
OCEAN

Plymouth

New
Hampshire

Rochester

New
York

Manchester

Manchester

Newfane

2

Massachusetts

Massachusetts
Bay

Sturbridge

Boston

Provincetown

Cape Cod
Bay

Rhode
Island

Connecticut

Nantucket

Rhode Island
Sound

1

Greenwich

New England Overview Map

	New Hampshire Beckons
	Sturbridge & The Connecticut Shore
	Route 7 & Much More
	Byways of Coastal Maine
	Cape Cod, Nantucket, Newport & Martha's Vineyard

0   100 Miles

0   100 KM

Contents

Dedicated to our dear friend, Roland,

who shares with us his passion for

New England— its people, its places, his home.

Cover Painting: Alyce's Dunscroft-By-The-Sea, Harwich Port, MA

Authors: Karen Brown and Jack Bullard.

Editors: Clare Brown, Karen Brown, June Eveleigh Brown, Debbie Tokumoto.

Illustrations: Vanessa Kale.

Cover painting: Jann Pollard.

Maps: Rachael Kircher-Randolph.

Technical support: Andrew Harris.

Copyright © 2010 by Karen Brown's Guides, Inc.

Distributed by National Book Network, 15200 NBN Way, Blue Ridge Summit, PA 17214, USA. Tel: 717-794-3800 or 1-800-462-6420, Fax: 1-800-338-4500, Email: custserv@nbnbooks.com

A catalog record for this book is available from the British Library.

ISSN 1535-4059

Introduction

Because of its history, its special relationship with the sea, its back roads and scenic beauty, its changing seasons, and the great diversity between traveling the coast and the valleys and mountains, New England is a wonderful travel destination at all times of the year—though many consider that it is most glorious in the fall. New England is comprised of the six states in the northeast corner of the United States. The upper portion of New England encompasses Maine, New Hampshire, and Vermont; while Connecticut, Massachusetts, and Rhode Island make up the lower portion. The traveler to New England, more often than not, visits either the northern three states or the lower three, since touring the entire region, with all its many and diverse attractions, requires a considerable investment of time.

About Inn Travel

We use the term "inn" to cover everything from a simple bed and breakfast to a sophisticated resort. A wide range of inns is included in this guide: some are great bargains, others very costly; some are in cities, others in remote locations; some are quite sophisticated, others extremely simple; some are decorated with opulent antiques, others with furniture from grandma's attic; some are large hotels, others have only a few rooms. The common denominator is that each place has some special quality that makes it appealing. The descriptions are intended to give you an honest appraisal of each property so that you can select accommodation based on personal preferences. The following pointers will help you appreciate and understand what to expect when traveling the "inn way."

BATHROOMS

While the majority of guestrooms have connecting or *ensuite* bathrooms, you will want to make certain when you make your reservation. Some inns offer guestrooms that share a bath with other rooms, or rooms that have a private bath but locate it down the hall. We usually do not specify whether the bath is equipped with stall-shower, tub-shower, tub only, or Jacuzzi; so you will need to ask about that, too.

BREAKFAST

A welcome feature and trademark of many inns is their morning repast—many cookbooks have been authored and inspired by innkeepers. Breakfast is almost always included in the room rate, and the "coffee cup" icon on the hotel's page will confirm this. Although innkeepers take great pride in their delectable morning offerings, know that breakfast can range from a gourmet "waddle-away" feast (as proudly described by one innkeeper-chef) to muffins and coffee. Sometimes breakfast is limited to a Continental in your room or a hot breakfast with others in the dining room, and sometimes both. Breakfast times vary as well—some innkeepers serve a hot breakfast at a specified time, while others replenish a buffet on a more leisurely schedule. Breakfasts are as individual as the inns themselves and are something to look forward to each morning.

If you have any special dietary requirements, most innkeepers will gladly try to accommodate your needs. Not having a fully stocked refrigerator as a restaurant would have, innkeepers usually plan a breakfast menu that features one entree and have those ingredients on hand. Therefore, it is best to mention any special requests at the time of making your reservation, both as a courtesy and from a practical point of view, so that the innkeeper can have on hand items such as special, low-fat dairy products, egg substitutes, sugar-free syrups, etc.

CANCELLATION POLICIES

Although policies vary, inns have only a few rooms and when a reservation is made, the owner/innkeeper counts on receiving that revenue. Most inns usually require you to cancel at least a week in advance of the arrival date, and some inns charge a small fee if the reservation is cancelled in order to cover their administrative costs. If you cancel within a specified number of days prior to your planned arrival, you may be required to pay the first night if the room cannot be re-rented. Some inns have even more stringent policies, so be sure to inquire at the time you make your reservation.

CHECK-IN

Inns are usually very specific about check-in time—generally between 3 and 6 pm. Let the innkeeper know if you are going to arrive late and he will make special arrangements for you, such as leaving you a door key under a potted plant along with a note on how to find your room. Also, for those who might arrive early, note that some inns close their doors between check-out and check-in times. Inns are frequently staffed only by the owners themselves and that window of time between check-out and check-in is often the only opportunity to shop for those wonderful breakfasts they prepare, in addition to running their own personal errands.

CHILDREN

Many places in this guide cater only to adults and do not welcome children, or welcome children only over a certain age. They cannot legally refuse accommodation to children, but, as parents, we really want to stay where our children are genuinely welcome. We would always recommend that you inquire about the inn's policy when making your reservation. In the inn descriptions on our website (*www.karenbrown.com*), we have an icon that indicates at what age children are welcome.

COMFORT

Comfort plays a deciding role in the selection of inns recommended: firm mattress, a quiet setting, good lighting, fresh towels, and scrubbed bathrooms. The charming decor and innkeeper will soon be forgotten, if you do not enjoy a good night's sleep and comfortable stay. Be aware, however, that some inns in areas with hot summers, especially those in older buildings, do not always have the luxury of air conditioning. If air conditioning is of prime importance to you, look for the appropriate icon at the bottom of the description and verify that the inn has it when making a reservation.

CREDIT CARDS

Whether an establishment accepts credit cards is indicated at the bottom of each description by the symbol 🔲. Even if an inn does not accept credit card payment, it will perhaps request your account number as a guarantee of arrival.

CRITERIA FOR SELECTION

It is very important to us that an inn have charm. Ideally an inn should be appealing—perhaps in an historic building, beautifully decorated, lovingly managed, and in a wonderful location. Few inns meet every criteria, but all our selections have something that makes them special and they are situated in enjoyable surroundings. We have had to reject several lovely inns because of a poor location. Many are in historic buildings, but remember that the definition of "historic" may depend on the century in which the state came into being. Many inns are newly constructed and may be in buildings built to look old. Small inns are usually our favorites, but size alone does not dictate whether a hostelry is chosen. Most are small, but sometimes the only place to stay in a "must-visit" area is a splendid, larger establishment of great character and charm. We have tried to include properties with a variety of size, decor, and ambiance to suit a variety of tastes and pocketbooks.

ICONS

Icons allow us to provide additional information about our recommended properties. We have introduced the following icons in this guide to supplement each property's description. For easy reference, an icon key can also be found on the inside back cover flap. ❄ Air conditioning in rooms, ⊥ Beach nearby, ☕ Breakfast included in room rate, 🐾 Children welcome, ♨ Cooking classes offered, 💳 Credit cards accepted, 🔺 Dinner served upon request, ☎ Direct-dial telephone in guestroom, 🐕 Dogs by special request, 🛗 Elevator, 🏋 Exercise room, @ Internet access available for guests, � Mini-refrigerator in rooms, 🚭 Some non-smoking rooms, P Parking available (free or paid), 🍴 Restaurant, ☘ Spa (treatments/massage etc.), 🏊 Swimming pool, 🎾 Tennis, 📺 Television with English channels in guestrooms, 💒 Wedding facilities, ♿ Wheelchair friendly, W Wireless available for guests, ⛳ Golf course nearby, 🥾 Hiking trails nearby, 🐎 Horseback riding nearby, ⛷ Skiing nearby, 🏄 Water sports nearby, 🍷 Wineries nearby.

MEMBERSHIP AFFILIATIONS

If a property is a member of either Select Registry or Relais & Châteaux, we reference this on the hotel description page. These associations impose their own criteria for selection and membership standards and have established a reputation for the particular type of property they include.

PROFESSIONALISM

The inns we have selected are run by professional innkeepers. We recommend only inns that offer privacy for their guests, not places where you would have to climb over family clutter to reach the bathroom.

RESERVATIONS

The best way to make a reservation is changing. We used to just pick up the phone and call, but with the advent of the worldwide web, it is now possible to view many properties, including the bedrooms, "on line" and then make a reservation electronically. Email links are published on the individual hotel pages on the Karen Brown Website. Phoning is still a good way to discuss the various differences in available accommodation and the inn's policies. As a courtesy to the innkeepers, however, keep in mind that staff is often limited, and during certain periods of the day, such as the breakfast hour, they are busier than others—flipping pancakes, checking out guests, helping plan activities. Also, inns are often homes, and you might be waking up the innkeeper if you call late evenings or early mornings. Another convenient and efficient way to request a reservation is by fax. If the inn has a fax, we have noted the number in the listing next to the telephone number. As a final note: when planning your trip, be aware that the majority of inns in this guide require a two-night stay on weekends and over holidays.

RESPONSIBILITY

Our goal is to outline itineraries in regions that we consider of prime interest to our readers and to recommend inns that we think are outstanding. All of the inns featured have been selected solely on their merits. Our judgments are made on the charm of the inn, its setting, cleanliness, and, above all, the warmth of welcome. Each property has its own appeal, and we try to present you with a very honest appraisal. However, no matter how careful we are, sometimes we misjudge an inn's merits, or the ownership changes, or (unfortunately) sometimes inns just do not maintain their standards. If you find an inn is not as we have indicated, please let us know and accept our sincere apologies.

RESTAURANTS

A bonus to staying in a New England inn is that of dining in its restaurant. Your meal will be a great one and will feature regional fare ranging from seafood like lobster, clams, and bluefish to the wild game of pheasant and quail. The heritage of New England is turkey, and Thanksgiving dinners generally include the presentation of this bird with a variety of family stuffing recipes, from oyster and corn bread, to traditional herb bread with seasonings. At the end of a day of touring, you will find that the fireplace in the inn's tavern, and another in the dining room, will lure you to both warmth and good dining. If a property has a restaurant, it is indicated by the fork and knife icon. In the inn descriptions on our website (*www.karenbrown.com*), we have an icon that indicates which meals are served.

Lobsters: Second only to lighthouses, lobsters are considered one of New England's premier attractions. Who could imagine a trip to New England without stopping for a lobster roll dripping in melted butter or donning a bib to indulge in a freshly cooked crustacean plucked right out of the shell? Seventy percent of lobsters harvested in New

England are from Maine. It is said that New Englanders can easily taste the difference between a lobster caught off the shores of Maine versus Massachusetts—the distinction is said to be a reflection of the water and temperatures. For full appreciation of this regional delicacy, it is interesting to note a few facts about lobster. Of the thousands of eggs that are hatched from a single lobster those that do not cling to the jellylike mass at the end of the female's tale will be lost to sea and awaiting predators. Lobster eggs take almost nine months to develop and even then, of the thousands that cling to the mother, very few survive. They spend much of their early life hiding on the ocean floor until they are large and strong enough to protect themselves. Lobstermen must adhere to minimum size standards when they cultivate their catch. Although, once cooked, lobsters are all red in color, surprisingly, when alive, they vary dramatically from greenish-brown with an orange underside to blue, red, white and yellow-spotted.

A few tips about eating lobster: Always wear a bib! Twist off the claws. Separate the tail by bending it back until it breaks away from the body. Break the flippers off the tail. Snap off the flipper. Use any method of preference for pushing the tail meat out and in removing meat from the joints. The small legs are good eating—remove the meat by sucking it out. Remove the inner body from the shell. There is some good meat in this section also. Crack each claw with a nutcracker to facilitate removing the meat. Enjoy and savor this delicacy!

If you decide to purchase lobster directly from the fishermen and not simply order it off a restaurant menu, one cost-saving tip: lobsters with just one claw (termed culls) usually cost a fraction of those with two claws; result in more tail per poundage, and make the delicacy more affordable.

ROOM RATES

It seems that many inns play musical rates, with high-season, low-season, midweek, weekend, and holiday rates. We have quoted the 2010 general range of rates, regardless of season, for two people (singles usually receive a very small discount) from the lowest-priced bedroom to the most expensive suite including breakfast. The rates given are those quoted to us by the inn. Please use these figures as a guideline and be certain to ask at the time of booking what the rates are and what they include. We have not given prices for "special" rooms, such as those that can accommodate three people traveling together. Discuss with the innkeeper rooms and rates available before making your selection. Of course, some inns are exceptions to our guidelines, and whenever this is the case, we mention the special situation (such as breakfast not being included in the rate). Please be aware that local tourist taxes are not included in the rates quoted and can be very high.

SMOKING

Most inns have extremely strict non-smoking policies. A few inns permit smoking in restricted public areas or outside, but, in general, it is best to assume that smoking is not appropriate. If smoking is of great concern, be sure to ask the hotel specifically as to their policy about smoking in the garden, on the deck, or in a specially designated public area.

SOCIALIZING

Inns usually offer a conviviality rarely found in a "standard" hotel. The gamut runs all the way from playing "cozy family" around the kitchen table to sharing a sophisticated, elegant cocktail hour in the parlor. Breakfast may be a formal meal served at a set hour when the guests gather around the dining-room table, or it may be served buffet-style over several hours where guests have the option of either sitting down to eat alone or joining other guests at a larger table. Then again, some inns will bring a breakfast tray to your room, or perhaps breakfast in the room is the only option. After check-in, many inns offer afternoon refreshment, such as tea and cakes or wine and hors d'oeuvres, which may be seen as another social opportunity.

Some inns set out the refreshments buffet-style where guests are invited to meander in and out, mixing or not mixing with other guests as they choose. Others orchestrate a more structured gathering, often a social hour, with the innkeeper presiding.

WEBSITE

Please visit the Karen Brown website (*www.karenbrown.com*) in conjunction with this book. Our website provides updated information, trip planning assistance and services, updates, the ability to create a personalized itinerary, new discoveries, traveler reviews, restaurants, recipes, reader reviews, blogs, forum, color photos, interactive links, the opportunity to purchase goods and services that we recommend (rail tickets, car rental, travel insurance, etc.), and one-stop shopping for our guides, associated maps and watercolor prints.

Most of our favorite places to stay are featured with color photos, direct website, and email links. Also, we invite you to participate in the Karen Brown's Readers' Choice Awards. Be sure to visit our website and vote so your favorite properties will be honored.

WHEELCHAIR ACCESSIBILITY

If an inn has at least one guestroom that is accessible by wheelchair, it is noted with the symbol ♿. This is not the same as saying it meets full ADA standards.

About Itineraries

Though the same thread of "Yankee" (as defined by many) culture is woven throughout all six states, there are distinctive differences between the states themselves. Within each state, there are areas that are markedly different in terrain, weather patterns, and tourist attractions. These differences make for delightful trips. This book guides you on journeys that show off this diversity, and gives you the opportunity to choose the experiences you most want to have.

Boston: A Grand Beginning describes our recommendations for what to see in this wonderful gateway city to New England. Five detailed driving itineraries (*Sturbridge & The Connecticut Shore; Byways of Coastal Maine; Cape Cod, Nantucket; Martha's Vineyard & Newport; Route 7 & Much More, and New Hampshire Beckons*) describe routes through the various regions of New England, so that you can choose a journey through an area that fits both your time and travel constraints. The itineraries are outlined on the hotel state maps found at the front of the book in the color map section and on the individual, more detailed, black-and-white map that precedes each itinerary. The overview map will help you visualize the routes of the various itineraries as they navigate a course through the New England states. Tailor these itineraries to meet your own specific needs by leaving out some sightseeing if time is limited, or linking several itineraries together if you wish to enjoy a longer vacation.

Though several itineraries use Boston as their point of origination, and this is a logical starting point for travel to Cape Cod and the Berkshires, they may be accessed at any point en route and from any of the various points at which you may arrive in the northeast. Your entry into New England will probably depend on your destination—Manchester, New Hampshire—for ease of access into Maine, New Hampshire, and Vermont; Providence, Rhode Island—for visiting Cape Cod, the islands of Nantucket and Martha's Vineyard, and the small but activity-rich areas of Rhode Island; Hartford, Connecticut—for trips to the western portions of Connecticut and Massachusetts, and north into Vermont and New Hampshire; and Albany, New York—for alternative access to the western parts of New England. Although New York City is located at least an hour's drive (more if you travel during congested commuter hours) from Connecticut and the start of the itinerary travels up the western side of New England, its airports may provide the best airfares and schedules for the international traveler, as well as the more distant U.S. traveler.

ANTIQUING

If you have a passion for antiquing, you might already know that New England is full of treasures to satisfy almost any desire to start or add to a collection. Most of the antique shops in New England are small and privately owned, but in the last several years, "collectives" have become very popular. These are group shops representing a few antique dealers, or maybe as many as a hundred dealers. In the larger shops, there is a greater chance of finding the elusive object you are searching for. Antiques are generally divided into objects of significant value and collectibles, the latter having less dollar value, but not necessarily of less interest-value to the buyer. Fortunately, in New England there is a wealth of both antiques and collectibles, and the challenge is finding the shops in which those treasures you have always wanted will be waiting for you. To aid you in this, a good reference is Sloan's *Green Guide to Antiquing in New England,* a compendium of 2,500 shops. Since no dealer can be familiar with the value of all objects in all categories, and generally has items in stock not within his general line of expertise, you may have an opportunity to purchase an overlooked treasure at a real bargain.

CAR RENTAL

Our itineraries are designed for travel by car. If you are staying in any of the major cities at the beginning of your trip, it is not necessary to pick up a rental car until you leave the city or just before any day trips you can make only by car, since public transportation systems are so convenient and all of the cities are great for walking. Ask your hotel if there is a car rental office nearby—if so, you might find out if that particular company can give you rates as competitive as any other. If you are lucky, as with some of the rental companies, you might even have your car delivered to your hotel. There is no question that the less time you have to spend getting to your car and then turning it in at the end of your trip, the happier you will be. Inquire when you make your car reservation about all the add-on charges, and do not be surprised at how much they increase the total rental cost. Do check to see if your home or car insurance or your credit card will provide you with coverage in the event of an accident.

DRIVING TIMES

New England is not particularly large—in the central portions six hours of driving will generally take you from east to west or from south to north, unless you stretch out New England and try to go from southern Connecticut to the tip of Maine (more like a ten-hour trip). We have indicated in our itineraries a daily pace that we believe will make for a pleasant and comfortable trip, allowing you time to enjoy not only the scenery, but also the historic sights along the way. Allow more time if you want to do a lot of shopping, or if you have a special interest in any particular area.

FALL FOLIAGE

While routes are picturesque in any season, our driving itineraries weave through some gorgeous regions, where the richness of your day will be matched not only by the color of the foliage, but also by each passing farm with pumpkins and gourds piled high, and cornstalks tied to fence posts. Fall Foliage highlights are referenced in the introductory pages of each itinerary, but if you were to choose the most traditional Fall Foliage route, you might want to consider the itinerary, *New Hampshire Beckons*.

New England is special at any time of the year, but there is simply nowhere on earth where you can experience nature's changing colors as you can here. When the days become shorter, the nights turn cool, the first frost coats the lawn, and the roof shingles sparkle with their early-morning ice, New England prepares for the magic season of fall foliage. Trees, shrubs, flowers and weeds all begin the transformation that changes their color from green to multiple hues of red, orange, and gold—and a million shades in between. It is simply a time of magic! It is also the time when nature performs a brilliant display reminiscent of fireworks on the fourth of July. It is a time to be in New England.

Fall foliage is generally at its peak in the first two weeks of October after the first bite of cold temperatures, and seems to be best when there has been the proper amount of rainfall during the spring and summer. This season of changing colors generally begins in the far northern reaches of New England (unless you happen to be on a winding lane in the Connecticut valley alongside a quiet pond where the cold air of the night has settled in and painted everything in sight with a vivid brush of intensity). The turning of the colors generally wends its way southward, unless it happens to turn west, or unless you happen to be on the peak of a mountain enjoying views for miles around. Remember, each rule about the timing of fall foliage has an exception.

This is a special time in New England. Unless the weather is unusual, it will perform as it has for hundreds of years. Do not worry excessively (or perhaps at all) about being on exactly the perfect road at the precise moment when the foliage achieves its peak and the golden and red leaves fall from the trees. Generally, plan to be in New England between mid-September and mid-October—farther north in the middle of September, and in Massachusetts and Connecticut in the month of October.

Reservations: The northeast's fall foliage is without a doubt one of the most popular tourist attractions in the U.S. Finding places to spend the night is sometimes difficult, so reservations are a must. Hopefully, you will be able to find a place to suit your preferences among the inns recommended in this guide. If there is no room available, ask the innkeeper for his or her recommendation of an alternative accommodation—most innkeepers recommend only places where they themselves would stay, so you will be safe with their suggestions. Nonetheless, making a reservation as soon as you book your airplane ticket or plan your road trip is well advised.

MAPS

A total of five colored maps are to be found at the front of the book. The overview map outlines our recommended driving itineraries as they cross through the New England states. The overview is followed by a series of four detailed maps that show the itinerary routings, and places to stay by geographic state groupings. Fronting each itinerary is a black-and-white map that outlines the suggested route, detailing sightseeing suggestions and roads. These are simply renderings and not necessarily to scale. For detailed trip planning, it is essential to supplement these with comprehensive commercial maps. Rand McNally maps are available for purchase on our website, *www.karenbrown.com.*

PACING

At the beginning of each itinerary, we suggest our recommended pacing to help you decide the amount of time to allocate to each one. The suggested time frame reflects how much there is to see and do. Use our recommendation as a guideline only. Choreograph your own itinerary based on how much leisure time you have, and whether your preference is to move on to a new destination each day or to settle in and use a particular inn as your base.

WEATHER

There is a saying in New England "If you don't like the weather, just wait a few minutes." While the weather may be changeable, there are certainly some guidelines that will be helpful to the traveler in planning a trip. In the winter months of December through March, you can expect everything, from snow and ice to sleet and freezing rain. Temperatures often get down to zero and below, and there may be days, even weeks, when there is little snow and just brisk cold weather. Traditionally, in the latter half of January, there is even a period of warm weather, deceiving everyone into believing that winter is over. The spring months of April, May, and June are wonderful—with all of New England sprouting forth with bulbs of every description, and flowering shrubs and trees. The newness of everything with the green freshness of spring is hard not to love. However, occasionally in the spring there is a taste of winter weather that will remind you that the decision to bring a coat on your trip was indeed a very good one. Summer is a lazy time of year and generally has lovely weather, but there will be rain showers. Summer can also get hot and humid—on those days you will welcome the pair of shorts and short-sleeved shirt that you brought, and you will be grateful that your rental car and hotel are air-conditioned. Many a traveler will say that New England is best in the fall when the days are long and warm, the evenings are cool, and the foliage begins to turn.

Introduction–About Itineraries

Boston: A Grand Beginning

Boston, the economic and intellectual center of New England and, historically, America's cradle of liberty, is the stage on which much of the drama of the earliest years of our country took place. It is here that the Colonies, which evolved into the present United States, were first established. The capital city of Massachusetts, Boston was first settled in the 17th century, but it was the 18th century that saw the growing rift between the English Parliament and the colonists in what was referred to as the Bay Colony. Many of the historic sites and buildings in Boston, and the towns surrounding it, are associated with this period of separation from the Crown.

Recommended Pacing: Plan to spend at least three nights and four full days in Boston, and you will be able to choose among the many things to do and come up with a program tailored to your interests. Touring Boston is not only desirable, but also necessary to fully appreciate New England's historical and cultural importance.

Beacon Hill, Acorn Street

Getting Around: Boston is a wonderful city to explore on foot and it has an efficient public system, so it is also easy to explore the city by its subway, locally referred to as the "T". Visit Park Street station (one of the main downtown stations) to obtain a map of the color-coded subway lines and information on Boston Passports, which provide unlimited subway travel for 1, 3, 5, and 7 days. If you plan to take day trips to Lexington or Marblehead, you can do so from North Station (on the subway system). For further information: *www.mbta.com.*

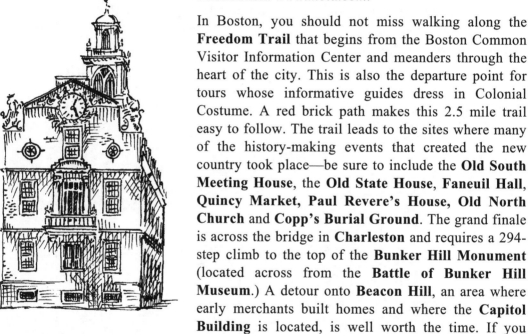

In Boston, you should not miss walking along the **Freedom Trail** that begins from the Boston Common Visitor Information Center and meanders through the heart of the city. This is also the departure point for tours whose informative guides dress in Colonial Costume. A red brick path makes this 2.5 mile trail easy to follow. The trail leads to the sites where many of the history-making events that created the new country took place—be sure to include the **Old South Meeting House**, the **Old State House**, **Faneuil Hall**, **Quincy Market**, **Paul Revere's House**, **Old North Church** and **Copp's Burial Ground**. The grand finale is across the bridge in **Charleston** and requires a 294-step climb to the top of the **Bunker Hill Monument** (located across from the **Battle of Bunker Hill Museum**.) A detour onto **Beacon Hill**, an area where early merchants built homes and where the **Capitol Building** is located, is well worth the time. If you would like to do some shopping as a break from all the history, just walk across the Boston Common and proceed, with credit card in hand, down **Newbury Street**, where you find the city's finest boutiques, art galleries, antique shops, and some of the city's best restaurants.

Charles Bullfinch, one of the principal architects of many of Boston's historic buildings, completed the **State House**, with its golden dome, in 1786. Nearby, another example of his talent, the **Harrison Gray Otis House**, today serves as the headquarters of **SPNEA** (Society for the Preservation of New England Antiquities). Throughout New England, there are 37 houses and gardens owned by SPNEA, displaying the furnishings and decorative arts of the region's past. Telephone 617-227-3956 or visit their website at *www.spnea.org* for information on these historic properties.

Back Bay, with its commercial and shopping areas, begins at the **Boston Common**, a 50-acre park in the center of the city. The adjacent **Public Garden** (the first public botanical garden in the country), with its guide-pedaled swan boats and wonderful duck statues found along its network of paths, is a treat for children who have read and loved *Make Way for Ducklings*. Not to be missed in Back Bay are **Copley Square**, **Trinity Church**, and the **John Hancock Tower**, from whose 60th-floor observatory you get splendid views in all directions. **Commonwealth Avenue** retains much of the grandeur of a residential street with its center mall lined with elm trees.

In the colorful part of Boston known as the **North End**, there are many Italian bakeries, restaurants, and street markets. Its narrow cobbled and brick streets descend down to the Inner Harbor and its string of wharves. The Freedom Trail travels through this district with the **Paul Revere's House** and the **Old North Church** key points of interest. Periods, as well as some original pieces, decorate the 17th century Paul Revere home and informative docents are present in each room to enhance your self-guided tour. In his lifetime, Paul Revere was a silversmith (the Revere bowl), established a bell and cannon foundry supplying ammunition to the navy. Revere's role as one of the patriots who bravely took on the cause to defeat the British, was immortalized when Henry Wadsworth Longfellow wrote (many years after Revere's death), *The Midnight Ride of Paul Revere*. His historic ride of April 18, 1775 actually began from across the river where he hid awaiting confirmation that the British were indeed leaving the city to arrest rebels and seize munitions in Lexington and Concord. From the riverbank he could see the belfry of the Old North Church (definitely worth a visit) where lanterns were to signal the departure of the British (one if by sea, two if by land). Paul Revere was one of three riders on that historic night who successfully warned their fellow patriots before being captured by British patrol. (Next door to the Paul Revere home, his cousin's home, the **Pierce-Hichborn House** is a wonderful example of 18th century architecture.)

Boston's **financial district** is centered around one of its major transportation hubs, South Station. Within a few blocks' walk are the Aquarium, Chinatown, the theater district, and many shopping opportunities in the larger department stores.

Boston, home since the early years to some of our nation's most prominent educational, medical, and research institutions, is equally famous for its cultural activities. Here you find important international museums including the **Museum of Fine Arts** and the **Isabella Stewart Gardner Museum**. While each is very different from the other, they both have world-renowned art comparable to the best museums anywhere. In the Museum of Fine Arts, our favorite galleries would include those devoted to American and European art; but major collections of Asiatic, Egyptian, Nubian, and Near-Eastern artworks, as well as sculpture and photography, are there to enjoy. Housed at the neighboring Isabella Stewart Gardner Museum are incredible pieces of art (Rembrandt, Sargent, Titian, Raphael, Botticelli, Van Dyke, Degas), sculpture, tapestries and furnishing. Every piece of art was carefully positioned by Mrs. Gardner herself who fulfilled a dream, begun with her husband, to create a museum whose intimate display would enhance the visitor's experience and appreciation. The museum was also built incorporating architectural pieces acquired all over the world—staircases, ornate ceilings, windows, fireplaces. The rooms and hallways of each level wind around and open onto a central core and an ornate, first floor garden whose plantings change seasonally. The exterior of the building is non-descript, but the interior walls that embrace the garden look like an Italian villa turned inside out! Concerts are held regularly in the Tapestry Room. Just south of the city, reachable via public transportation, is the **Museum at the John Fitzgerald Kennedy Library**, which houses the archives of the former president.

For children, there are two museums of particular note: The **Boston Museum of Science**, located by the Charles River, offers an array of educational exhibits that invite active participation in the world of science and technology. (This museum is fascinating and I urge you to make time for it in your program.) The **Children's Museum** at Museum Wharf is a wonderful, interactive, educational museum that will delight adults as well as children, and has an area for toddlers and preschoolers.

The **Boston Symphony Orchestra**, one of the world's most famous, performs throughout the fall, winter, and spring seasons in Symphony Hall and during the summer at Tanglewood in the Berkshires. The **Boston Pops**, with its programs of lighter music, performs in summer at Symphony Hall and in free concerts on the Charles River Esplanade. There is nothing like a summer night under the stars listening to music with a picnic supper. Boston has a **theater district** just south of Boston Common and not far from the financial district—most of the theaters are on Tremont and Boylston Streets. Here you can find many pre-Broadway and current Broadway shows, as well as a ballet company, which performs seasonally.

Back Bay Skyline and the Charles River

Across the river, neighboring **Cambridge** is home to **Harvard University** (the nation's oldest university), **Radcliffe College**, and the **Massachusetts Institute of Technology**. Around these academic communities has developed a maze of commercial and residential neighborhoods, artists' studios, and theaters. On the Harvard campus, sites worth visiting include **Harvard Yard** with its student residential buildings, **Memorial Church**, **Harvard Museums of Cultural and Natural History**, and the **Botanical Museum,** which houses the world-renowned collection of Blashka glass flowers. These pieces were created between 1877 and 1936, and represent more than 780 species of flowering plants—an absolute must for garden enthusiasts. To this day, no one has been able to recreate the processes used in producing these magnificent examples of floral beauty.

For adults and children alike, the **New England Aquarium** is a special place to visit. Its center exhibit is a four-story 187,000-gallon ocean tank re-creating a Caribbean reef, and there are exhibits encouraging children to handle crabs, sea urchins, and starfish.

The *USS Constitution*, the oldest commissioned warship afloat, which participated in a number of sea battles in disputes between the American colonies and the British, is berthed in Charlestown, and reached by public transportation or a very long walk.

There are many other varied attractions for the visitor to Boston. More information can be obtained from the **Greater Boston Convention and Visitors Bureau** located at 2 Copley Place, Suite 105, at the intersection of Tremont and West Streets (1-888-SEE BOSTON, *www.bostonusa.com*). Full descriptions and details of the hotels we recommend in Boston are given in the *Massachusetts Places to Stay* section of this book.

Cape Cod & Nantucket

- Orientation/Sightseeing
- Itinerary Route
- -- Ferry Route

Wilmington
Danvers
Salem
Concord
Minute Man NHP
Marblehead
495
Sudbury
Cambridge
Malden
Boston
Massachusetts Bay
20
Framingham
Quincy
Cohasset
Needham
95
Weymouth
3A
Norwood
Marshfield Hills
140
1
95
3
Milford
MA
24
Duxbury
Mansfield
Plymouth
Provincetown
495
44
Cape Cod Bay
Taunton
Middleborough
3
Cape Cod NS
295
Cape Cod Canal
Sagamore Bridge
Eastham
44
Pawtucket
140
Sandwich
Orleans
Providence
Wareham
Yarmouth Port
Brewster
RI
136
Buzzards Bay
6A
Dennis
Warwick
Fall River
195
Barnstable
Chatham
95
6
Hyannis
1
New Bedford
Buzzards Bay
Wakefield
114
Woods Hole
Falmouth
Nantucket Sound
Newport
Vineyard Haven
Oak Bluffs
Gay Head
Edgartown
Wauwinet
Menensha
Nantucket
Rhode Island Sound
Siasconset
Block Island

Cape Cod, Nantucket,
Martha's Vineyard & Newport

Travel south from Boston—to the coastal villages and fishing harbors of Cape Cod, out to the enticing islands of Nantucket and Martha's Vineyard, on to the gracious mansions of Newport—and back to Boston. Along the way, you have ample opportunities for antiquing, and you will come to love the weathered architecture that gave its name to the "Cape" style of building. The north shore of the Cape along Route 6A is my favorite. It is much quieter, less populated, and much less commercial than the towns along Route 28 to the south, and there is a real sense of community here. In the warm months, flower gardens thrive on Cape Cod, especially roses, which seem almost to engulf the houses in early June.

Nantucket

Recommended Pacing: The routing for this itinerary is also outlined on Map 2 (in the front section of the book). This itinerary can be comfortably followed in its entirety in six or seven nights, though you can, of course, adapt it to fit your individual interests. On day one, head south along the coastal route; visit Hingham, Duxbury, Plymouth, and stay overnight in Duxbury. On day two, cross the Sagamore Bridge and stay overnight in Sandwich. On day three, drive along the north side of Cape Cod to the Cape Cod National Seashore and the artist community of Provincetown, spending the night in Orleans, Eastham, or Chatham. Day four takes you south along the coast to Hyannis, where you take the ferry or fly to the islands of Nantucket or Martha's Vineyard. One day (minimum) on each of these islands provides time to see the villages and to absorb the culture of the seafarers who arrived as early as the 18th century. On day six, a flight or boat trip back to Hyannis and a drive to Newport, Rhode Island provide an opportunity to see the grand summer cottages of the "rich and famous" residents, built in the first quarter of the 19th century. Spend the night in Newport, and then a second night, if your interest in touring the mansions of Newport has absorbed an entire day. From Newport, head north back to Boston, stopping off en route to explore Providence, the capital of Rhode Island.

The Cape Cod Canal is only an hour's drive from Boston if you take the Southeast Expressway out of Boston and pick up Route 3 to the Cape. The bridge onto Cape Cod can also can be reached via the winding Route 3A, a slower road, which takes you through the coastal communities whose history and charm will make their way into your heart. (Note that the towns located along the 3A and Cape Cod are best and most easily visited outside commuter hours.) From Boston, follow signs onto the Southeast Expressway (I-93) to Quincy; and then take either the faster Route 3, or the more leisurely Route 3A, to the Sagamore Bridge and the beginning of the Cape.

On Route 3A, the towns of **Quincy**, **Cohasset**, **Duxbury**, and **Plymouth** are quaint: their main streets have been traveled for the last two centuries by horse, carriage, and now sport utility vehicle. Quincy, previously referred to as **Braintree**, was the birthplace of John Adams, our second president, and his son, John Quincy Adams who served as our country's sixth president. What was their birth home, as well as a home purchased later that was much grander and more appropriate to his station in life, are now part of the National Park Service. It is worthwhile to stop in Plymouth at the historical sites of **Plymouth Rock**, where the Pilgrims first landed and see the replica of *Mayflower II*, the ship that brought the Pilgrims to Plymouth in 1620, and **Burial Hill**, the graveyard where many of the first settlers are buried. It is interesting to note that the fear of Indians at the time was so great that in order to disguise their dwindling numbers, settlers were buried in the dark of the night. The last gravestone dates to 1620. Take a stroll down Leyden Street, the oldest street in New England, and look across to Clark's Island, where the sick were once quarantined. Handsome, old homes still line the street, seemingly very little has changed from days gone by. You can almost envision someone walking down the street with a lantern, signaling the island that the mail and supplies are on the way, and to meet the boat at the halfway point. There are two museums, the **Mayflower Society Museum** and the **Pilgrim Hall Museum**.

Located three miles north of town on the Plymouth waterfront, the **Plimoth Plantation** is an absolutely incredible, living history museum that is a "must-see" and warrants no less than a half-day's visit. A re-creation of a 1627 Pilgrim village with homes, storehouses, animal pens, and fields planted for harvest stretch up the hillside from the water's edge and also includes the neighboring Wampanoag Indian community—**Hobbamock's Homesite**. To give you a perspective of time, the Mayflower landed seven years earlier than the date of this village, and Boston would not be founded for another three years after. If you have had an opportunity to visit Sturbridge or Williamsburg, they would not be settled for another 100 years. The docents that live and work at Plimoth Plantation are not just day actors, but rather, termed Time Travelers, who have dedicated years to studying a particular character. Admission to Plimoth Plantation is to experience their world. Talk with them about their passage, their hardships, their battles, their joy, and their lives. I promise you will believe you have traveled back in time. Note: It is possible to purchase an admission ticket valid for the Plantation, the Homesite and the Mayflower II. For more information, visit *www.plimoth.org*.

The **Sagamore Bridge** spans the **Cape Cod Canal**, which is used by shipping and pleasure craft to avoid circumnavigating the entire Cape on journeys between Boston and the coasts of Rhode Island, Connecticut, and states to the south. This is your entrance onto **Cape Cod** with its scenic character and unique charm. Almost immediately after crossing the bridge, exit Route 6 (the continuation of Route 3) onto Route 130, then 6A to the town of **Sandwich,** an excellent place to stop for the night (be sure to make advance reservations in season). The town is a charming one for wandering the streets and has two outstanding museums. The **Sandwich Glass Museum** (closed in January) displays the glass produced in Sandwich between 1825 and 1888—lamps, candlesticks, tiebacks, doorknobs, vases, and much more, which have become collectors' treasures. The **Heritage Plantation Museum,** founded with the generous contributions of the Lily family, has collections of early-American historical artifacts and folk art. There are extensive collections of firearms, cars, as well as folk art and an old-fashioned carousel. On the museum's grounds is an extensive rhododendron garden, which blooms each year from mid-May to mid-June—a "must" if you have an interest in gardening.

Leaving Sandwich, get onto Route 6A, the northern route along the upper coast of Cape Cod. It is a delightful road to follow as it winds its way through the lovely, historical towns of **Barnstable**, **Yarmouth Port**, **Dennis**, and **Brewster**. These old seafaring communities with their lovely main streets, beautiful homes, and colorful harbors make for a wonderful day of browsing, antiquing, and for just absorbing the atmosphere of the Cape. Continuing north through the towns of **Orleans** and **Eastham**, you come to the **Cape Cod National Seashore,** where you can take a fabulous dunes tour from April through October—a perfect way to see the ever-changing face of the sand dunes of this portion of the Cape. Farther on, at the tip of the Cape, is the artist community of **Provincetown**. **Chatham**, protected by the sandy, offshore barrier of Nauset Beach, remains an active fishing port.

Head south and travel along the south shore of Cape Cod on Route 28, which brings you into the more commercial area of the Cape—more traffic, more shops, and more restaurants, but many inns and places to visit. **Hyannis** is the major shopping center for

Cape Cod's residents and the **summer home** of former president **John F. Kennedy**, where there is a small museum of photographs of the Kennedy family on summer vacations.

Before you return to the mainland, take the time to visit the enchanting islands of Nantucket and Martha's Vineyard. Leave your car in the parking lot at any one of the various departure points (Hyannis, Woods Hole, Falmouth, or New Bedford) from which airplane or ferry services (but not necessarily both) are available. Some ferries are catamarans and make very fast trips. The frequency of both air and ferry service depends on the season and the weather (on the day I was to go to Nantucket, fog prevented me from flying and I ended up taking the one-hour ferry from Hyannis). You can fly to Nantucket or Martha's Vineyard from Hyannis (the best and most frequent service), Providence, and Boston with Cape Air (800-352-0714), Island Airline (508-228-7575), and US Airways (800-428-4322). Ferries to Nantucket run from Hyannis (alternative departure points include Harwich Port and Martha's

Nauset Light House, Eastham

Vineyard). Hy-Line (508-778-2600) has a one-hour, high-speed catamaran, and the Steamship Authority runs a high-speed catamaran and other boats that take somewhat longer (508-495-FAST).

Ferries to Martha's Vineyard leave from Falmouth, Hyannis, Woods Hole, New Bedford, and Nantucket. I suggest that you ask the staff at the inn where you are planning to stay for their recommendation of the best and fastest routes.

The two offshore islands of Nantucket and Martha's Vineyard were major whaling industry seaports from 1740 to 1830. The wealthy tradesmen who were associated with this very profitable venture built many of the magnificent homes along the streets of the seafaring ports of both islands.

Nantucket is perfect for exploring on foot or by bicycle, (bicycles may easily be rented from one of the many shops near the ferry landing). The **Nantucket Historical Association** sells combination tickets to the historic houses and museums it manages, which include the **Whaling Museum**, the **Old Mill** (a 1746 windmill still being used to grind corn), **Old Gaol** (the original jail with its four cells), and the **Oldest House** on the island. Tickets are available at any of these locations. Along the town of Nantucket's cobblestoned, elm-shaded Main Street are many shops, art galleries, and very good restaurants, the latter specializing in the locally caught seafood. Of particular note are the **Three Bricks**, three stately mansions built by a wealthy merchant for his three sons. Nantucket is one of my all-time favorite places—I have been there in the summer; I have enjoyed a vacation in a rented cottage in October; and I have spent a New Year's weekend there. Each occasion was very special. Nantucket is simply one of those destinations whose ambiance and charm vary with the mood of the season—it is improved only by your having more time to spend there.

When it comes time to leave Nantucket, go on to Martha's Vineyard by boat or by plane, or return to the mainland.

Martha's Vineyard has a greater number of villages, so unless you are going to restrict your visit to the village where the ferry docks, you will either have to rent a car (my suggestion if you are planning to make more than just a brief visit) or take taxis to reach the various parts of the island. Of course, you can also rent a bicycle, but remember that the villages, which appear to be so close together on the map, are really several, to many miles apart. If you fly to Martha's Vineyard, you will need to rent a car since the airport is some distance from the island's points of interest.

The ferry (from Wood's Hole, Hyannis, Falmouth, or Nantucket) will bring you into one of the three principal townships on Martha's Vineyard. Vineyard Haven, Oak Bluffs, and Edgartown are distinctly different from one another, although they are all fishing villages. **Vineyard Haven**, the principal entry point to the Vineyard and a source of rental cars or bicycles for touring the island, has a group of shops and restaurants, but very quickly changes into a rural landscape stretching along the coast with homes built in the 19th century. There is particular charm in the settlement of **Oak Bluffs**, a meeting place for Methodists in the late 19th and early 20th centuries. Around the meeting ground and the tabernacle that was built for these religious gatherings, a colony of small, wooden cottages decorated with gingerbread (Victorian lace-like) trim were built and painted in wonderfully vivid colors. **Edgartown** was the seaport from which the whalers left to hunt the elusive whale, and the island's mansions were built in this area. Be sure to visit **Gay Head** with its clay cliffs, which have stood high above the sea for the last 100 million years—their colors and majesty are memorable.

Returning either by boat or by plane to the mainland, drive west on Route 28 through Falmouth, picking up Route 25, which in turn connects to I-195. Look for the exit to Route 136 south and then Route 114 into **Newport**, Rhode Island. The homes built there in the 19th century for the wealthy to escape the oppressive summer heat of the south became the center of a social life never seen before or since. Today many of these homes are open to the public and tours give you a glimpse of the opulence of a bygone era. You can tour many of these homes. If you plan to visit several, purchase a ticket that will allow you to visit two or eight of them. Among the "must-visit" mansions are: The Breakers, home of Cornelius Vanderbilt, The Marble House, built for William Vanderbilt, The Elms, and Rosecliff, used for the filming of *The Great Gatsby*. For details and tickets call 401-847-1000.

Take a bracing walk along the oceanfront, which hearkens the image of those halcyon days. This is a very special experience and you should plan to take an hour or several hours (perhaps as I did with a bottle of wine, some cheese, and a loaf of good bread) to enjoy this oceanfront path. With the ocean on one side and the fabulous homes on the other, this is a memorable experience. Today, many festivals take place in Newport including a music festival during the summer months.

Leaving Newport, head back north on Routes 114 and 136 to I-195 into **Providence**. With a concerned effort to bring back the ambiance of yesteryear, Providence is quickly becoming one of New England's most popular cities because of its historical charm. This is the capital city of Rhode Island. Three rivers weave a course through the heart of town and segment the key districts: the university quarter, the business, convention center and mall, and the seat of government with its **Capitol Building** and **State House**. The educational institutions of **Brown University** and the **Rhode Island School of Design** are located in a tree-shaded, residential neighborhood where there are many small cafés, bookstores, and little shops. At the Rhode Island School of Design, there is a museum with collections ranging from medieval to contemporary pieces; and in the nearby **John Brown House,** you can take a guided tour of this 18th-century brick museum with its fabulous collection of furniture belonging to the family. Business is the focus at the heart of town with the convention center, larger hotels, principal shopping mall and the Capitol Building dominating the northern hillside. If your visit falls on a weekend night in summer, you will be fortunate to experience **Waterfire**. A crowning tribute to Providence's renaissance, Waterfire is a living sculpture. An award-winning creation by sculpturer, Barnaby Evans, Waterfire pays homage to the importance of fire in human civilization as depicted in Greek mythology. Volunteers clad in black, act as fire tenders and ply the waters of the Woonasquatucket and Moshassuck Rivers in boats named after the gods, traveling from one of the 42 braziers to the next, igniting the wood set in the sculptures, sparking bonfires that crackle above the water passage. With a backdrop of enchanting music and the aromatic fragrance of wood smoke, this is a hauntingly memorable experience.

Leaving Providence, drive north on I-95 to Route 128, the circumferential route around the city of Boston, and follow the signs to Boston. This is about an hour's drive, unless you hit rush hour.

If you plan to connect with another of the itineraries in the southern part of New England, drive southwest from the Providence area on I-95 along the coast of Connecticut into the area of the Connecticut River Valley.

Sand Dunes on the Massachusetts Shore

Sturbridge & Conn. Shore

Orientation/Sightseeing

Itinerary Route

MA

Concord
Minute Man NHP
Lincoln
(126)
Lexington
Arlington
Cambridge
Malden
Boston
Needham
Norwood (1)
(122)
Worcester
(20)
(495)
Auburn
(90)
Milford
(146)
(24)
Mansfield
Palmer
Springfield
(20)
Sturbridge
Southbridge
(495)
(84)
(169)
(295)
Pawtucket
Providence
(44)
(44)
(395)
(6)
(6)
CT
RI
Warwick
(136)
Fall River
(2)
(102)
(95)
(114)
Colchester
Jewett City
Norwich
North Stonington
Hope Valley
Newport
East Haddam
(11)
(164)
Old Mystic
Kingston
(9)
Deep River
(9)
Chester
Essex
Ivoryton
(95)
Old Lyme
Mystic
Stonington
Westerly
(1)
Rhode Island Sound
(1)
Old Saybrook

33

Sturbridge & the Connecticut Shore

This itinerary takes the traveler from Boston to Lexington and Concord, sites of historical events that led to the founding of the Colonies, and from there, westward to Sturbridge Village and south to the Connecticut shoreline, with a visit to Mystic Seaport. This is an especially good route for those with children, since the historical sites have guides who theatrically depict the events that took place in days of yore.

Mystic Seaport

Recommended Pacing: (The routing for this itinerary is also outlined on Maps 1 and 2 at the front of the book.) The Lexington and Concord portion of this itinerary is an easy day trip from Boston, since this area is only about an hour's drive from the city. Alternatively, you can overnight here or go on to Sturbridge, a little less than an hour away, and sleep there. Plan to spend one full day in Sturbridge before heading for the Connecticut shore, about an hour and a half beyond Sturbridge. You will definitely want to include at least one night based on the coast in order to adequately explore the towns of Essex, Old Lyme, and Mystic with its wonderful "living museum," Mystic Seaport.

Fall foliage touring in this area is ideal for those who want to do a day trip to see what New England is so famous for. There is no prettier area for seeing color in the trees than in the towns to the west of Boston. Couple the history of this area with the beauty of the countryside as the leaves begin to turn, and you have a very special itinerary. This foliage trip can also be the beginning of a visit to areas beyond the towns west of Boston, down into Connecticut, and to the shore towns along the Connecticut River.

Today, Lexington and Concord are residential suburbs of Boston, but their place in history has linked them together for over 200 years. It was here, in April 1775, that the Colonial troops fought with the British in skirmishes that eventually led to the **American Revolution**. That story comes alive in the preservation of the sites and monuments, and in the annual April 19th re-creation of those important events. In areas now designated as national parks, guides relate the events that led to the revolution giving the visitor, young and old, a graphic understanding of what took place during that momentous time. Perhaps the most famous story is that of **Paul Revere's** horseback ride from Boston to Lexington and Concord—to warn of the impending attack by the British—which enabled the colonists to meet the challenge and drive them back.

To reach Lexington, leave Boston on Storrow Drive and then follow signs to Route 2, which takes you from Boston west through Cambridge and Arlington. Exit Route 2 in Arlington on Route 60 to Route 2A, which will take you into the center of **Lexington**. Lexington's village green, with its several monuments to the April 19th route of the

The Old North Bridge

British who fled back to Boston, is surrounded by lovely homes. There are a few shops and restaurants where you can refresh yourself after walking around the historic area.

Leaving Lexington, continue along Route 2A to **Concord** and visit the area where the battle at the **Old North Bridge** between the British and the Minutemen took place. The **Minutemen**, so called because of their willingness to pick up arms on a minute's notice to defend against injustices inflicted by the British government, drove the British soldiers back through Lexington and on to Boston. At the **Old North Bridge Visitor Center** there is a replica of the "bridge that arched the flood" and a national park ranger recounts the story.

Sturbridge & the Connecticut Shore

The **Minuteman National Historic Park** between the towns of Lexington, Lincoln, and Concord has a Minuteman Visitor Center showing a movie that re-creates that period.

The **Concord Museum**, in the town center, houses 19 galleries with furnishings of the revolutionary period and the century that followed. What is particularly interesting in this museum is that each room represents a different period. As you tour these various rooms, guides explain the evolving style of decoration and life as it was lived at the time. Other interesting stops include **Orchard House**, home of Louisa May Alcott, author of *Little Women*, the home of the poet **Ralph Waldo Emerson**, and **Walden Pond** where Henry David Thoreau lived and wrote. **Sleepy Hollow Cemetery**, the ancient burial ground for many of these famous citizens, is a suitable finale to the Concord tour.

From Concord, Route 126 leads south to the Massachusetts Turnpike (I-90), which is the fastest way to reach **Sturbridge**, less than an hour away. The town itself is worth a stop. Beautiful, old houses line the common or central lawn, the old tavern still serves fine food in an ambiance of the past, and the cemetery with tombstones that date back hundreds of years identify and lend tribute to many of the original settlers. On the outskirts of town is the **Old Sturbridge Village**, a living-history museum; you should allow a full day to explore the re-creation of life as it was lived in the first half of the 19th century. Costumed actors inhabit the village by day, wandering the streets, staffing the stores, and tending to the tasks of yesteryear. They bring history to life.

Sturbridge & the Connecticut Shore

There are more than 40 staffed exhibits, homes, craft shops, mills, and farm buildings on more than 200 acres of fields and farmland. Among my favorite buildings is the clock gallery where many different types of timepieces are on display. In addition to the one-room schoolhouse, the mills, and the demonstrations of shoemaking and cooking over a wood fire, there are seasonal exhibits of sheep shearing, apple pressing, and maple sugaring. For children, there is a special educational program providing hands-on activities. Be sure to wear comfortable walking shoes.

From Sturbridge, the scenic Route 169 leads south toward the Connecticut shore. However, if time is of the essence, I recommend Route 20 from Sturbridge northeast to Auburn, picking up I-395 south to Jewett City, and then Route 164 into **Mystic Village Seaport**, a stop that appeals to both parents and children alike. Ever since the 17th century, Mystic has been the area's center of shipbuilding and of maritime commerce. It is now a museum village depicting life as it was in this earlier time. At the visitor center a movie is shown that introduces you to the town—an excellent way to begin your visit. Many clipper ships were built in this port in the middle of the 19th century and here you find several examples of the vessels of that era. Of the three fully rigged sailing craft moored at the docks, particularly interesting—and open for tours—is the *Charles W. Morgan*, the last of the 19th-century whaling ships surviving today. Do not miss the shops of the craftsmen who made the materials used in the construction and the sailing of these vessels. There is a **Children's Museum** where you can enjoy the activities and games played on board ship.

In the **Stillman Building**, visitors can watch a ten-minute film describing the adventure of whale hunting on the open sea.

If you have time, a drive through the **Connecticut River Valley** is most relaxing. To reach the towns along the Connecticut River, take I-95 south to Route 9 north, and exit immediately for Essex. The valley has along its banks a number of lovely Colonial seafaring towns where white clapboard homes, churches, and town greens are still very much in evidence. There are old shops and pubs, and a number of art galleries reflecting the love that so many artists have for this area. Be sure to visit **Essex** and drive the broad tree-lined main streets of **Lyme** and **Old Lyme**. In fact, a highlight in terms of sightseeing and well worth a visit is the **Florence Griswold Museum**, located in Old Lyme and considered by many to be the birthplace of American Impressionism. A prosperous ship builder, Captain Robert Griswold built what is now the museum as a home for his bride. However when the family fell on hard times after the Civil War and with the popularity of transport by steam engine competing with the sea-faring vessel, to save the home it was converted to a school and then later a boarding house. Florence Griswold was left to maintain the family home at a time when the American School of Landscape Painting was established in town. Many of the artists who came here to paint settled into the Griswold boarding house with Florence mothering them all—retrieving brushes, praising work, putting up with the crazy lifestyle of this bohemian group of painters. Evidenced by the number of paintings of which she is the subject, some of America's finest painters had a great fondness for Ms. Florence. In Old Lyme you will want to visit her home and the grounds and gardens of her home that served as inspiration for many a canvas, the Robert and Nancy Kriebel Gallery, and The William Chadwick studio. (*www.flogris.org*, tel: 860-434-5542.)

If time allows, it is also fun to note that in season, there is a steam train running from Essex to **Chester** (about an hour's trip) enabling you to enjoy the Connecticut River Valley at its best. A riverboat trip from **Deep River** to **East Haddam** either can be a separate trip or combined with the train excursion. In the town of East Haddam, during the months of April through December, the **Goodspeed Opera House** is the home of musicals being previewed for the legitimate theater and revivals of some of America's most beloved plays.

You have several options at the end of this itinerary: return to Boston going northeast on I-95 along the Connecticut and Rhode Island coasts through Providence (about two and a half hours); go north to I-91 to visit northern New England; or travel west on I-95 along the coast of lower Connecticut to Norwalk, where you can join the itinerary *Route 7 & Much More* through the western part of Connecticut, Massachusetts, and Vermont. If you are leaving New England, continue southwest along the I-95 to the airports of La Guardia and John F. Kennedy.

Sturbridge & the Connecticut Shore

Richmond
Waitsfield
Chelsea
110
113
10
4

Burlington
89
Shelburne
Warren
89

VT
Woodstock
Plainfield
NH

Bristol
100
Barnard
Windsor
Vergennes
7
73
Mendon
Bridgewater Corners
Goshen
4
Addison
Brandon
Chittenden
Ludlow
103
Chester
35
Weston
Grafton
West Townshend

NY
30 Dorset
11
Jamaica
30
10
Newfane
Chesterfield
2
202
Manchester
Mt. Equinox
5
91
Arlington
West
Greenfield
Old Bennington
Dover
Deerfield
20
Bennington
2
North Adams
MA
Northampton
Palmer
84
Williamstown
Adams
Holyoke
44
7
Jacob's
Pillow
Pittsfield
Lee
90
202
Hartford
Richmond
8
Simsbury
Lenox
Tanglewood
Stockbridge
Ashley
Great Barrington
Falls
44
10
CT
Sheffield
Norfolk
5
Canaan
63
Litchfield
Salisbury
Waterbury
Cornwall
Washington
15
1
Bridge
202
84
95
New
Milford
7
New Haven
Danbury
Stratford
Ridgefield
Westport
New
Norwalk
Canaan

Route 7 & Much More

● Orientation/Sightseeing

⟨ Itinerary Route

41

Route 7 & Much More

A trip to New England should include a drive along the western edge of the region through the states of Connecticut, Massachusetts, and Vermont. Fortunately, Route 7 follows the contours of this western edge almost exactly and is the backbone of this itinerary. The "much more" portion comes in when you cross the Green Mountains to visit the towns of Newfane, Townshend, and West Townshend. If you are interested in antiques, there is no drive with more "opportunities" waiting than this one. If what appeals to you is the charm of countryside, field, and farm; the rural character of this route will delight you. Pretty, little towns appearing around bends in the road after miles of countryside present farmhouses, stately mansions, and summer cottages—each with its own brand of charm. Plan to be in one of these towns to share the experience of Memorial Day or the Fourth of July; when the schoolchildren parade, the girl and boy scouts march, the high-school band plays, the hardware store staffs a float, and the fire engine screams its presence.

Route 7 & Much More

Recommended Pacing: (The routing for this itinerary is also outlined on Maps 1 and 3 at the front of the book.) Allow five nights to complete this itinerary, four if you do not cross over the Green Mountains but continue up Route 7. Spend the first night in the northwest corner of Connecticut in Norfolk. Then the following day, continue north across the border into Massachusetts, luxuriating in the beauty of the Berkshires. Settle for the night in Stockbridge or Lenox. Continue north to Williamstown, and then into Vermont to overnight in Manchester or Dorset. Cross over the Green Mountains and visit the towns of Newfane, Townshend, and West Townshend. Plan to spend the night in one of these towns where there is an inn that is certain to appeal to you. On day five, conclude this itinerary either by driving north and east to Woodstock, or to Shelburne with its wonderful museum.

It is important to realize that the number of miles to be driven during any one of these days is not great—to emphasize the point they are noted below (all approximate):

Norwalk to Norfolk—80 miles
Norfolk to Stockbridge—30 miles
Stockbridge to Manchester—70 miles
Manchester to Townshend—40 miles
Townshend to Woodstock—65 miles
Townshend to Shelburne—160 miles

This itinerary has no prescribed "sightseeing" or "timetable," rather, it affords the opportunity to "experience" New England. You set the specifics. You can decide to meander along at a leisurely pace—pause in front of the post office and walk through the village; look at the plaque that dates a home; go into the local drug store where, if you are lucky, there will be a row of counter stools to sit and have an ice-cream soda. Wander into the antique stores for the experience of seeing your grandmother's pitcher or the old kitchen spatula. Buy a postcard to send to a friend, a gift for a loved one, or a memento to take home.

If your trip is focused on fall foliage, there can be no better route to follow than this one, for as the leaves of the trees change from green to red, yellow, and orange, you can follow the line of frost and the magic of a countryside in vivid color.

This is New England at its best. This is not the New England where great events of history shaped the founding of the Colonies, or the New England where you walk the beach and squiggle your toes in the sand, dodging the breaking waves. This is the heart of the New England states: where farmers grew their crops, where school was in one room, where the inns usually had a pub, and where having a meal at the place you slept was customary.

Join Route 7 at its southernmost point in **Norwalk**, Connecticut. If you have just completed the itinerary that ends in the Connecticut River Valley, it will take no more than two hours to reach Norwalk and to begin the route north. If shopping in an upscale suburban community is what you feel like during the morning, go to **New Canaan** on Route 106 and visit galleries, antique stores, and other high-end shopping. New Canaan is the home of the **Silvermine Guild of Artists** with studios for studying and creating many different forms of art. Every May and June the Guild exhibits works by its members. Taking Route 106 from New Canaan back to Route 7 will put you on the path to Ridgefield, which will be the second detour—and you have hardly begun! **Ridgefield** is only an hour north of New York, but you would never know it from the rural character of this lovely town. Old trees line the streets and front the gracious homes, many of which date back to the 18th and early 19th centuries. Here you will find the **Aldrich Museum of Contemporary Art**, where changing exhibits display the work of today's contemporary artists.

Back on Route 7, proceed north through Danbury and above New Milford take Route 202 to **Litchfield**. With its village green and surrounding homes dating back to the 18th century, there is no prettier town in all of Connecticut. The **Litchfield First Congregational Church** is an architectural treasure, and if you are traveling here in the autumn, the church framed by the seasonal color of the trees will be one of your most memorable photographs.

If you especially like impressionist art, you might want to consider a detour east from Litchfield to visit a wonderful, private art collection that includes Edgar Degas, Édouard Manet, Claude Monet and James Whistler. **The Hillstead Museum**, once a private home and a wonderful example of Colonial Revival architecture, offers a tour that includes a guided visit of 19 intact period rooms filled with art and antiques. Located in the village of Farmington, to reach the Hillstead Museum, travel east from Litchfield on Route 118 which merges with Route 4. (*Closed Mondays and holidays, www.hillstead.org, tel: 860-677-4787.*)

Return north on Route 63 to South Canaan and Canaan, then drive west on Route 44 to **Salisbury**, yet another charmer.

Cross into Massachusetts and in the towns of **Ashley Falls**, **Sheffield**, and **Great Barrington**, you find a bounty of antique shops. Referring to a local guide, available in most of these shops in the Route 7 area, will enable you to concentrate on those stores most likely to have the treasure missing from your collection. If you are not an antique

The Berkshires

lover, enjoy the towns—stop and wander about, have coffee or a bite to eat at one of the local eateries, and just absorb the charm. Ashley Falls is tiny, Sheffield is mid-size, and Great Barrington tends to be the "papa bear" of these three towns and the convenient center with a hardware store and larger supermarkets.

Just 7 miles north of Great Barrington is **Stockbridge**, that grand old dame of the Berkshires. Whether you stay here or in one of the surrounding towns matters not, for there is much to do in this area. The village of Stockbridge, with its broad Main Street, lovely old trees, and one beautiful old home after another, is worth a full day. At the top of the list is a visit to the **Norman Rockwell Museum**, which houses the largest collection of the work of this famous American artist. Many pieces were used on the covers of the *Saturday Evening Post* and his depictions of everyday life ring true and close to home with any viewer. Smiles are difficult to repress! In a totally different vein is **Chesterwood**, the estate of Daniel Chester French, the creator of the monument to the Minutemen in Concord, Massachusetts and, more importantly, the sculpture of Abraham Lincoln in Washington, D.C. If you want to enjoy the music of the Boston Symphony Orchestra at the **Tanglewood Music Festival**, held each summer since the 1930s, then you need to make plans to extend your stay. There are several halls in which these musical events take place, but there is nothing like sitting on the lawn with a picnic supper and a bottle of wine for a relaxing summer evening enjoying beautiful music. This is an experience not to be missed. Also in this area are the **Jacob's Pillow Dance Festival**, the **South Mountain Concert Festival**, and summer theater at the **Berkshire Playhouse** in Stockbridge. The **Williamstown Theater** is a little more than 30 miles to the north, also on Route 7.

Head north toward the border of Massachusetts and Vermont. Along the way plan to visit the **Hancock Shaker Village**, located outside of **Pittsfield**, and then (one of my all-time favorites) the **Sterling and Francine Clark Institute** in **Williamstown**. This treasure, built by its donors in a town far away from urban centers that at the time might be threatened by war, has collections ranging from the Renaissance to the great American painters of the 19th and 20th centuries. There are also displays of furniture and porcelain, and (my particular favorite) a wonderful collection of English and American silver. Do find the time for this visit as it is an extraordinary one—a major museum in a spectacular countryside setting.

Leaving Williamstown, cross into Vermont and continue on to **Old Bennington**, a charming village dating back to the 18th century and steeped in Colonial history, which lies 9 miles to the west of the commercial town of **Bennington** on Route 9. Allow time for the walking tour (maps available at the Chamber of Commerce) including the **Old First Church**, the **Bennington Battle Monument**, and the **Grandma Moses Schoolhouse**, where you can see several paintings of the well-known artist who started painting at the age of 70 and continued painting until she was 101.

As a fan of folk art, I find that the primitive-style paintings of Grandma Moses with their naïve renderings of farm and country life (particularly those in winter) to be extraordinarily charming.

Continuing north on Route 7 brings you into the town of **Arlington**. If traveling between May and November consider stopping at the **Norman Rockwell Exhibit** located on Route 7-A. A display of his artistry, particularly the work he completed while he lived here from 1939 to 1953 is on display in the former 19th century church. Of special, sentimental interest, local townspeople who posed as models for the numerous Saturday

Evening Post Covers work the exhibit and orchestrate a reunion each May. (*Tel: 802-375-6423.*)

At this point, from Arlington, take Route 7A towards Manchester, detouring for a short side trip along the scenic Equinox Skyline Drive, a 5½-mile drive to the top of **Mount Equinox**, the highest point in the Taconic Range. Views from the summit are especially wonderful in the fall when the foliage is at its best. **Manchester** and **Manchester Center** have lovely old homes sitting along their main streets. One of these beautiful estates, **Hildene**, was built by Mary and Abraham Lincoln's only son to make it to maturity. He fell in love with the area and at the turn of the 20th century, purchased 500 acres and built what he termed his ancestral home. It is possible to tour the home and gardens. Also, an exhibition of our 16th president's personal artifacts is now on display here and referred to as *The Personal Abraham Lincoln.*

In Manchester Center, there is now a grand array of brand-name outlet shops. From Manchester Center, follow Route 30 for 8 miles into **Dorset**, a small village with lovely, white clapboard homes, church, and village green (a favorite of mine). Whether you are visiting in winter with the town dressed in white, in summer with the fragrance of freshly mown grass in the air and the Dorset Playhouse presenting summer theater, or in fall when frost coats the pumpkins and turns the leaves into magical colors, you are in for a special treat when you visit Dorset.

Leaving Dorset, you pass through more of the same bucolic countryside—farms and fields, rolling hills and valleys, rushing streams, sturdy stone walls, and towering trees—a photographer's paradise at any time of the year. Take Route 11 to Londonderry and turn south on Route 100 to **Jamaica**, **West Townshend**, **Townshend**, and on to **Newfane**. Retrace your steps back to Townshend and head north to **Grafton**, **Chester**, and **Ludlow**. This winding and relatively narrow route will enhance your appreciation of the special, unique qualities of Vermont villages. The **Green Mountains** are home to some of New England's oldest and most famous ski areas—many a youngster has learned ski technique here. Each mountain has its own distinctive style of skiing and skiers often will have their favorite. Studying the individual ski area descriptions of elevation, number of trails, degree of difficulty, and overall size should make a decision easier as to which to visit. As always, the mid-week package lift ticket is the most economical way to enjoy skiing on any mountain. Do not count these areas out at other times of the year—many of them run their ski lifts for visitors in the fall when the foliage can be enjoyed from a unique perspective on high.

From Ludlow, you can easily conclude this itinerary in **Woodstock** by driving north on Route 100 to West Bridgewater then turning east on Route 4. Ever since the 18th century Woodstock has been a magnet for merchants, professionals, and those who wish to live in a sophisticated community. The homes, of many architectural styles, are a legacy of those prosperous citizens. Today this village is not only the commercial center for this area of Vermont, but also provides upscale shopping in its many stores and galleries.

If you are staying with this itinerary, turn west from Ludlow to Route 7 following it north towards **Burlington** on Lake Champlain and detouring along the way to visit **Mendon**, **Chittenden**, and **Goshen** before arriving in **Shelburne**. Be sure to visit the **Shelburne Museum** with its incredible collection of folk art and displays of the crafts, furnishings, art, and tools used in the early years of the 20th century. The complex consists of 37 buildings on a 45-acre setting that is open from late May to late October. A visit to this museum is all but a must, if you can add this extra day to your itinerary. There is the Circus Parade Building, the Shelburne Railroad Station, the *Ticonderoga* (a side-wheeler steamship), the Stencil House displaying decorative wall stenciling, the Colchester Reef Lighthouse with its collection of marine art, the Stagecoach Inn, and the Electra Havemeyer Webb Memorial Building with a re-creation of rooms from the Webbs' Park Avenue apartment. With this small sampling of the contents of the Shelburne Museum, you can see that it would be easy to spend more than one day exploring even a portion of what is here for your enjoyment. You can overnight either in the Shelburne area or nearby **Warren** or **Waitsfield**.

This itinerary ends here, but if your travel time permits, consider continuing to the east and spending time in New Hampshire.

Marblehead Harbor, Maine

Waterville

ME

Bethel

Waterford

Augusta

Farmingdale

Bucksport   Hancock

Seasport   Blue Hill   Hancock Point

Belfast   Bar Harbor

Deer Isle   Northeast Harbor

Sunset   Penobscot   Southwest Mt.

Camden   Bay   Harbor   Desert
Island

Waldoboro

Damariscotta

Wiscasset   Newcastle

Rockland

Thomaston

Acadia NP

Durham

Bridgton

Fryeburg

Lewiston

Brunswick

Freeport

Bath

Port Clyde

New Harbor

Boothbay
Harbor

Monhegan
Island

Portland

NH

Sanford

Rochester

Durham

Exeter

Goose Rocks

Cape Porpoise

Kennebunkport

Kennebunk Beach

Wells

Ogunquit

York

Portsmouth

Hampton

Salisbury

Newbury Port

Rowley

Ipswich

Rockport

Essex

Gloucester

Salem

Marblehead

Cambridge

Boston

Weymouth

MA

Marshfield Hills

Massachusetts
Bay

ATLANTIC
OCEAN

Byways of
Coastal Maine

● Orientation/Sightseeing

⌇ Itinerary Route

- - Ferry Route

51

The Byways of Coastal Maine

There are many wonderful itineraries in New England and none is more different than the trip up the coast of Maine with its rugged beauty and picturesque charm. In the lower portions of the coast, the seaside villages are all relatively near the road, while above Portland the geology of the ice age created long fingers into the sea as the ice retreated, and you have to travel miles down winding backcountry roads to reach the tips of some peninsulas. What makes this itinerary so special is the fact that your pace is, by necessity, very leisurely since the roads wind from one lovely town or harbor to the next. You could not drive fast if you wanted to—and, believe me, you will not want to. For those who want to venture off the coast, north to the Moosehead Lake Region, a special detour is suggested that will allow you to experience the untouched beauty, and wilderness of the Maine Highlands—and hopefully afford sightings of Maine's mascot, the Moose.

Recommended Pacing: (The routing for this itinerary is also outlined on Map 4, as well as briefly referred to on Maps 2 and 3—all at the front of the book.) There is no perfect way to follow this itinerary. Where you spend your time will be dictated by your personal interests. Allow a minimum of six nights—five, if you do not visit Salem and Marblehead. If you choose to visit Salem and Marblehead, spend your first night here. Day two takes you to Rockport and Gloucester and the small villages in the northeastern part of Massachusetts. After which you enter New Hampshire and quickly cross over the Merrimack River into Maine, where you stay overnight in the area of York or Kennebunkport. Continue north through Portland and Bath to the lovely village of Wiscasset and spend the night there. The following day, your drive takes you through Rockland to Camden, a favorite spot on the Maine coast and one of the most charming towns in which to spend the night. Conclude your itinerary in Bar Harbor with a two-night stay, allowing time to explore the Acadia National Park. If exploring some of the Nation's last untouched wilderness appeals, and seeing Moose peaks your interest, consider continuing your journey north and inland to the Moosehead Lake Region as detailed at the end of this itinerary. You will want to add a minimum of two additional nights based in Greenville in order to discover the beauty of the region; take advantage of this sportsman's paradise: cross-country skiing, hiking, fishing, whitewater rafting, canoeing, kayaking and of course, scouting for Moose.

Magnificent, old trees sit beside the roads with their branches hanging over the passing vehicles; houses are white and old barns have mellowed with the weather to soft browns and grays; and, everywhere, there are views down saltwater inlets, views that change with the rise and fall of the ocean tides. These wonderful trees open their bright, green leaves later in the spring than in the more southerly parts of New England, as winter and its snowy ground cover continues its hold in this northern territory. It has said that to plant before the last full moon in May (generally around Memorial Day weekend) is foolish indeed, as there is always that one last frost which will nip your early gardening enthusiasm.

Fall foliage along the coast of Maine is often interspersed with the Maine pines, which tend, in the more southerly areas of the State, to predominate. It is only when one reaches north of Portland that the traveler gets the best of both, the craggy coast with its tiny inlets and sparkling blue waters, and the rippling colors of trees as they begin to turn into brilliant, autumn colors.

As you travel on the back roads and byways of Maine, be sure to stop at the farm stands which open in the late spring with strawberries, garden peas, and sweet peas, and continue into the bounty of summer produce, and then in the fall with the arrival of pumpkins, Indian corn, and interestingly shaped gourds.

However, before you reach this magical coast of Maine, you must take the time to visit Salem and Marblehead, where history buffs will find much to enjoy while walking the streets and learning about the lives of the citizens who lived in these communities over two centuries ago. Rockport and Gloucester offer visitors the opportunity to see the arts, antiques, and scenic harbors that make this part of Cape Ann so charming. Leave Boston on I-93 north, turning onto the circumferential Route 128 and I-95. Shortly after you have turned east on I-95 and are headed towards the north shore of Massachusetts, you find signs that will take you, via Route 114, towards Salem and Marblehead.

Salem, famous in the late 17th century for witchcraft hysteria, is well known now as the home of the **Peabody Essex Museum**, a superlative museum where you can easily spend several hours viewing the exhibits on the maritime history of the Massachusetts Bay Colony. The focus is on objects collected by the ship captains of Salem on their voyages delivering the colony's goods to the capitals of Europe and Asia. Of particular note is the Asian export art collection (decorative art made in Asia for export to the West), considered to be the most complete of any in the world, featuring 17th- through 19th-century decorative and utilitarian objects used in homes and businesses. There is also a great collection of maritime art, as well as a focus on Asian, Oceanic, and African art, and Native American arts and archaeology. The **Witch Museum** offers exhibits and a sound and light show with vignettes of the witch trials of 1692. **Chestnut Street** is lined with mansions built by ship captains that reflect the wealth of that era and the shipping trade. Salem is also famous as the home of the **House of Seven Gables**, where tours bring to life the scenes from Hawthorne's famous novel of the same name. **Pioneer Village** (open from May through October) is a re-creation of buildings that existed in the early days of the settlement of Salem. There are houses with thatched roofs, dugouts, and a wigwam. Interpreters dressed in costume explain the daily life of Salem's early settlers.

A visit to the North Shore would not be complete without a drive to **Marblehead**, and a walk in the historic district dating back to the 17th and 18th centuries when Marblehead's harbor was, as it is today, a hive of activity. In fact, Marblehead is known as the sailing capital of New England. On summer weekends, you can see sailing yachts of every size and description racing and cruising in the waters of the harbor and nearby ocean from many vantage points.

If you have spent the night in the Salem and Marblehead area, you will now be facing the choice of a second day on the North Shore or moving onward into Maine. I recommend that you drive to **Gloucester** to visit **Beauport**, the **Cape Ann Historical Museum**, and, if time permits, the **Hammond Castle Museum**. My favorite of these three is Beauport, the 40-room home designed and decorated by Henry Davis Sleeper. Beauport is open from May to September and guided one-hour tours are available. If decor is of interest to you, this visit would be one you will never forget. This is one of the many fine houses that are owned by the **SPNEA** (Society for the Preservation of New England Antiquities) and a tour of several of these properties throughout New England would be well worth an itinerary all of its own. For details contact SPNEA at 617-227-3956, or visit their website at *www.spnea.com.*

After you leave Gloucester, take Route 127A to **Rockport**. This part of **Cape Ann** is the site of an artists' colony and its galleries. Surrounding shops are very busy during the summer months with visitors enjoying the scenery of the old fishing village and harbor. In the harbor, one scene of an old fishing building and wharf has become so famous that it is known as "Motif # 1" to artists around the world.

Leaving the Cape Ann peninsula on Route 133, you drive through the town of **Essex**, famous for its several antique shops, where you may find some treasure to take home. If traveling on a Wednesday or Thursday between May and September, you would be well rewarded to detour out to **The Great House** on the 2,100-acre **Crane Estate**. Presiding over rolling hills, quiet woods, open meadows, salt marshes, and miles of sandy beach and estuary islands, this 59-room mansion was built by Richard Crane and is preserved as a National Historic Landmark. (Note: the gate house of the Crane Estate has guestrooms available to travelers. See the Hotel Section for its description and more information.)

From Essex, Route 133 connects to Route 1A through the town of Rowley and onto **Newburyport** with its magnificent High Street, another town made famous by its shipping history and the homes of those associated with that very prosperous trade.

Exit the Maine Turnpike (I-95, the fast interstate highway) onto Route 1 (the road that connects one old historical town to the next) as soon as you can. The exit from the turnpike in York is a perfect place to begin this journey. In this lower part of Maine you will find yourself less than a mile from the coast, so driving in and out of the little coastal villages is quick and easy. If you can begin this itinerary in Maine with a drive through **York** and **York Harbor**, it is a nice way to start to relax and see the sights, and experience the sounds and smell of the ocean. You will also begin to see some color in the foliage of the deciduous trees in these charming villages. There are a number of **antique shops** all along Route 1. Lower Maine has several collectives (where several dealers, rather than one, display their merchandise) in the York area.

Continuing north from the Yorks brings you to **Ogunquit**, which, in the language of the American Indian tribe of the Algonquins, means "beautiful place by the sea." The long, narrow harbor is especially scenic, and while you may not see the lobster boats depart early in the morning, you can catch them returning in the afternoon with a following of inquisitive sea gulls seeking a free dinner. Because of the attractiveness of this area, many artists settled here—the subjects for their art are everywhere. The Ogunquit Playhouse offers theater performances on summer evenings.

Traffic along Route 1, as you drive north to Wells, can be especially tedious—even more so on a foggy or rainy day, when all the tourists are searching for entertainment and are visiting the concentration of outlet shops at the southern end of this route. I would suggest, if possible, avoiding this drive at the beginning or the end of the beach day, when those who have spent the day on the sand and in the ocean find their way to restaurants, grocery stores, and back to their overnight accommodations.

In the town of **Wells** there is a real concentration of antique shops offering formal and country furniture and decorative objects. Just north of Wells, Route 9 breaks off to the town of **Kennebunkport**, and I strongly recommend that you drive into "the Port," as the locals call it. This is a storybook village, but was originally a fishing port. In the fall, the ancient trees on its main streets pour forth with gorgeous colors of red, yellow, orange, and everything in-between. You can still see the lobstermen go out to sea each day to empty their traps and to bait them for the next day's catch. Kennebunkport has become a tourist Mecca, especially for its shops. To absorb the charm of this town with its lovely stately homes and elm-tree-lined streets, allow time to include a walking tour of the town center. Afterwards, find a spot to have a cup of New England clam chowder or a Maine lobster. One of the sights outside the town is the **Wedding Cake House** on Route 9A, which, as the stories go, was decorated with all manner of gingerbread trim by a sea captain who was called to sea immediately after his wedding.

Just north of Kennebunkport, taking Ocean Avenue first east and then north from the village, you come to the **summer home** of the 41st president of the United States, **George Bush**. Shortly thereafter, along Route 9, you reach **Cape Porpoise**, which exudes all the ambiance of a tiny fishing community with houses set on hills looking down on its lobster boats and other small craft. It is tiny and will take only a short time to visit, but it is charming. Make sure to take the time to drive through the village and out to the point from which you can see the lighthouse just off shore. Back on Route 9, you continue north a few miles to a barn on your left with a clock tower and a somewhat confusing sign on your right that points to the beach called **Goose Rocks**. With one tiny store, this beach is a magnificent 2-mile-long stretch of sand—a rarity on the rocky coast of Maine.

If you are able to linger here, you become immediately aware that the tides on this northeast coast rise and fall 10 feet or more with each change of tide, so the beach you walk at low tide will become much narrower as the tide comes in. If you put a toe into the water, you quickly learn that swimming on the coast of Maine takes a degree of courage!

Portland Head Lighthouse

From Goose Rocks, drive north on Route 9 to Route 1 north, and then take I-95 onward to Portland. With its population of about 65,000, the city of **Portland** is the largest town you come to as you go northward along the coast. The port is an important one for the fishing industry and the city has become the center for commercial business in northern New England. This is a city that is perfect for sightseeing on foot since all the interesting spots are within a short distance of one another. There is also an advantage to walking as the pace allows you to study the architecture and permits the occasional glimpse into a hidden garden here and there. The downtown area of Portland has been revitalized and many of the historical buildings have been rehabilitated. There are many great restaurants and lots of shopping in boutiques known for their handcrafts. Portland has a great

The Byways of Coastal Maine

historical area and is a regional center for the arts. The **Museum of Art** focuses on artists of the state of Maine, and there are wonderful paintings by Winslow Homer, Andrew Wyeth, Edward Hopper, and John Marin. For those interested in seeing more of **Casco Bay**, there are seasonal, daily trips by boat to view the islands, though it is not always possible to disembark.

From Portland, you can take a ferry to Nova Scotia; but unless your time is very limited, I suggest you continue a little farther north by car along the coast to Bar Harbor. This is well worth the time, and from there it is a much shorter sea trip to reach the maritime provinces.

About 12 miles northeast of Portland, off the I-95, is the town of **Freeport**, made famous by the **L. L. Bean store** that is open 24 hours a day. Here you can find everything from a canoe or camp stove to a ski cap. This famous institution has now expanded into selling almost anything you can use in your home. Freeport has also become home to more than 120 brand-name outlet stores of every type which have been very cleverly and appealing incorporated into the heart of the old downtown. If shopping is your thing, this is the place to "shop till you drop." Of greater interest to me is the **Desert of Maine**, a phenomenon of former forest where the winds of time have laid bare more than 500 acres of sand, now formed into sand dunes—in an area nowhere near the sea. To reach and view this phenomenon (open from early May until mid-October), take I-95 to exit 19 and then drive 2 miles west on Desert Road.

North of Freeport is the community of **Brunswick**, home of **Bowdoin College** and the **Bowdoin College Museum of Art** with its collections of early-American portraits and (annually from mid-May until mid-August) a display of the paintings, etchings, and memorabilia of the artist Winslow Homer. The particular focus of much of his work was the coast and lore of Maine, so this becomes a topical experience for those interested in the work of this very famous American artist.

Just north of Brunswick, Route 1 begins its coastal-hugging path toward Bar Harbor, still 150 miles to the north. Long fingers of land stretch out into the sea, and a trip down any of these will bring great pleasure as you meander along winding, tree-lined roads between one small fishing village and the next. The village of **Bath** has been a shipbuilding center for hundreds of years, and its harbor hosts the relics of schooners from long ago. You can see ships in dry dock being repaired, in mothballs, or in the process of being built. As you view the wide harbor, it is easy to imagine a time when commercial ships sailed from this port to the European capitals, the Far East, and to the West Indies. In Bath, a visit to the **Maine Maritime Museum**, with its exhibits on coastal life, the shipbuilding industry, and the commerce of Maine, would provide an interesting diversion for both adults and children. There is a movie on the lobster industry, as well as exhibits in a sail loft. During the summer, you can take a boat ride on the **Kennebec River** to observe the boat-building industry as it exists today.

From Bath follow the Route 1 a short distance to the intersection of Route 127 and turn south to **Georgetown** and on to **Reid State Park**. Here you will find wonderful dune beaches as well as tidepools for exploration—a great picnic spot. Continue from Reid State Park to **Five Islands** to visit a charming fishing harbor and the picturesque **Hendricks Head Lighthouse**.

Proceed north across the bridge to the town of **Wiscasset**, one of my very favorite villages in all of New England—I especially love its long street leading down to the water. There could be no prettier village in which to take in fall foliage that Wiscasset. Magically, the natural beauty of the homes along its streets are enhanced that much more when the colors of fall foliage play off the sparking white clapboard exteriors. This is a community with tree-lined streets, white churches, and lovely old homes dating back to the 18th century. It is also a terrific and popular center for antiquing, with an emphasis on country things rather than formal. In the winter, the pace is slower with the fickle weather, and some dealers open and others not.

Beyond Wiscasset, you are now in one of the most famous of all Maine regions— **Boothbay Harbor**. With a year-round population of only a couple of thousand, this is an area that can absorb the summer residents, the visitors staying the night, and those who will simply be passing through on the way north or south. This is one of the larger towns in the region and from here there are many options for boat cruises and excursions. Be sure to venture beyond the town and explore the roads that hug the water's edge. A favorite drive is to follow Scenic drive (Route 96) east and then south to **Ocean Point**. Lovely residences enjoy this exclusive real estate and from here one can easily look out to **Burnt Island Light House**. If traveling with children and for an insight into Maritime Heritage, you might consider an excursion (departures from pier 8 in Boothbay Harbor) out to Maine's ninth lighthouse. Refurbished, actors play the role of lighthouse keepers, are dressed in costume and stage an ambiance of days of old. (*Tours July and August, 10 minute boat ride, two hour tour, www.balmydayscruises.com*)

As you explore, this coastal region charm is at every bend in the road, as one scenic vista opens onto yet another and as one lovely old farmhouse with attached great barn and old faded-color siding leads to the next. Extraordinarily special are the little inlets from the sea with water shimmering so brightly that it almost blinds the eyes, wonderful green trees lining the banks. These saltwater extensions of the ocean bring the sights, sounds, and smells right up to the highway. With a dock here and there and a boat tied up, perhaps with a morning check of the lobster pots, this is a scene that will bring out your camera to capture a delightful memory. From the early spring green of new leaves signaling the end of winter, through the summer grasses and multicolored wildflowers, to the colors of fall, this is Maine at its best. Take the time to rent a bike and meander along the country roads that connect the little villages in the Boothbay area. Or at least park in a town or two, leaving your car under a red sugar maple so that you can smell the fall in the crisp air and collect a few leaves to press between the leaves of a book back home. There is no end to their shapes and colors; and by the time you have picked up a handful of chestnuts, you will be wondering how to roast them over a fire back home. To all of this, add the flavors of seafood from the neighboring waters, especially lobster served boiled or stuffed, cold or hot with melted butter, and your visit is something special. While I was visiting, not only did I have my fair share of lobster in every form, but I also enjoyed the seasonal local clams, oysters, and Maine shrimp.

If you are interested in islands and the charm they provide, you can take a boat trip from Boothbay Harbor, New Harbor, or Port Clyde to **Monhegan Island**. Lobstering is the island's principal trade. The large number of artists who spend the summer here and work in the area augments the island's population. There are miles of trails for the hiker, and spectacular views from practically every vantage point. Any photographer would find that a visit here provides more subject matter than there is film.

Working your way north again along Route 1, you will come upon **Newcastle** and, just north of it, **Damariscotta**. Both are seafaring villages with restaurants, shops, and overnight accommodations. Everything is informal here, and you find the down-east Maine resident to be as special in his accent as in his friendliness.

A detour south from Newcastle to the tip of the peninsula will reward you with yet another charming fishing town, **New Harbor** with its colorful harbor and old fort, **Fort William Henry Colonial Pemaquid**, and Maine's most photographed lighthouse at Pemaquid Point. Built in 1827 on a rocky ledge, **Pemaquid Point Lighthouse** is indeed very picturesque.

Rockland, with its almost 8,000 population, is the next town of size. It has all the hustle, bustle, and commercial activity of a modern seaport from which lobsters are shipped throughout the world. Here you find the **Farnsworth Art Museum**, which is almost a required stop because of its 19th- and 20th-century paintings by Fitzhugh Lane and a large collection of paintings by members of the Wyeth family, who traditionally summered in Maine. Their ability to capture local Maine scenery and everyday events in oil and watercolor makes a visit to this museum a rewarding experience.

Farther north on Route 1 is another of my favorite towns on the Maine coast—**Camden**, which surrounds a protected harbor full of windjammer schooners moored on summer weekends, as well as gorgeous yachts cruising the waters of **Penobscot Bay**. This is a harbor of constant activity—an artist's dream from any angle. At the head of the harbor, high on the hill, is the **Camden Library**. From its windows and terraces, there are unforgettable views of all that lies below. In the fall when the foliage turns to red and gold, this view makes for one those indelible memories of your fall foliage trip. Be sure to leave time to drive on the back streets of Camden to see the displays of color and the fall gardens with their brilliantly colored chrysanthemums, asters, and other fall flowers. **Main Street**, lined with white mansions and more New England churches, is a great place to stop for lunch if your meandering around the town has you there at that hour. Enjoy the lovely architecture of the homes around you. There are art galleries, shops, and restaurants. In summer, window boxes and flowers thrive in the day's sun and the evening's cool temperatures. It would be difficult to think of a nicer place to stay than this delightful town. There is a good, little walking guide available locally, which I urge you to follow, for it will greatly enhance your visit. Also of interest, Camden is the host harbor for many seafaring schooners on which you can take a week's or few hours' cruise along the spectacular coast, either helping with the sailing or relaxing and soaking up the sun on deck.

As you leave Camden, given an extra half hour and a beautiful day, we recommend you take a short detour that will reward you with some memorable views. Just on the northern outskirts of town watch for a left hand turn to **Mount Battie** and **Camden Hills State Park**. This road winds to the top of the hill and affords some of the most incredible views of the harbor, bay and town.

From Camden travel northward along the coast through the towns of Belfast, Searsport, and Bucksport. From Route 1 take Route 175 south, and Route 15 down to **Deer Isle**, **Sunset**, and the incredible harbor of **Stonington**, one of the most photographed harbors anywhere. An old whaling town settled long ago by the Portuguese its main street now boasts a number of quaint restaurants, galleries and shops. After visiting Stonington, take Route 175 north to the delightful village of Blue Hill—the heart of this Blue Hill peninsula. There are small restaurants, lots of antique shops, art galleries, and places that will entice you through their front doors to look for a treasure to extend the memory.

There is no way to return to the highway without taking another country road, but the Blue Hill Peninsula is wide enough to allow a different view from its eastern side. After the town of Ellsworth, you leave Route 1, taking Route 3 down into Mount Desert Island

Mount Desert Coastline

and the **Acadia National Park**. This park is an unforgettable experience and will cap your trip on the Maine coast, well worth the effort of getting there. Plan on at least one overnight in this area if you intend to spend any time in the Acadia National Park (we have inn recommendations in Bar Harbor and Northeast Harbor). The smallness and compactness of this area allows for easy visiting of all that there is to do.

Mount Desert Island is about 108 square miles in size, its beauty lying in its granite quarries, mountains, pine forests, and freshwater lakes. From high on top of any of its mountains are panoramic views over the park and the surrounding islands. There are rocky mountains with exposed granite, and charming plants that seem determined to make the most of a short-lived season. Bright and diminutive wildflowers, blueberries, and plants with colorful leaves and berries will reward your camera with yet another photo opportunity. You can tour the park by car, guided bus, bicycle, or horse and carriage. You will want to linger and stop often, so I urge you to arm yourself with informational materials available at the National Park Headquarters and head off on your own.

Be sure to find and follow **Loop Road**, the park's main attraction, as it winds its way along the coast and up to Cadillac Mountain. There are many places to park, to gaze, to photograph, and to smell, and many birds to watch in this ever-changing landscape. Be sure to get to the top of **Cadillac Mountain** for the spectacular views. (Take a windbreaker with you to protect you from the chilly breezes.) Other points of interest include **Otter Cliffs** and **Thunder Hole**—the water rushing into this narrow cavern with the changing tide sounds like thunder. If you have time, be sure to walk the **Beach Cliff Trail**, and visit **Bass Head Light** and other areas of the national park located in the **Schoodic Peninsula**. In the fall, what you will find here is not the towering maples and other deciduous trees with their brilliant foliage, but rather the beauty of small rock-hugging plants and the deep reds and russets that beacon forth from their tiny leaves. One of the most spectacular plants for fall color is the wild, Maine blueberry bushes—blushing with the brilliance of their unforgettable, red color.

A visit to the village of **Bar Harbor** is more enjoyable in the summer when you will find it alive with activity and summer residents. After Labor Day, the pace in this part of Maine slows down and the night begins to turn frosty with everything covered with dew. The smells of fall are very special and the clear crispness can almost be tasted. In the winter, many of its shops are closed. However, then the pace is slower, and there is a special, quiet charm without the crowds. In the late 19th and early 20th centuries, Bar Harbor became a fashionable alternative to Newport, Rhode Island. Summer homes are grand beyond your wildest imagination and driving around Bar Harbor and down to either **Northeast Harbor** or **Southwest Harbor** will take you back to another era.

If you are traveling to Maine to see fall foliage, you will need to plan to be traveling (normally) by late September, as fall color comes early here in this part of the Northeast.

This itinerary officially ends at Bar Harbor and from here you can consider a number of options. You can always retrace your route south, perhaps taking advantage of I-95 that efficiently covers the distance between Bangor and Boston. Because of its location, Bar Harbor would also serve as a good beginning to other journeys onward to Nova Scotia by boat. Another suggestion, by heading west from Bar Harbor, you can take an alternative route across Maine into New Hampshire and Vermont, visiting the more northern areas of the **White and Green Mountains**. Herein lay small New England towns where farming and milk production are the principal industries, and where being off the beaten track is not an inconvenience, but rather a wonderful bonus. These small New England towns truly paint a picture and provide a poetic sense of New England, and there is much joy in finding an inn with a cozy fireplace, a nice dining room, and congenial hosts. And finally, if you want to extend your journey and venture further north into the upper reaches of Maine and the Moosehead Lake Region (possibly when enroute to Quebec), consider the following suggested extension to this itinerary.

The Byways of Coastal Maine

The **Moosehead Lake Region** is just one district of the Maine Highlands and its natural beauty, many rivers, lakes and mountains make it an outdoorsman's paradise and provide the traveler with unique experiences. At the heart of the region is a lake of the same name, whose outline when viewed on a map, remarkably does indeed look like a moose head with those distinctive antlers! Maine's largest lake, Moosehead Lake is forty miles long and 420 miles around and has an intricate shoreline that weaves in and out to afford some spectacular bays, coves, beaches and even embraces a few islands. At the southern tip of the lake is **Greenville**—the closest to a metropolis for miles around! In fact approximately 20 miles north of Greenville when traveling north on either side of the lake, roads are gated and there is restricted access into the wilderness area. There is actually talk of converting and preserving this magnificent region of northern Maine into one of the nation's largest national parks.

There is no doubt that a visit, and a stay in the Moosehead Lake Region with Greenville as a base would provide the traveler with unique experiences. From here you can venture forth to explore the region. Where else can you stay in one locale and go dog sledding, ice fishing, whitewater rafting, snowmobiling, cross-country or downhill skiing, canoeing, kayaking, participate in a moose safari, and have a guide instruct you in the fine art of fly fishing? Seaplanes are a popular mode of transportation in these northern parts, but if you are driving in the back woods on unpaved roads, a four-wheel-drive vehicle is good insurance that you will arrive at your destination.

We were intrigued by the notion of moose sightings and happened to be traveling at the prime time—late spring, early summer. Moose are famous for making unexpected, cameo appearances and if you are lucky, you just might see one with or without the aid of binoculars. Moose are definitely prevalent as is evidenced by the over 1,000 accidents and fatalities attributed last year to cars colliding with moose... so be careful! Part of the blame falls on the moose whose vision is limited to about 25 feet. Also, in the Moosehead Lake Region, moose outnumber people (tourists!) by 3 to 1. Nevertheless, if you are determined as we were, there are a few key guidelines to enhance your chances of a sighting.

With the exception of the lighthouse, there is no other image more symbolic of Maine than the moose. The fact that it is the state animal and appears as on the state seal is proof that the local residents are also enamored by this adorable, gangly creature. A large male may measure as long as 10 feet, stand 7 feet tall and weigh three-quarters of a ton. Cute and big, they are the largest antlered animal in North America and the largest member of the deer family in the world.

Observing moose in their natural habitat is exciting. Luckily for the moose-seeking traveler, the best times for sightings are also the best times for visiting Maine—late spring/early summer and in the fall. In the springtime, craving sodium that has been depleted from their bodies after the long winter, moose are attracted to the roadsides where salt remains from winter spreading; and with a weakness for tender, sodium-rich aquatic plants they are often seen at a pond or body of water. In late September and early October moose are on the prowl because it is mating season and because the bulls can also be very aggressive in their pursuit and mistake anything moving for an alluring cow a good zoom lens might be the preferred and conservative means of a "close up" viewing.

In general, Moose are nocturnal animals and the best times to sight them are early mornings or at dusk. You can venture forth to inlets and wooded areas by private car. In pursuit of moose it is possible to go off-road on many of the logging roads, but be alert for logging trucks, who like moose are bigger than you are! It is also possible to hire a guide and explore by canoe, kayak or seaplane. Regardless of the means of pursuit, remember to be careful. Although, moose are not considered dangerous, they are massive and you do not want to startle them. It is important to note that cows are very protective of their young and bulls are very aggressive in the mating season.

As a recommendation for the best areas considered for sightings are to simply explore the main roads and back roads around Moosehead Lake. From Greenville take Route 6 and then 15 to Route 201 in **Jackman** and follow it to Sandy Bay township at the Canadian border. Or, travel Lily Bay Road from Greenville, traveling northeast, for approximately 20 miles and watch for moose at any point along the way. If you have gotten to **Kokadjo** and still have not seen any or enough, head to lazy **Tom Bog** just past Kokadjo—this bog is very popular with local moose! If you want to make a day of moose watching, drive to Rockwood, a town north of Greenville, from which you can then venture to **Mount Kineo** for some hiking, exploring and moose watching.

As a final note, moose definitely prefer shady, wet areas and so definitely focus your search around beaver flowages, marshes and swampy areas; logging areas where there is young growth as well as broccoli fields. Get a good map; pack binoculars and a picnic and hopefully, along with some patience, you will be well rewarded. However, even if you are not fortunate to see a moose, in the pursuit it is guaranteed that you will see and experience some absolutely gorgeous wilderness. Although, centuries have passed since this region was settled by the Penobscot tribes and this was where early European settlers first landed in the mid-1700s it remains rugged, untouched and wild.

From Greenville your options are to continue your journey north to the Canadian border, travel east to New Hampshire or return south to the Maine Coast and on to Massachusetts. When here you will feel isolated from any sense of civilization, so it is very interesting/comforting to note that in terms of distance and time you are just 1½ hours' drive from Bangor, 2½ hours from Portland and 4½ hours from Boston.

If returning south, consider extending your journey just a bit further north on the 15/6, traveling the east side of Moosehead Lake and at The Birches follow the 15/6 west to Jackman Station. Regarded as one of Maine's scenic highways, from Jackman travel Interstate 201 south in the direction of Waterville and the junction of the Maine Turnpike, I-95. This loop first north and then south from Greenville has also been recommended as one of Maine's most beautiful routes during the spectacular fall foliage.

The Byways of Coastal Maine

New Hampshire Beckons

New England is special at any time of the year, but there is simply nowhere on earth where you can experience nature's changing colors as you can here. When the days become shorter, the nights turn cool, the first frost coats the lawn, and the roof shingles sparkle with their early-morning ice, New England prepares for the magic season of fall foliage. Trees, shrubs, flowers and weeds all begin the transformation that changes their color from green to multiple hues of red, orange, and gold—and a million shades in between. It is simply a time of magic! It is also the time when nature performs a brilliant display reminiscent of fireworks on the fourth of July. It is a time to be in New England. This itinerary weaves a journey through the backroads of New Hampshire to experience the splendor and glory of New England's fall foliage.

Recommended Pacing: (The routing for this itinerary is also outlined on Map 3 and partially on Map 4, at the front of the book.) Two nights will enable you to cover the entire itinerary *at a leisurely pace* unless you decide to make this itinerary the center of your trip into this part of New England. The focus of this itinerary is the road trip north into Conway and North Conway—the heart of the Green Mountains. It provides the opportunity to explore several different spurs, then return to the main route of the itinerary. Deciding which of the spurs to pursue is analogous to having to choose one of your children, so let our descriptions guide you to the different alternatives. No matter which one(s) you choose, you will have a wonderful time. Let your day be open to new experiences and vistas and you will be many times rewarded. Plan to use Boston or the Boston area as your point of departure going north on Route 95 through the northern part of Massachusetts into New Hampshire, where you will pick up Route 4 in Portsmouth, and then Route 16 north on the Spaulding Turnpike toward Rochester, and finally, north into the heart of New Hampshire.

To the west of Route 16 lies the grand Lake Winnipesaukee, at the southern portion of which is the town of Wolfeboro, the center of much boating activity on the lake, and the summer home for many who live in the cities of New England. This is a very popular area for vacationers, as there is nothing more idyllic than a week or two at the edge of a lake, swimming off the dock, fishing with your kids, or going out in a boat to explore the lakes' many coves and tributaries.

If you have resisted the temptation to go to Lake Winnepasaukee, just continue along Route 16 on the very scenic route leading into **Conway** and **North Conway.** Whether you are traveling to enjoy the wintertime activities of the ski country of New Hampshire; the beauty of the unfolding spring with the flowering daffodils; the bounty of summer with the town fairs, the markets, summer theater, antiquing, or the fabulous colors of Fall—you are the beneficiary of the many attributes that typify New England. In these mountain towns, you will find a ski area or two that will be running chair lifts during the fall season. This is a glorious way to rise above the trees and to gaze down, at first to the areas below you, and then from the top of the mountain to the vistas of the surrounding countryside. In many instances, these vistas include a blue lake lying below a swath of color, as if an artist were painting a brightly lit canvas.

The Conways, Conway and North Conway, and just to the north of them, the town of Jackson, are ideal locations for you to find a place to stay a night or two, and from which to take day trips into the surrounding countryside. From the Conways, there are three routes, resembling fingers, heading into the western portion of northern New Hampshire. An excellent daytrip takes the northern finger out of North Conway, returning in the evening via the middle finger. This northernmost finger follows Route 16 to **Jackson** and **Gorham**. Turn west at Gorham to connect with Route 2 to **Lancaster**, at which point pick up Route 116 south to **Littleton** and then east through **Bethlehem.** Follow Route 302 through **Twin Mountain**, **Bretton Woods**, **Crawford Notch**, **Hart's Location**, and **Bartlett** to **Glen**. Here you pick up Route 16 south, which returns you to North Conway.

An alternative to this more northern spur is to leave Conway via the "lower finger," turning west just south of town on Route 112, known as the **Kancamagus Highway**. This road rises through the **White Mountains** and is simply beautiful. It twists and winds, rises and falls, making every beautiful, scenic mile one to remember. The road ends in **North Woodstock** and from this point you head north via the I-93 to **Franconia**, **Bethlehem**, **Lower Waterford**, and **St. Johnsbury**, where you can leave the itinerary to travel south into Massachusetts on I-91, or continue on Route 2 to **Montpelier**, the capital of Vermont. The recently remodeled state capital building is wonderful to tour.

This is the end of this itinerary, but certainly not the end of things to do in this area. If your plans call for a return to the Boston area, you can use one of the previous routes to reach Route 93, which will speedily bring you back south to either Route 2 or further south to Route 90, the Massachusetts Turnpike, and into Boston itself.

New Hampshire Beckons

Connecticut
Places to Stay

The unspoiled Connecticut River Valley, with its delightful, historic river towns founded in the 17th century, is one of the most scenic areas in the state. None of these towns is more charming than Essex, and there is no more enchanting place to stay there than The Griswold Inn, known for its historic dining rooms with their collections of marine art, cozy atmosphere, and fine seasonal cuisine and drinks. A stunning wine bar features small plate menus, with over 50 wines by the glass and an extensive bottle list. Lively music, ranging from dixieland, banjo and swing music to sea shanties, is featured nightly in the handsome, award-winning Tap Room. A hostelry since it opened in 1776, it also offers appealing accommodations—the owners have created in the guestrooms a level of charm and comfort that, like the dining rooms, makes for instant relaxation. The air-conditioned, pine-floored rooms and suites are located in five buildings on both sides of the street. I stayed in a long, narrow suite above two shops with a great window seat looking out into the courtyard. The first floors of these separate buildings house little gift shops where you can find that perfect gift to take home. Essex's attractions include the Connecticut River Museum, a steam train and riverboat ride, or taking a stroll along the quaint old riverfront. *Directions:* From I-91: exit at 22 south, follow Rte 9 south to exit 3 for Essex and the inn. From I-95: exit at 69, follow Rte 9 north to exit 3.

❄ ☕ 🏊 💳 ☎ @ P ⏐⏐ 🎿 ⚓ 🚶 👫 🍷

THE GRISWOLD INN
Innkeepers: Joan & Doug Paul
36 Main Street
Essex, CT 06426, USA
Tel: (860) 767-1776, Fax: (860) 767-0481
31 Rooms, Double: $132–$300
Restaurant: closed Christmas
Open: all year, Credit cards: all major
Select Registry

Only a few inns anywhere in the world can begin to approach the level of accommodation and service offered by the Homestead Inn. Proprietors Thomas Henkelmann, a world-class, European-trained chef, and his wife Theresa, a truly talented designer, present the best of tradition and contemporary style. From the moment the valet opens your door, to the welcoming greeting you receive as you enter the small and charming lobby, the magical experience of your visit to the Homestead begins. The bedrooms have been ingeniously designed in the best of traditional decor with touches of spirit and whimsy that can only make you laugh and the colors used are bold and bright. Be prepared for interesting lamps, wall sconces, and artwork carefully selected to be part of the integrated scheme; be prepared for bathrooms with heated tile floors, for brilliantly colored wall tile, for interesting accessories, and for top-of-the-line amenities. The restaurant, Thomas Henkelmann, softly lit with candles and its tables set with silver and fine china, provides cuisine of extraordinary caliber. There's nothing here that has been left to chance —absolutely every detail has been well thought out. This is a real winner: one of those treasures that must be experienced. *Directions:* From I-95, take exit 3, go left at the end of the ramp to the second light, and turn left onto Horseneck Lane. At the light turn left onto Field Point Road. The inn and restaurant are on the right.

❄ ✗ 💳 ☎ @ W P ⅋ 🚭 ⚤ ♿ ⚓ ⅋

HOMESTEAD INN–THOMAS HENKELMANN
Innkeepers: Thomas & Theresa Henkelmann
420 Field Point Road
Greenwich, CT 06830, USA
Tel: (203) 869-7500, Fax: (203) 869-7502
11 Rooms, Double: $250–$395*
7 Suites: $495*
*Breakfast not included: $16–$22
*Service: 20%
Closed: 2 weeks in Mar, Credit cards: all major
Relais & Châteaux

Originally constructed in the 1880s as the home of an ivory comb and keyboard manufacturer. The inn has lovely gardens and a fountain within a native woodland in Ivoryton, one of three villages that make up the town of Essex. The magnificent Copper Beech tree in front of the inn gives it its name. In the main house are four beautifully restored guestrooms, each air-conditioned, two with fireplaces; and in the renovated Carriage House there are nine rooms with whirlpool baths, TVs, and lovely decks. I especially loved the feeling of these Carriage House rooms with their soaring ceilings and exposed original beams. Bathrooms have been remodeled with extensive use of marble, heated floors and European accessories. The bedrooms are beautifully appointed and with their large size are particularly gracious with sitting areas and writing desks. The decor in this inn may be traditional but the guest has all the amenities that guarantee a restful stay and a return visit. The inn's award-winning restaurant features sophisticated French food served at tables set with linens, fresh flowers, and sparkling silver. It's warm and inviting. *Directions:* From New Haven, drive east on I-95 to exit 69, travel north on Route 9 to exit 3, then west for 1¾ miles to the inn.

❄ 🍺 🛝 💳 ☎ 🐾 @ P 🍴 🖼 🐕 🛌 🏌 🚶 ⛷

COPPER BEECH INN
Innkeepers: Barbara & Ian Phillips
46 Main Street
Ivoryton (Essex), CT 06442, USA
Tel: (860) 767-0330, Fax: (860) 767-7840
Toll Free: (888) 809-2056
13 Rooms, Double: $165–$375
Restaurant: open Tue thru Sun
Open: all year, Credit cards: all major
Select Registry

The Stonecroft Country Inn is located on a winding country road adjoining a nature preserve and provides the visitor with a true escape from the pace of busy times. The inn has ten bedrooms, some in the historic 19th-century house and the rest in The Grange, which houses the inn's restaurant. Fireplaces abound and there are whirlpool tubs for your enjoyment. There's a wonderful blend of luxury and simplicity, where everything that the guest could want is anticipated and always right at hand. Rooms in the main house bear their historical heritage, and they do it well. They are comfortable and attractive, with French country fabrics and warm, cozy charm. Every amenity is available. In the newer building there are four rooms on the first floor and two suites on the second; these are extra spacious, with cathedral ceilings and over-sized bathrooms. When you add a first-class restaurant with a European-trained chef, this inn makes for a great getaway retreat. The restaurant is particularly charming in its décor and its views, and tables are nicely set apart from one another. It is just a few minutes to drive to the nearby attractions, but the inn is so inviting that you might just stay put and enjoy the peacefulness of that which surrounds you. The restaurant is open by reservation only so be sure to call if you plan to dine there. *Directions:* Take I-95 to exit 89 and then turn left if coming from the south or right if coming from the north for 3¾ miles to the inn.

STONECROFT COUNTRY INN
Innkeeper: Cathi Clayton
515 Pumpkin Hill Road
Ledyard, CT 06339, USA
Tel: (860) 572-0771, Fax: (860) 572-9161
Toll Free: (800) 772-0774
10 Rooms, Double: $150–$300
Restaurant: closed Mon, by reservation only
Open: all year, Credit cards: all major
Select Registry

The Steamboat Inn is an exceptional little hotel with an idyllic location right on the water with glorious views of the river. The entry, at the back, is small but handsome in a nautical theme of teaks, with an oar taking up the length of a side brochure display and a gorgeous, large stained glass of a colorful steamboat hanging above the reception desk. The five first-floor bedrooms, (all but one with river views, four with kitchenettes), have spacious bathrooms and double Jacuzzi tubs. Upstairs, six slightly smaller guestrooms enjoy wood-burning fireplaces and Jacuzzi tubs. All the rooms are sentimentally named for famous Mystic ships from the schooner days. We were able to see two bedrooms, both on the second floor: Mystic, which is very handsome with a mahogany four-poster queen bed, fabrics in blue, off white and red with a comfortable sitting area facing the fireplace. The Marie Gilbert is a very pretty room in rich blues and creams with a white-painted four-poster bed angled to maximize the view out of one long wall of windows, sofa, light-pine table, and lovely fireplace. Also on the second floor is an attractive common room where guests can help themselves to tea and coffee and where they enjoy evening sherry. A deluxe Continental breakfast of fresh juice, fruits, baked goods, cheese and hard-boiled eggs is served each morning. *Directions:* On the west side of the drawbridge overlooking the river and wharf.

❄ ☕ ✍ 💳 ☎ @ W ⅄ P 🏃 👫 🌊 🍷

STEAMBOAT INN
Innkeeper: Kathryn R. Abel
73 Steamboat Wharf
Mystic, CT 06355, USA
Tel: (860) 536-8300, Fax: (860) 536-9528
11 Rooms, Double: $125–$300
Minimum Stay Required: weekends
Open: all year, Credit cards: all major

On the eastern approach to Mystic, just before the famous bascule bridge over the scenic Mystic River, sits a lovely, historic hotel that affords reasonably priced accommodation, a warm welcome, and comfortable rooms in five separate buildings. The location is ideal for walking to just about everything. The reception is housed in the oldest building where guestrooms are found on three levels overlooking Main Street or back courtyard parking. The attention to decor and comfort is impressive in these nicely sized rooms, which enjoy reproduction period beds, writing desks, inviting armchairs, and armoires concealing TVs. Our bathroom was simple but prettily wallpapered. Rooms are also found in the historic 1865 House next door, also fronting the main street. Behind it in two wings of rooms built about 20 years ago, the Stonington and Noank Houses, which, in addition to standard double rooms, also have guestrooms that can accommodate two double beds—perfect for families. A replica of an existing building, The Hoxie House houses rooms with water views, fireplaces and oversize bathrooms with whirlpool tubs. A Continental breakfast is set out in the hospitality room or guests are welcome to take it back to their rooms. A restaurant is conveniently located in the main building. *Directions:* From I-95 take exit 90 or exit 89 to Route 1 into downtown Mystic. The inn is located one block east of the drawbridge.

❄ 🍵 🧺 💳 ☎ @ W P ⅼ ⅼ ♿ ⚓ 🧍 👫 🏇 💃

WHALER'S INN
Owners: Paul Connor, Bill Griffin & John McGee
Innkeeper: Richard Prisby
20 East Main Street
Mystic, CT 06355, USA
Tel: (860) 536-1506, Fax: (860) 572-1250
Toll Free: (800) 243-2588
40 Rooms, Double: $109–$199
8 Suites: $169–$269
Open: all year, Credit cards: all major

Not far from the Mystic Seaport is a small inn with eight guestrooms in two buildings: one a former bookstore where the keeping room, with its original fireplace and lovely old paneling, dates back to 1784, and behind this a carriage house built in 1988. This is a simply furnished inn where each guestroom has a queen bed (five have canopies), antique quilts, its own sitting area, and a private bathroom (one is across the hall from the bedroom). Three rooms have wood-burning fireplaces, two have whirlpool tubs, three have gas fireplaces, and several have stenciling on the walls. Since this was once the Old Mystic Bookstore, each of the rooms is sentimentally named after a New England author and contains the works of that author as well as a synopsis of the author's life, which the innkeeper has thoughtfully provided. Michael Cardillo was trained at the Culinary Institute of America and breakfasts are his special creation and a time to show off his talent in the pleasant breakfast room with its fireplace and bay window. In addition to the Seaport, nearby are the Aquarium, the USS Nautilus Submarine Museum, and the casinos, and an hour away lies Newport, Rhode Island with its famous mansions. Mystic and its neighboring towns offer many attractions, among them antique shops, restaurants, and many festivals. *Directions:* From I-95 take exit 90 to Route 27 north 1½ miles to the third intersection. Turn right. The inn is across from the Old Mystic Post Office.

❄ ☕ 💳 @ W P 🍴 🚭 🌺 🐾 ⚓ 🚶 🏇 🍇

OLD MYSTIC INN
Innkeeper: Michael Cardillo
52 Main Street
P.O. Box 733
Mystic (Old Mystic), CT 06372, USA
Tel: (860) 572-9422
8 Rooms, Double: $135–$215
Minimum Stay Required: Weekends May to Oct
Dinner packages available, Oct to Apr
Open: all year, Credit cards: all major

To stay at Manor House is to visit a grand home built a century ago and as you approach the front door along the winding driveway, it's somehow easy to imagine that earlier life. When you walk through the door into the large hallway from which rises a grand staircase, you're sure that you are about to experience a romantic retreat. As the surroundings begin to come into focus, you're aware of incredible architectural details and then you notice the exquisite Tiffany stained-glass windows in the dining room and living room. I stopped, I stared, and I thought how wonderful it was to be a guest in this home. The comfortable guestrooms are all furnished with period antiques. I stayed in the room that was originally the master bedroom—its sitting area in front of the fireplace would have been a good place to linger longer than time permitted. Some rooms have fireplaces, some have private balconies, some have oversized Jacuzzis or soaking tubs. From the many windows, views encompass lawns, gardens, and countryside. When I arrived I was welcomed by the smell of baking bread, an enticing prelude to the delicious breakfast which includes pure local maple syrup. *Directions:* Take I-84 to the exit for Route 8 north at Waterbury. At the end of Route 8 (Winsted) take Route 44 west to Norfolk.

MANOR HOUSE
Owner: L. Keith Mullins
Innkeeper: Michael Dinsmore
69 Maple Avenue
Norfolk, CT 06058, USA
Tel: (860) 542-5690, Toll Free: (866) 542-5690
9 Rooms, Double: $130–$255
Open: all year, Credit cards: all major
Select Registry

One of the most charming villages in Connecticut must be Old Lyme where the Bee and Thistle Inn was built as a private home in 1756. Its second owners found its location too close to the road; so they moved it back from the wide main street of this village to its present gracious setting with a welcoming curved driveway, adding enhancements such as the lovely sunken garden which you should stroll around. In the late 1930s this home was transformed into an inn, now updated to offer 11 guestrooms. From the welcoming front hall there's a lovely carved staircase that takes you up to the tastefully decorated bedrooms on the upper floors, all decorated in Colonial style, with flowered wallpapers, quilts, and Oriental rugs. The rooms, with sitting areas and full bathrooms, have everything that a guest might want. The inn is noted for its award-winning restaurant and wine list, and the several dining rooms with their individual fireplaces are as attractive as the common areas where guests are invited to relax while staying at the inn. Readers of Connecticut Magazine voted this restaurant the most romantic in the state. I stayed here over 20 years ago and find everything about this inn to be as charming today as it was then. *Directions:* From I-95 traveling south, take exit 70, turn right off the ramp to the third building on the left. Traveling north on I-95, turn left off the ramp and right at the second light, go to the end of the road, then turn left to the inn.

✳ 🛋 🧺 📇 ☎ P ‖ 🐕 ⚓ 👫 ⚓ ❦

BEE AND THISTLE INN
Innkeepers: Linnea & David Rufo
100 Lyme Street
Old Lyme, CT 06371, USA
Tel: (860) 434-1667, Fax: (860) 434-3402
Toll Free: (800) 622-4946
11 Rooms, Double: $140–$275*
*Service: $8.00 per room, per night
Open: all year, Credit cards: all major
Select Registry

Ridgefield is a glorious country town in the mid-western corner of Connecticut and the West Lane Inn is perfectly situated for explorations of the area. The inn is set graciously in an elegant 19th-century estate, surrounded by an expanse of lawn and garden. There's a grand terrace spanning the front of the building—a great place to sit and read with a cup of tea. The air-conditioned guestrooms have queen four-poster or king-sized beds (some have 2 queen-sized beds), private baths, some fireplaces and every amenity a guest might want. There is also a cottage housed in a separate building that has 3 deluxe rooms with kitchenettes—perfect for extended stays. Flowered wallpapers are used extensively, adding to the rooms' charm and comfort. Built in 1849 the West Lane Inn combines the charm of an intimate country inn with every convenience of a large hotel: satellite TVs, VCRs, wireless internet access, 24-hour telephone service, voice mail, hair dryers, refrigerators, laundry service, and then some. A complimentary continental and an à la carte menu is served in the breakfast room or on the terrace, weather permitting. Restaurants abound, including their neighbor, one of Connecticut's finest, Bernard's serving French cuisine. *Directions:* From New York City take the West Side Hwy to Saw Mill River Parkway to exit 6; turn right on Rte 35 east for 12 miles to the inn.

❄ ☕ ⚒ ♨ CREDIT ☎ @ W Ⴤ P ⊘ 🚶 🖼 🏃 👫 ⛷ ⚓ ♟

WEST LANE INN
Innkeepers: Maureen Mayer & Deborah Prieger
22 West Lane (Route 35)
Ridgefield, CT 06877, USA
Tel: (203) 438-7323, Fax: (203) 438-7325
18 Rooms, Double: $170–$450
Open: all year, Credit cards: all major

The Simsbury 1820 House is located in one of those wonderfully charming Connecticut towns with wide streets, sweeping green lawns, and homes that cluster along the main street near the post office, the general store, and other conveniences. The history of these towns dates back to the 17th and 18th centuries when life was indeed simpler. Inns like the Simsbury 1820 House provide today's traveler with a sense of "home away from home" and a place to relax while vacationing or working in the area. The guestrooms, with king or queen beds and private bathrooms, are all decorated in the same palette of soft blues and whites, but there is no "hotel" feeling in this property at all. The inn is unique in that it offers its guests a small dining room with a limited but excellent menu. Monday through Thursday nights, the chef prepares dinner—a wonderful option for those who would prefer at the end of the day to stay put rather than to go out to find a restaurant. My dinner was excellent and was topped off with a mocha pecan tart with whipped cream that was nothing short of decadent. The Simsbury 1820 House also has several beautifully furnished private function rooms for dinners, weddings, and other gatherings. *Directions:* From I-91 take exit 35B to Route 218 west. Follow Route 218 to 185 west. Turn right onto Route 10 north—the inn is about 1 mile along on the left.

SIMSBURY 1820 HOUSE
General Manager: Jan Losee
731 Hopmeadow Street
Simsbury, CT 06070, USA
Tel: (860) 658-7658, Fax: (860) 651-0724
Toll Free: (800) 879-1820
34 Rooms, Double: $99–$229
Restaurant: open to guests only, Mon to Thu
Open: all year, Credit cards: all major

The Inn at Stonington, overlooking the water in the picturesque village of Stonington, is a relative newcomer to the hospitality world but it exhibits all the features, amenities, and charm a traveler would expect in an inn with many years of experience. The living room, graciously decorated with seating areas and a fireplace has windows that capture the magic of the waterfront activity, a bar off one end and an area where breakfast is served daily as well as a nightly wine & cheese social. On the top floor guests have the use of a sitting room overlooking the harbor, and downstairs, below the bedrooms, is an exercise room. While the 18 bedrooms are individually decorated, most particularly varying in style of bed, they have in common their comfortable furnishings, seating areas, nice linens, and up-to-the minute bathrooms with all the amenities. Rooms have fireplaces and most have Jacuzzis to add to the pleasure of your visit. The work of local artists is shown throughout the inn. Within a short walking distance you find restaurants, antique shops, boutiques, and several coffee houses. Boaters will appreciate the inn's 400-foot deepwater dock. *Directions:* Traveling north or south on I-95, take exit 91 to the end of the ramp—turn right if traveling north and left if traveling south. Continue for ½ mile to North Main Street where you turn left for 1.6 miles to Route 1. Cross Route 1 to the first stop sign, turn left then right at the next stop sign, driving 6/10 mile to the inn.

INN AT STONINGTON
Innkeeper: Susan L. Irvine
60 Water Street
Stonington, CT 06378, USA
Tel: (860) 535-2000, Fax: (860) 535-8193
18 Rooms, Double: $150–$445
Open: all year, Credit cards: all major
Select Registry

When we passed through the gates of the Mayflower Inn, we felt as if we had been transported from bucolic New England to a European country estate. While the mood is European, the inn and the town boast a strong American heritage. The village was settled by descendants of the original Mayflower party and in its early days the inn hosted such distinguished guests as Eleanor Roosevelt. The Mnuchins wanted to create the ambiance of the finest European auberge and traveled France and England to collect art and antiques that now enrich the decor. Set on 28 acres, the inn houses 25 luxurious guestrooms and suites and anticipates and provides for guests' every possible want and need. From the moment you enter you are embraced by the warmth, elegance, and richness of the ambiance. We arrived on a Saturday afternoon and found the setting and mood enviable: guests were reading, sleeping, writing, or enjoying hushed conversations in front of log fires crackling in intimate sitting areas, salons, and the library. A few guests were already studying the dinner menu over a drink in the cozy bar and the critically acclaimed restaurant was elegantly staged. Stay here and take advantage of the beautiful grounds, the fitness center, pool, cross-country trails, and the endless walks. Let yourself be transported to another world. *Directions:* Located off Rte 47 on the northern outskirts of the village of Washington, just south of the junction with Rte 109.

❄ ⚡ 💳 ☎ 🏌 @ W Ⓨ P ⑪ ❀ ≋ 🎿 ⑆ ⑇ 🚶 ⚲ ⛵

MAYFLOWER INN
Owner: Michael Gallegos
Innkeeper: John Trevenen
Box 1288, 118 Woodbury Road
Washington, CT 06793, USA
Tel: (860) 868-9466, Fax: (860) 868-1497
19 Rooms, Double: $500–$800*
11 Suites: $950–$1600*
*Breakfast not included: $6–$12
Open: all year, Credit cards: all major
Relais & Châteaux

Every once in a while a really wonderful inn is created from an historic structure by a group of very talented artists. Such is the Inn at National Hall: where all imaginable comforts are augmented by a staff and level of service both always present yet unobtrusive. Every conceivable amenity is available and there are extra-special touches such as slippers at turn-down time, little readings to take to bed, the next day's weather forecast, and suggestions of things to. This is a great, fabulously decorated inn and you are tempted to cancel all plans just for the privilege of staying here—and that is exactly what I did. I stayed in a corner suite with mustard-painted walls, expansive river views, a king bed with a paisley corolla canopy, and a desk. Painted on the bathroom wall were whimsical trompe l'oeil monkeys, which reflected in the mirrors. This inn has polish, charm, wonderful furnishings, and it uses whimsy in its decor to create an enduring memory of a time spent in total comfort. Westport, just an hour from New York, is a very sophisticated community and this inn complements the town perfectly. *Directions:* From New York: take the I-95 to exit 17 and turn left to Route 33 for 1½ miles. Then after three traffic lights turn immediately right to the inn. From Merritt Parkway: leave at exit 41, drive south toward Westport, and in about 2 miles you find the inn on the left.

❄ ☕ 🛒 💳 ☎ @ W Y P ⚓ ♿

INN AT NATIONAL HALL
Manager: Marco Degl'Innocenti
Two Post Road West
Westport, CT 06880, USA
Tel: (203) 221-1351, Fax: (203) 221-0276
Toll Free: (800) 628-4255
8 Rooms, Double: $325–$405
8 Suites: $545–$850
Open: all year, Credit cards: all major

Maine
Places to Stay

Picture yourself standing on the sweeping porch looking out over the pool down to the water through the towering pine trees; imagine that morning cup of coffee as you watch the activity on the sea and the changes in the water's reflections; conjure up your perfect bedroom with its lovely four-poster bed, one you have to climb into and from which you can gaze out through the windows to the sea—this can be a reality with a stay at the idyllic Inn at Bay Ledge. All the bedrooms in the main house of this inn are spacious, welcoming, and attractively decorated and those on the second floor benefit from spa tubs and private decks. There's a long living room with a grand piano for entertaining and breakfasts are sumptuous whether enjoyed in the pretty sunroom or at tables on the expanse of the porch. Tucked in the woods on the other side of the street are three summer cottages that are very cozy in their rustic, mountain decor. Named Bear, Moose and Deer, rough-hewn woods are used in the original furnishings, all commissioned in Maine. The Inn at Bay Ledge as the name implies enjoys an incredible location on a ledge above its own 450 foot stretch of private beach. A steep trail climbs down to the beach and the impressive, natural formation titled, Cathedral Arch. *Directions:* Before the town of Bar Harbor, take Route 3 on Mount Desert Island for 5 miles. Opposite the Best Western, turn onto Sand Point Road and drive for ¾ mile to the inn on your left.

THE INN AT BAY LEDGE
Innkeepers: Jack & Jeani Ochtera
150 Sand Point Road
Bar Harbor, ME 04609, USA
Tel: (207) 288-4204, Fax: (207) 288-5573
10 Rooms, Double: $175–$475
Open: May to Oct 19, Credit cards: MC, VS
Select Registry

The Ullikana and The Yellow House are now referred to as the Inns of Ullikana. The Tudor style Ullikana, built in 1885, is one of the few remaining original cottages in Bar Harbor. Though located within an easy walk of all the town's activities, it provides a quiet haven near the water's edge. The 16 rooms, all with king or queen beds, are situated in either the Ullikana or in the very pretty, Victorian, The Yellow House. Both old-fashioned homes boast big rooms and cross ventilation. The Ullikana was owned by a Boston Ship merchant and its common rooms are of a dark wood—appropriate to the era in which the inn was built—and the furnishings of the period are an integral part of the inn's mood and setting, complimented by an incredible display of diverse and interesting art. Painted in colors appropriate to an oceanside town in summer, some rooms have views of the water and the boating activity for which Bar Harbor is so well known. There's also a cottage where you can settle in with your entire family. Lots of country pine is used in the decor of guestrooms located in The Yellow House. Rooms are airy, attractive and enjoy the use of first floor sitting rooms. Regardless of where you stay, breakfasts are served either in the dining room of the Ullikana or in its garden, which is delightful during the summer months. *Directions:* Take Route 3 to Bar Harbor, turn left onto Cottage Street, right on Main Street, then left after the Trust Company building.

INNS AT ULLIKANA
Innkeepers: Helene Harton & Roy Kasindorf
16 The Field
Bar Harbor, ME 04609, USA
Tel: (207) 288-9552, Fax: (207) 288-3682
16 Rooms, Double: $125–$340
Open: May to Nov, Credit cards: MC, VS
Select Registry

Nestled in the shade of the pretty trees that line historic West Street, the Manor House Inn is an attractive, mustard-yellow with green trim, three-story home with shuttered windows, steep pitches and angles to its roof, and lovely wide verandas. Built in 1887 as a lavish 22-room residence, Manor House has now been authentically restored to its original splendor and is listed on the National Register of Historic Places. The grounds are lovely and the common room on the first floor with Victorian style furnishings is inviting. Guestrooms, all with private bathrooms, are found in the original Manor House, the two Garden Cottages, the original Chauffeur's Cottage, and the Acadia Cottage, which was constructed in 2000 to provide an additional four luxurious rooms. Breakfast begins with freshly baked blueberry muffins and breads, fresh fruit, and cereals, followed by a hot dish such as ham-and-cheese baked omelet or baked blueberry-stuffed French toast. Manor House's in-town location is only moments from the water and just a few more moments away from all of Bar Harbor's restaurants and galleries. Access to Acadia National Park with its many attractions is less than a mile away. *Directions:* Take Route 3 south and just as you enter Bar Harbor turn left onto West Street (the first cross street). Manor House is three blocks down on the right.

❄ ☕ 🛎 💳 @ W Y P 🚭 🖼 ⚓ 🚶 👥 🐴 ⚓

MANOR HOUSE INN
Innkeepers: Stacey & Ken Smith
106 West Street
Bar Harbor, ME 04609, USA
Tel: (207) 288-3759, Fax: (207) 288-2974
Toll Free: (800) 437-0088
16 Rooms, 2 Cottages, Double: $155–$265
Open: mid-Apr to end-Oct
Credit cards: all major
Select Registry

The Blue Hill Inn, located right in the heart of a picture-perfect coastal village, has a history stretching almost back to when the town was chartered in 1789. It was first settled in 1762. Both the town and inn offer the classic New England hospitality of yesteryear. Exceptionally comfortable with a charming innkeeper, the inn has provided lodging since 1840. Two separate stairways, off either side of the cozy central living room warmed by a large open fireplace lead to myriad accommodations—eleven bedrooms. A luxury suite, the Cape House, is in a separate building. The attractive first floor king (or twin-bedded room), number 1; dramatic number 4 at the top of the stairs with handsome four-poster king bed against a dark floral backdrop; or the very pretty back corner room number 8 with a four-poster bed embraced by windows on three sides—it is hard to select a favorite. The house was built in two stages; evidenced by two front doors, two entries and three stairways. Note the "Mortgage Button" (applied when fees were paid) on the end post of one stairway dated in the 1830s. Each evening the inn serves wine, cocktails, and hors d'oeuvres. Breakfast offers a choice of five entrees. *Directions:* Take Maine Turnpike (I-95) to Augusta, exiting at Route 3 east to Belfast, continuing east through Bucksport. Take Route 15 south to Blue Hill. Bear right at Blue Hill Inn sign on Route 177 east, then left at the fork to the inn down the hill on the right.

❄ ☕ ⚚ ♨ 💳 ☎ @ W P 🍴 🚭 ⚞ ⚕ ⚓ 🚶 🎿 ⚵

BLUE HILL INN
Innkeeper: Sarah Pebworth
40 Union Street
P.O. Box 403, Blue Hill, ME 04614, USA
Tel: (207) 374-2844, Fax: (207) 374-2829
Toll Free: (800) 826-7415
9 Rooms, Double: $155–$205, 2 Suites: $175–$205
Cape House Cottage: $175–$295 daily
Cape House Studio: $160–$270 daily
Closed: Nov to mid-May, Credit cards: all major
Select Registry

Everyone should experience the pleasure of staying on the Maine coast where the casual life of a small village is imbued with the charm of the surrounding sea and the activities of those who make their living on that sea. When you're driving to Boothbay Harbor, and then on to East Boothbay, along winding country roads with glimpses of water through the foliage of lush green trees, you are aware that this is quintessential Maine. To enjoy this area to the fullest you can do no better than to relax in the Five Gables Inn, one hundred plus years old with its great wrap-around porch on a hill, overlooking the sea with boats just waiting for a sail to be raised for a day of exploration along the craggy, rocky coast. This inn has a great common room with a wood-burning fireplace and several tables in front of big water-view windows. There are 16 bedrooms, all but one with views of the water. Number 10, furnished with a queen pencil-post bed, is a corner room that catches the morning sun and has water views in two directions. Room 14, the inn's largest bedroom, is under a gable. It has a king bed, bath with shower, wood-burning fireplace, and a seating area with great views of the harbor. Mike and De are charming hosts and guests will profit from Mike's culinary talent and passion. *Directions:* Take Rte 1 to Rte 27 south to Rte 96 through East Boothbay. Turn right at the yellow blinking light onto Murray Hill Road for ½ mile to the inn on the right.

FIVE GABLES INN
Innkeepers: Mike & De Kennedy
107 Murray Hill Road
P.O. Box 335
Boothbay Harbor, ME 04544, USA
Tel: (207) 633-4551, Toll Free: (800) 451-5048
16 Rooms, Double: $140–$235
Open: end-May to mid-Oct, Credit cards: MC, VS

Set on a hillside above the charming port of Boothbay Harbor is a wonderful inn, Topside–The Inn on the Hill. With a lawn that overlooks the sea, it commands some of the finest views the town has to offer. The handsome three-story main house, in tones of grays and white with a great wrap-around porch, caught our attention. Converted from a 19th-century sea captain's home, the inn has been completely renovated by its wonderful new owners, Ed and Brian. The décor is intentionally understated and simple blinds dress the windows to minimize any competition with the panoramic views. Soft muted colors wash the walls and compliment the attractive fabrics and furnishings. Area rugs and Oriental carpets top the beautiful old pine floors. A nautical theme appears in artwork and photos on the walls. Attractive guestrooms are found in all three buildings. Rooms in the main house have their own individual character and are more "styled". Those in the two additions, Windward and Leeward, are ideal for those seeking a casual, coastal experience. Facing the bay, all guestrooms in Windward enjoy both a front and back porch with a mix of one or two beds. Rooms in Leeward are a bit larger with refrigerators, larger closets, and more distant views. A bountiful breakfast is served in the main house dining room. Guests enjoy lounging in front of the fireplace in the inviting living room. *Directions:* From Coastal Rte 1 just north of Wiscasset, follow Rte 27 south 11 miles to Boothbay.

🛋️ 🏃 💳 🐕 ♿ @ W P 🚭 🖼️ 🕴️ 👫

TOPSIDE –THE INN ON THE HILL
Innkeepers: Ed McDermott & Brian Lamb
60 McKown Street
Boothbay Harbor, ME 04538, USA
Tel: (207) 633-5404, Fax: (207) 633-2206
21 Rooms, Double: $155–$225
Minimum Stay Required: 2 nights on weekends
Open: May 15 to Oct 31, Credit cards: all major

Listed in the National Registry, the Camden Maine Stay is a grand old New England home dating from 1802. It was actually built by Alden Bass, a direct descendant of John Alden, who came over on the Mayflower. Camden is one of those picturesque towns surrounded by hills from which you peer down onto a harbor of schooners and boating activity—for me as mesmerizing as staring into a star-filled evening sky. The Camden Maine Stay is delightfully decorated and shipshape in every respect, and you'll find any one of the rooms to be totally comfortable for as long as you can stay. There's a variety of accommodation both in the main house and the attached carriage house, from the two-bedroom Amelia Huse Suite with its own sitting room to my favorite, the cozy Carriage House with its private patio overlooking the spectacular gardens that buffer one from any sense of reality. There is no such thing here as a room that I would not love to stay in for nights on end. Two inviting parlors provide guests with comfortable places to relax and chat with one another. There's also a sitting room with fireplace, TV, and DVD player and, of course, a porch—the kind that makes New England inns so very special. A huge Aga stove warms the kitchen and bakes all the wonderful food that you'll enjoy at breakfast. You can walk to everything in town and the innkeepers are happy to steer you in the right direction for all the places to visit in the area. *Directions:* The inn is three blocks north of the village.

CAMDEN MAINE STAY
Owners: Roberta & Claudio Latanza
22 High Street
Camden, ME 04843, USA
Tel: (207) 236-9636, Fax: (207) 236-0621
8 Rooms, Double: $110–$295
Minimum Stay Required: Weekends in season
Open: all year, Credit cards: all major
Select Registry

When love of innkeeping and fine cuisine come together in an inn located in one of the most charming of all seaside towns, you can be assured of a memorable visit. With Mary Jo, her artistic eye giving the inn its elegant decor, and Michael adding his incredible culinary talent; both combine to provide superb hospitality. The inn's eight rooms and six suites are furnished lovingly. The Tea Cup Suite showcases Mary Jo's collection of tea cups. Bright and cheerful, a skylight over the bed adds to the enjoyment of early-morning reading while curled up under the sumptuous comforter. Other rooms are found either in the main house, the Carriage House or The Manor House—all spectacular and individual in their furnishings and include comfortable seating for those times when you want to relax in the privacy of your own room. The dinner I enjoyed was a feast including a seared five-spice quail, Maine lobster ravioli with diver scallops and lobster tail, and a hot raspberry soufflé served with a chambord crème anglaise. After such a wonderful meal, relaxing in the living room in front of the fire was the frosting on top of a perfect evening. Everything is close by with the main street just outside the front door (triple glazing does much to subdue the sound). During the winter the inn runs cooking classes and Michael has his own cookbook—it is spectacular, like everything these two do. *Directions:* Take I-95 to Route 1 to Camden. The inn is on the left at 41 Elm Street.

❄ ☕ ✄ ♨ ▦@ W P ❚❚ ✿ ⚓ 🎿 👫 🐎 ⛷ ⚓ ❦

HARTSTONE INN
Innkeepers: Michael & Mary Jo Salmon
41 Elm Street
Camden, ME 04843, USA
Tel: (207) 236-4259, Fax: (207) 236-9575
Toll Free: (800) 788-4823
12 Rooms, Double: $105–$190, 9 Suites: $175–$270
Minimum Stay Required: Weekends
Open: all year, Credit cards: MC, VS
Select Registry

Pilgrim's Inn, an historic 1793 Colonial building, overlooks Northwest Harbor and a picturesque millpond on Deer Isle in Penobscot Bay. The setting is magnificent and the views of the flowering gardens and pond behind the inn are enchanting, and immediately and totally relaxing. Easy to spot, the inn is painted a handsome barn red. Inside the decor is warm and inviting with furnishings respecting the island's history and character with pine floors, wonderful heavy old beams, several large fireplaces, and antique furnishings. Warm Colonial colors enhance the cozy feeling of comfort. Twelve lovely guestrooms, a couple with gas stoves, are found in the main house. If you are traveling with children, consider one of the three complete cottages for a longer stay. The Whale's Rib Tavern, featuring American cuisine and fresh local ingredients, offers a diverse menu with something for everyone. The restaurant is located in a rustic barn with hand-hewn beams, vaulted ceiling and windows that frame the idyllic water setting. The inn is a good base for visiting Acadia National Park and Isle au Haut (40 minutes by ferry). At its doorstep you can hike, bike, and go boating. There's a great gallery just up the corner from the local library. *Directions:* From Boston take I-95 north to Augusta and Rte 3 to Belfast, then follow Rte 1 north to Rte 15. Turn right onto Rte 15 (south), heading for Deer Isle through the Blue Hill Peninsula. In the village turn right onto Main St. (Route 15A).

PILGRIM'S INN
Innkeepers: Tom Lawless & Tina Oddleifson
P.O. Box 69
Deer Isle, ME 04627, USA
Tel: (207) 348-6615, Toll Free: (888) 778-7505
12 Rooms, Double: $109–$209
3 Cottages: $239 daily
Restaurant: dinner only
Open: mid-May to Oct, Credit cards: all major
Select Registry

Distinguished by its beautiful stained-glass sign and landscaped gardens, the Linekin Bay Bed & Breakfast is a very attractive, white clapboard, two-story home whose front wrap-around porch is decorated with hanging plants and overflowing window boxes. To fully appreciate the setting, continue around to the back where the lawn sweeps down to the bay. Enter the property from the front porch to the welcome of owners, Marti and Larry. Leaving behind their former careers in teaching and law enforcement, they easily and naturally adapted as innkeepers of this 1878 historic property. Off the entry on one side is a wonderful front parlor, the other side leads to the breakfast room and a glass-enclosed back sitting room. The Holbrook Suite, dramatic and spacious, is located on the first floor with its own private porch. It has a four-poster king bed and looks out through large picture windows to the lawn and water. The other three rooms are found by climbing the steep entry stairs and also enjoy views to the water. Rhapsody in Blue is to the right and Crooked Chimney is to the left; both enjoy views to the water. Whispering Rose overlooks the front garden, but climb to its romantic loft where its A-frame window faces the idyllic back view. *Directions:* From north traveling Route 1, turn right after Wiscasset Bridge to Route 27 toward Boothbay Harbor. Continue 12 miles and turn left at the one traffic light in town onto Route 96/Ocean Point Road; travel 3.9 miles.

❄ ☕ ✍ 💳 ☎ @ W P 🚫 🏕 ⚓

LINEKIN BAY BED & BREAKFAST
Innkeepers: Marti Booth & Larry Brown
531 Ocean Point Road
East Boothbay (Boothbay Harbor), ME 04032, USA
Tel: (207) 633-9900, Toll Free: (800) 596-7420
4 Rooms, Double: $145–$155
2 Suites: $175–$195
Open: all year, Credit cards: MC, VS

L.L. Bean introduced outlet shopping to Freeport and numerous retailers have followed with their offerings housed in the quaint buildings lining the charming village streets. The Harraseeket Inn, built in 1895, boasts a longer history of welcoming travelers who have simply sought the beauty of Maine and gracious warmth of this inn's hospitality. A town where the Harraseeket River meets the Casco Bay, this is a sportsmen's paradise. As a novice, you can take advantage of L.L. Bean's outdoor discovery schools that teach kayaking, fly casting, archer and day shoots—returning at day's end to the luxury and comfort of an elegant hotel. With two dining rooms, The Maine Dining Room is located beyond the elegant entry and tempts travelers with a menu committed to local and organic produce and wild regional specialties, complimented by an incredible wine list. The Broad Arrow Tavern is more casual, painted a cozy green with a hunting theme décor—the centerpiece being the buffalo head. Handsome fabrics and reproduction pieces decorate the comfortable, well-appointed guestrooms. I especially loved #203 that enjoys a cozy bedroom warmed by a pot belly stove that steps up from the entry sitting room and a wonderful bath with large Jacuzzi tub. Although, the hotel boasts 84 rooms, it feels more intimate with the personal attention of the hotel's incredible staff. *Directions:* Take Exit 20 off I-95 to Main Street.

❄ ☕ 🛶 💳 ☎ 👫 🛗 🍽 @ W P ⏹ 🚭 ☘ ≈ 🖼 🐾 ♿ ⚓ 🚶 🏃 ⛷ 🚣

HARRASEEKET INN
Innkeeper: The Gray Family
162 Main Street
Freeport, ME 04032, USA
Tel: (207) 865-9377, Fax: (207) 865-1684
Toll Free: (800) 342-6423
84 Rooms, Double: $195–$305
Open: all year, Credit cards: all major

Blair Hill Inn is a stunning three-story mansion set high on a hillside with breathtaking views of Moosehead Lake and the wilderness of northern Maine. Built in 1891 as a gentleman's farm, it has been meticulously restored and opened as an inn by Dan and Ruth McLaughlin. Upon stepping through the main door, warmth and beauty abound: a magnificent circular entryway, then tall pocket doors open into the grand living room whose huge windows frame the million dollar view. A beautiful fireplace, one of seven, centered between two sets of French doors warms the elegant seating area and a baby grand piano is nearby. The front porch, which runs the entire length of the home, again offers lake and mountain views beyond compare. The graciously refined dining room overlooks the water as well. On weekends a five-course, fixed price dinner is offered in this extremely romantic setting. A magnificent circular staircase leads to eight simply gorgeous guest rooms. All rooms are spacious, light-filled and extremely inviting. A favorite, number 1, is exquisite. There is a four-poster mahogany king bed, five large windows brimming with lake views, a wood burning fireplace, and a beautiful marble tiled bath that seemingly stepped off the pages of a design magazine. *Directions:* From Greenville continue towards Lily Bay following the east side of the lake on Lily Bay Road north.

※ ☕ 🎿 💳 🍸 @ W P ⑪ 🌱 🖼 ⚓ ⛵ 🚶 👫 🐎 🎿 ⚓

BLAIR HILL INN
Innkeepers: Dan & Ruth McLaughlin
351 Lily Bay Road
P.O. Box 1288
Greenville, ME 04441, USA
Tel: (207) 695-0224, Fax: (207) 695-4324
8 Rooms, Double: $275–$495
Open: all year, Credit cards: MC, VS
Select Registry

Magic is everywhere in this northern part of Maine—particularly at the Lodge at Moosehead Lake. It's hard to imagine anyone more devoted to seeing that guests experience all this part of Maine can offer: dogsledding, snowshoeing, snowmobiling, cross-country and downhill skiing, mountain biking, whitewater rafting, touring by plane, hiking, canoeing, or fly fishing in a secret stream or lake in summer. And where else can you go on a moose safari? The Lodge is situated above the lake and frames this magnificent setting. From the common rooms, dining room, or on the expanse of back porch, one is captivated by views overlooking the broad waterscape and islands of the largest lake in Maine. The five bedrooms and four suites are nothing short of fabulous. I stayed in the Bear Room in a hand-carved four-poster queen bed, with bears carved into and perched on its posts. There was a hand-carved bear bench at the foot of the bed, two different sitting areas, and a gas corner fireplace with chair nearby for gazing out at the lake. Twigs are used to create borders instead of moldings and to simulate picture hangings. The decor is clever and artistic, yet rustic throughout. *Directions:* Take I-95 to Newport, Route 7 north to Dexter, Route 23 north to Guilford then Route 15 north to Greenville.

❄ ☕ 💳 ⛺ @ W P ‖ 🚭 🌿 🖼 ⚓ ⚓ 🏃 🚶 🐎 ⛷ ⛵

LODGE AT MOOSEHEAD LAKE
Innkeepers: Linda & Dennis Bortis
368 Lily Bay Road
P.O. Box 1167, Greenville, ME 04441, USA
Tel: (207) 695-4400, Fax: (207) 695-2281
Toll Free: (800) 825-6977
5 Rooms, Double: $250–$395, 4 Suites: $375–$680
1, 2-bedroom Suite: $550–$680
Minimum Stay Required: 2 nights
Closed: Apr, Credit cards: AX, MC, VS
Select Registry

France in the middle of northern Maine? You can be sure that an overnight at this charming inn and dinner in its restaurant will transport you to Provence without any need for a passport as you walk through its gates into a garden oasis. Inside the inn the warm provincial colors of red and yellow are predominant in the common rooms and the dining room and are reminiscent of the south of France. The two suites, Les Baux and St. Remy, are particularly spacious with cathedral ceilings and sitting rooms; each has a bath with a clawfoot tub and shower. From each of the suites and the three rooms, you can walk out to a large deck where you can spend hours looking at the gardens and the towering pines in the backyard. Breakfast can be served on this deck or in the garden. There are beds of herbs growing for the foods of the kitchen, and perennial gardens providing continuous bloom. The lush green of the lawns and the white wicker furniture beckon one to take a book and be lulled to sleep while taking in the natural beauty. In the living room, there is a fireplace where you can await your table in the restaurant and contemplate the enticing menu. There's also a very attractive small bar which was stocked with every libation that your heart could desire. *Directions:* Route 1 northeast of Ellsworth to Hancock; the inn is on the right.

LE DOMAINE
Innkeeper: Beth Clark
1513 US Route 1
P.O. Box 519
Hancock, ME 04640, USA
Tel: (207) 422-3395, Fax: (207) 422-3916
Toll Free: (800) 554-8498
5 Rooms, Double: $150
2 Suites: $225
Open: Jun to mid-Oct, Credit cards: all major
Select Registry

The Crocker House Country Inn is a lovely, three-story, gray-shingle home trimmed in white and dating back to 1884. The setting on Hancock Point is very picturesque and quiet, and if you arrive by boat, it's just a short stroll over the hill from the harbor at Frenchman Bay. The current owners, the Malabys, have restored the property and created a warm and inviting ambiance both in the decor and welcoming service. Each of the guestrooms is individually and simply decorated; each has a country flavor and beds are topped with old quilts. Two bedrooms are located in the former carriage house, which also provides an additional common room and a spa. Guests have a lovely living room and two sitting rooms, one of which boasts a piano and live music on weekends. The inn is probably best known for its food, which you can enjoy in either of two dining rooms. The restaurant, open to both resident and non-resident guests, offers breakfast and dinner. Weekends a pianist offers some evening entertainment. Always busy and quite popular, the inn hosts many weddings, family reunions, and small business retreats. Attractions include a croquet court, clay tennis courts, antiquing, golf, kayaking, biking, and the fabulous Acadia National Park about 20 minutes away. *Directions:* From Ellsworth travel 8 miles east on Route 1, turn right on Point Road and go 5 miles to the inn (on the right).

CROCKER HOUSE COUNTRY INN
Innkeepers: Elizabeth & Richard Malaby
967 Point Road
Hancock Point, ME 04640, USA
Tel: (207) 422-6806, Fax: (207) 422-3105
11 Rooms, Double: $85–$165
Restaurant: dinner only
Open: Apr to Jan, Credit cards: all major

Being at the ocean's edge facing a wonderful sandy beach, a rarity in Maine, is just the beginning of the treats awaiting you at The Beach House. This 35-room inn is owned and managed by the proprietors of the spectacular White Barn Inn, located just a short distance away. The Beach House is coastside-elegant with its inviting living room with woven rattan chairs, oversized sofas, a large stone fireplace, and a large front porch where you can spend hour-after-hour just people watching. The bedrooms—standard, superior, and deluxe—have all the amenities any guest could desire; are cozy in size, and handsomely and subtly decorated in rich colors of beige, cream, black and gold. I especially liked room number 312, a front corner room with a king bed and ocean view. An extended Continental breakfast is served in what used to be one of the house's parlors with long windows facing the beach. In the afternoon, tea and cookies are set out and dinner is served at the White Barn. (There are also many good restaurants in Kennebunkport). The inn provides its guests with complimentary beach towels and chairs, bicycles, and canoes. During the winter holiday season, The Beach House offers packages that include dinner at the White Barn Inn. *Directions:* Take exit 3 to Kennebunk; follow Rte 35 south for 6 miles to Kennebunkport. At the intersection of Rtes 35 and 9, continue straight on Beach Ave. for 2 miles.

❄ ☕ 🚬 CREDIT ☎ 🛅 @ W P ♿ ⚓ 🎿 🚶 🐎 ⚓

THE BEACH HOUSE
Innkeeper: Corinne Heyl
211 Beach Avenue
Kennebunk Beach, ME 04043, USA
Tel: (207) 967-3850, Fax: (207) 967-4719
35 Rooms, Double: $189–$550
Restaurant at sister hotel, The White Barn Inn
Open: all year, Credit cards: all major

Ideally located within walking distance of the heart of Kennebunkport, straddling the riverbank where the river meets the sea, is the Breakwater Inn, Hotel and Stripers restaurant. An attractive gray-shingled building with the classic wrap-around white porch, the more historic 1800s inn houses the 20 guestrooms and the Stripers Restaurant. The restaurant runs the length of the building and overlooks the Breakwater's private beach and inlet. Featuring fresh seafood, a large aquarium is center stage. It is fun to watch the constant parade of boats heading in and out to sea. Also in the inn are a lovely back sitting room, lounge and bar. The appealing décor is very "coastal" with soft whites, blues and greens selected for walls and fabrics, and white painted furnishings set on light pine floors. Up the central stairs, rooms are comfortable and many enjoy window views and the sound of the lapping surf. Adjacent and housed in what was recently the Schooners Inn, the Spa offers 14 smaller rooms. At the entrance, a handsome sitting area steps down to a bar whose windows overlook the inlet. The guestrooms, named for Schooners, enjoy a soothing décor and comfortable sitting areas. Complimentary bikes, beach chairs and umbrellas. *Directions:* Take Kennebunkport Exit 25 from the Maine Turnpike (I-95); turn left on Rte 35 for 5.5 miles. Turn left at the light onto Rte 9, then right onto Ocean Ave. The inn is on the right after 9/10 mile.

❄ ☕ 🛷 💳 @ W � P 🍴 🚭 ❦ 🖼 ⚓ 🏌 🏄

BREAKWATER INN & SPA
Innkeeper: Lauren Schuyler
127, 131 & 133 Ocean Ave.
P.O. Box 560C
Kennebunkport, ME 04046, USA
Tel: (207) 967-5333, Fax: (207) 967-2040
38 Rooms, Double: $169–$729
Open: all year, Credit cards: MC, VS

Just outside the village of Kennebunkport, (a one mile walk, half of which is a gravel road), within an easy walk of the shops, galleries, and restaurants—is Bufflehead Cove, an inn set at the edge of a saltwater inlet. A narrow graveled drive delivers you to the doorstep of this property that enjoys an oasis on the water's edge. It can accommodate overnight guests with five guestrooms, a cozy living room, and a dining room. In the main house, I adore the Balcony Room which frames the water views, enjoys a private balcony, gas fireplace, king bed, and whirlpool tub. Nestled off on its own, the River Cottage has an upstairs bedroom with a downstairs living room and wood-burning fireplace, a deck with a water view, a kitchen, and a two-person spa. Also tucked away from the main house—absolutely gorgeous in luxurious decor, space and comfort—The Hideaway is a place to retreat to and hideaway. A delicious, lavish, full breakfast is served either in the dining room, on the porch by the water, or on the open sunny deck. The inn serves wine and cheese in the evening and the innkeepers will be glad to review restaurant options for dinner and make reservations for you. The personable dog, Lili, adds to the enjoyment of your stay. *Directions:* Leave the Maine Turnpike (I-95) at exit 25 onto Route 35 south. At the intersection of Routes 1 and 35, continue on Route 35 for 3-1/10 miles to the inn's sign on the left.

❄ 🍴 🛁 📺 🐕 W Y P ⚓ 🎿 👫 🐎

BUFFLEHEAD COVE
Innkeepers: Harriet & James Gott & son, Erin
P.O. Box 499
Kennebunkport, ME 04046, USA
Tel & Fax: (207) 967-3879
5 Rooms, Double: $155–$395
1 Cottage: $2310 weekly
Open: May to Dec, Credit cards: MC, VS

This 1804 Federal-style mansion was originally built by Daniel Walker as a wedding present for his daughter, Sarah, and her husband, the seafaring Captain William Jefferds. In 1996, the Bartholomew family restored this home and created a 15-room inn that was purchased by Erik and Sarah Lindblom in April 2005. After searching for 25 years, the Lindbloms, knew they found their "perfect inn" the moment they stepped in the door. All the rooms and suites have been renovated with the discerning traveler in mind; while preserving the original splendor and architecture of the federal style home. In addition to private baths, the rooms have air conditioning, remote-controlled CD players, and down-filled comforters. Some rooms have private porches, large showers, soaking tubs, or two-person whirlpool spas, and eight rooms have working fireplaces. Each afternoon guests are treated to a wonderful assortment of refreshments, which are served in the garden room. The inn is within a short walk of Kennebunkport with all its shops, restaurants, and historical sights, as well as the picturesque harbor and the activity of lobster boats. *Directions:* From the Maine Turnpike (I-95) take exit 19 to Wells. Drive east to Route 1, then take Route 9 to Kennebunkport to Pearl Street to the inn.

❄ 🛋 🚼 💳 ☎ 🐕 @ W P 🖼 ⚓ 🏌 🏃 ⛷ 🚣

CAPTAIN JEFFERDS INN
Innkeepers: Erik & Sarah Lindblom
5 Pearl Street
P.O. Box 691
Kennebunkport, ME 04046, USA
Tel: (207) 967-2311, Fax: (207) 967-0721
Toll Free: (800) 839-6844
15 Rooms, Double: $130–$375
Minimum Stay Required: 2 nights on weekends
Closed: Dec 24 to 26, Credit cards: all major
Select Registry

The town green sloping down from the Captain Lord Mansion to the river gives this stylishly decorated inn a very prominent position that befits its splendid interior. The decor is lavish, from the lovely wallpapers that adorn the walls in the halls to those in the bedrooms, each of which is named after a ship built here in an earlier era. Paintings in ornate frames hang everywhere—an obvious love of the owners who have searched long and hard to find the touches that make this inn so special. I stayed in the Cactus room with a king four-poster bed, gas fireplace, and a bath with double vanity and shower. Other bedrooms have canopy beds and whirlpool tubs for two. A delicious complete breakfast with a hot entree is served in the kitchen most mornings at two long tables where you have a good opportunity to meet and talk to your fellow guests. The parlor has a large fireplace that was burning warmly on the occasion of my visit and comfortable chairs in which to sit, relax, and have a good conversation or a cup of afternoon tea. Captain Lord Mansion is a quiet haven just a few minutes' walk from the heart of Kennebunkport with its many shops, activities, and restaurants. *Directions:* Take the I-95 (Maine Turnpike) to exit 25, go left on Route 35 for 5½ miles, then east on Route 9. Turn left over the bridge and first right in the square to Ocean Avenue. Go 3/10 mile and turn left into Green Street. The inn is at the top of the hill on the left.

❄ 🍽 🛴 💳 ☎ @ W Y P 🚭 🐾 ⚔ ⚓ 🕴 👥 ♿

CAPTAIN LORD MANSION
Innkeepers: Bev Davis & Rick Litchfield
P.O. Box 800
Kennebunkport, ME 04046, USA
Tel: (207) 967-3141, Fax: (207) 967-3172
Toll Free: (800) 522-3141
15 Rooms, Double: $199–$449
1 Suite: $299–$599
Open: all year, Credit cards: all major
Select Registry

The exterior of this beautiful 1860 Victorian, once home to sea captain Melville Walker with wraparound porches and impressive cupola, sets the tone for the style you find inside, where a magnificent suspended spiral staircase winds its way up from the entrance hall. The ground floor has been redecorated and the original oak floors refinished. There are six guestrooms in the main house. Captain's (16) enjoys a sitting area and the only king bed in the house, while room 12 is cozy with a gas fireplace. There are eleven cottages nestled on the grounds: number 3 benefits from a fireplace and kitchenette and number 6 with two separate bedrooms and a shared living room is popular with families. With so many variations of amenities be sure to discuss your preference for a gas fireplace, whirlpool tub, sitting room, or kitchenette when making reservations. If you stay in one of the cottages, you have the option of either coming to the inn for a full breakfast or having a breakfast basket delivered to your door. The Maine Stay is located a short walk from Dock Square, the center of activity in this little seaside village with charming shops and wonderful seafood restaurants. *Directions:* Take exit 25 from Maine Turnpike (I-95), turning left on Route 35 south. Go 5½ miles to Route 9, turn left, then go over the bridge and through the village to the stop sign. Turn right on Maine Street for three blocks.

❄ ☕ ✂ 🖼 **W P** 🚭 ⚓ 👤 👥 🐴 ⛷ ⚓

MAINE STAY INN AT THE MELVILLE WALKER HOUSE
Innkeepers: Judi & Walter Hauer
34 Maine Street
P.O. Box 500A, Kennebunkport, ME 04046, USA
Tel: (207) 967-2117, Fax: (207) 967-8757
Toll Free: (800) 950-2117
4 Rooms, Double: $129–$269, 13 Suites: $129–$319
10 Cottages
Minimum Stay Required: Weekends & Peak Season
Open: all year, Credit cards: all major
Select Registry

The Old Fort Inn is a beautiful 16-room inn offering elegance and tranquility. Surrounded by old estate cottages in one of Kennebunkport's most attractive residential neighborhoods, the inn has its own swimming pool and tennis court. The spacious and luxurious air-conditioned rooms—in the main building and in the circa-1880 converted carriage house—are stylishly decorated with antiques, fine fabrics, and attractive wall coverings. All guestrooms feature canopy or four-poster beds with down comforters and private baths. Some rooms have gas fireplaces and whirlpool baths. One room I visited had a fishnet canopy over the bed and was decorated in shades of gray and beige with black accents, an attractive color palette echoed in the bedspread. The inn has a separate large living room with a fireplace, comfortable chairs, and a view out to the pool and gardens. A lavish gourmet breakfast is served daily in the Great Room. The inn, in its own private, peaceful grounds of 15 acres, is just one block from the ocean, yet only 1¼ miles from the bustle of Kennebunkport's shops, galleries, and restaurants. *Directions:* Take the Kennebunk Exit, exit 25 from the Maine Turnpike (I-95), then turn left on Route 35 for 5½ miles. Turn left at the light onto Route 9 for 3/10 mile, then right onto Ocean Ave for 9/10 mile to the Colony Hotel (Kings Hwy.), where you take a left. Turn right at the T-junction and follow signs for 3/10 mile to the inn.

❄ ▬ ⚞ 🖾 ☎ @ W ▼ P ⊘ ≈ 🕴 🖾 ⟂ 🕅 👫 ⚓

OLD FORT INN
Innkeepers: Sheila & David Aldrich
8 Old Fort Avenue
P.O. Box M
Kennebunkport, ME 04046, USA
Tel: (207) 967-5353, Fax: (207) 967-4547
Toll Free: (800) 828-3678
16 Rooms, Double: $175–$450
Open: mid-Apr to mid-Dec, Credit cards: all major
Select Registry

Just beyond the historic town of Kennebunkport is the lovely White Barn Inn. Eighteen guestrooms and seven suites are found in the main building, pool house, and carriage house. Three absolutely gorgeous cottages enjoy their own secluded oasis on the wharf by the river's edge. All the rooms have been meticulously restored and furnished with period pieces with a great eye for detail. Plush amenities include fresh flowers, bathrooms with whirlpool tubs, thick robes, elegant toiletries, and wood-burning fireplaces. My room had softly painted walls and two comfortable upholstered chairs with an ottoman to rest my feet after a long day of walking around Kennebunkport. The restaurant is one of only five AAA five-diamond restaurants in New England. The special focus on locally caught seafood makes the ever-changing menu a real treat. Tables, set on wide plank boards staged in a room with a rustic ambiance, enjoy views through a spectacular window framing a lush, wooded garden. Complimentary bicycles are available for the short distance to the village or riding to the beach for a walk or a swim. If you prefer warmer water, try the heated pool. The nearby wildlife preserve is a great place to walk and enjoy the special beauty of Maine's rugged coast. *Directions:* Leave Maine Turnpike (I-95) at exit 25 for Kennebunk; take Rte 35 south for 7 miles to Kennebunkport. Cross the road at the light at Rte 9; the inn is ¼ mile on the right.

WHITE BARN INN
Innkeeper & Chef: Jonathan Cartwright
Innkeeper: Stuart Barwise
37 Beach Avenue
P.O. Box 560 C, Kennebunkport, ME 04046, USA
Tel: (207) 967-2321, Fax: (207) 967-1100
15 Rooms, Double: $395–$650, 11 Suites: $610–$950
3 Cottages
Restaurant: closed 2 weeks in Jan
Open: all year, Credit cards: all major
Relais & Châteaux

Just 4 miles north of Camden in the little village of Lincolnville Beach there's an inn sitting at the water's edge that provides an idyllic place for you to rest while listening to the water lapping at the shore and the wind sighing in the pines. The Inn at Sunrise Point, consisting of the main house with three bedrooms, five cottages and a loft, named after Maine's most famous writers and artists, offers luxurious guestrooms of great charm, all with private decks and all containing fireplaces. The Winslow Homer, The Fitz Hugh Lane, and The Rachel Carson cottages enjoy prime waterfront settings and the suite is so complete that one could move in and never move out. Bedrooms have either queen or king beds, bathrooms with large tubs, and plush robes. In the cottages there are two-person spa tubs, wet bars, and private decks. A full gourmet breakfast is served in the glass conservatory of the main house. This inn is nicely located for exploring all of the wonders of the Camden region, and at the end of a day of excursions, you can return to enjoy a glass of wine sitting by the fire in the cherry-paneled library. I can imagine nothing nicer than to rest in this setting for days, venturing out to the shops, the restaurants, and taking full advantage of the spectacular setting. *Directions:* Take exit 28 from I-295 in Brunswick. Follow Route 1 north to Camden. Continue through Camden, 4 miles farther on turn right at fire road #9.

INN AT SUNRISE POINT
Owner: Daina Hill
Innkeepers: Mary Ann (Mimi) & Captain Dave Barrett
P.O. Box 1344
Lincolnville Beach (Camden), ME 04843, USA
Tel: (207) 236-7716, Fax: (207) 236-0820
3 Rooms, Double: $300–$395
5 Cottages: $330–$595 daily
1 Loft Suite: $350-$695 daily
Open: Apr 10 to mid-Nov, Credit cards: all major
Select Registry

The Lucerne Inn is just down the hillside from Route 1A enjoying an incredible backdrop of sweeping hillside, towering mountains, lake, and forest. Open all year, this lovely roadside hotel offers comfortable accommodations, fine dining, and idyllic views in all seasons. An attractive, three-story, white clapboard inn whose roofline is pierced by chimneys and charming dormer windows, we discovered the inn in spring when the surrounding countryside was lush, green, and colored by wildflowers. The building core dates to 1812 and houses the reception, intimate salon bar with large river-rock wood-burning fireplace, and a restaurant that wraps around two sides of the building with tables enjoying the full expanse of window views. Saturday night guests enjoy the famous Sunday buffet. Guestrooms throughout have pretty fabrics and reproduction period furnishings. All rooms enjoy sitting areas in the main room or an adjoining room, gas fireplaces and standard bathrooms with whirlpool jets. Almost all enjoy sweeping views. Hard to distinguish the old from the new, I saw "new" room #27 which had a handsome, four-poster queen bed and #10 on the third floor in the main house with a lovely sitting area and fireplace. On the lawn below the inn is a large outdoor pool. Reputedly, the inn is haunted by a former resident who returned home to find his wife with a lover and ended all their lives. *Directions:* From Bangor, travel east on 1A to Lucerne.

❄ ☕ 🏌 💳 🏨 @ W P ⟍ 🚭 ≈ 🖼 👕 ♿ ⚓ 🏃 🚶 🚵

THE LUCERNE INN
Innkeepers: Rhonda & Steve Jones
Route 1a
2517 Main Road
Lucerne-in-Maine, ME 04429, USA
Tel: (207) 843-5123, Fax: (207) 843-6138
Toll Free: (800) 325-5123
31 Rooms, Double: $99–$219
Open: all year, Credit cards: MC, VS

The Newcastle Inn is a lovely country inn located in Maine's Mid-Coast region in the charming coastal community of Newcastle. The inn is as lovely inside as out and not long ago received a fresh look with new wallpapers, carpeting, and furniture. A very special touch is the living-room floor, which has been hand-painted in the most attractive of designs. Off the living room, an enclosed porch with beautiful views from its many windows is a great place to sit in the afternoon with a book, glass of wine or cup of tea. In summer enjoy breakfast on a deck overlooking the river or, sip a cocktail while you watch the beautiful sunset from an outdoor table. There are fourteen guest rooms. I stayed in a room on the third floor looking out to the water. While simply furnished, it was very comfortable with its floral wallpaper and upholstered chair where I enjoyed reading in the evening. The inn is centrally located for exploring all that this beautiful area of Maine has to offer. *Directions:* From Coastal Route 1 travel 6 miles north of Wiscasset Bridge. Turn right on River Road. The inn is on the right after half a mile.

❄ ☕ 🚼 💳 🐕 @ W P ⛵ ⚓ 🚶 👫 🏇 ⚓

NEWCASTLE INN
Owner: Julie Bolthuis
60 River Road
Newcastle, ME 04553, USA
Tel: (207) 563-5685, Fax: (207) 563-6877
Toll Free: (877) 376-6111
10 Rooms, Double: $165–$235
4 Suites: $200–$255
Minimum Stay Required: Weekends
Open: all year, Credit cards: AX, MC, VS
Select Registry

Hartwell House is located just outside Perkins Cove, one of those scenic Maine lobster-fishing villages. There are many inns in the region; yet Hartwell House, a lovely, traditional New England home, is valued as one of the nicest and is very elegant and ornate in its decor. The inn consists of two buildings facing each other across a street going down to the harbor. Set on an acre-and-a-half of lush green lawn and gardens, the elegant main building houses the common rooms: sun porch, dining room, and lovely sitting room. Attached to the main house with also seven guestrooms, two studio bedrooms step up to their own outside entrance. New spa tubs for two have been added in some rooms. Across the street all six bedrooms in the annex have a terrace or balcony and there are three suites. Off season, breakfast is offered in the main house; but in season guests are given a voucher for the neighboring restaurant, Swann House. Close to the inn is the Marginal Way footpath, one of the most picturesque spots on the coast of lower Maine. There is much to do here—fishing, golf, tennis, sailing, galleries, antiquing, and summer theater. *Directions:* Take exit 4 from the Maine Turnpike (I-95) north, turning left on Route 1 (north) for 4.4 miles. Turn right on Pine Hill, left on Shore, and go 2/10 mile to the inn. From the Maine Turnpike south, take exit 2, go left on Route 109, right on Route 1 for 6 miles, then left on Shore Road for 6/10 mile.

❄ ☕ 🛠 ♨ 💳 🔒 P ⑂ 🛋 ⚓ 🏃 👫 🐎 ⛷ 🚤 ⚓

HARTWELL HOUSE
Owners: Trisha & James Hartwell
312 Shore Road
Ogunquit, ME 03907, USA
Tel: (207) 646-7210, Fax: (207) 646-6032
Toll Free: (800) 235-8883
11 Rooms, Double: $140–$245
3 Suites: $175–$325
2 Studios: $140–$195
Open: all year, Credit cards: all major

A small city like Portland needs to have a great inn so that you can settle in to explore all that there is to do here for a day or two or three. The Pomegranate Inn is just the place, located in the historic district and within an easy walk of all the sights. Its totally conforming, external historical appearance belies the eclectic decorating that you'll find inside. The artwork—pictures and sculpture—demands your attention and your involvement. Whether you understand it or not doesn't matter—but you will love it just the same. The inn's eight rooms, including one suite and a garden room, are all beautifully decorated with antiques and show more of that eclectic touch with walls sporting hand-painted flowers. It would be hard to beat the carriage house with its own private terrace for real seclusion. Every room has a private bath, television, and some have fireplaces. This inn provides a different visual experience in a traditional setting and I think you'll like it as much as I did. A full breakfast is served in the dining room. *Directions:* From I-95 north take exit 44 to 295 N. Take exit 5 to route 22 E (Congress St.) Follow 22 E to the traffic light at the top of the hill. Take a right onto Bramhall St and bear left onto Vaughn St. Continue to the 4th intersection; turn left on Carroll St to the inn at the corner of Neal St.

❄ ☕ 🏍 💳 ☎ @ W P 🖼 ♿ ⛵ 🍴 🚶 👣 🦆

POMEGRANATE INN
Innkeeper: Leslie Cotrell Gregoire
49 Neal Street
Portland, ME 04102, USA
Tel: (207) 772-1006, Fax: (877) 421-0567
Toll Free: (800) 356-0408
8 Rooms, Double: $195–$295
Open: all year, Credit cards: all major
Select Registry

On a quiet residential street in Rockland sits the Berry Manor Inn, built in 1898 as an elegant residence and now a twelve-bedroom inn. The bedrooms, all large and with queen and king beds lavishly piled with mountains of pillows, are located on three floors, with four spacious and interesting accommodations in and around the eaves on the third floor. Room 1, once the boudoir for the lady of the house, is decorated in shades of moss, sage, basil, and dark quartz. It has a mahogany half-tester canopy bed, a double chaise, a working fireplace, and an attached private bath with a large two-person whirlpool tub and two shower heads. All bedrooms are equipped with individually controlled thermostats, air conditioning, fireplaces, telephones, high-speed internet access, and private luxury baths. The adjoining carriage house has been newly refurbished and provides four guest suites with spectacular bathrooms featuring whirlpool tubs and walk-in showers with body jets. Guests enjoy morning coffee in the library, a full gourmet breakfast in the large dining room at individual tables, and evening sweets (that include homemade pies made by our Mom who was featured on the Food Network) are provided in the well-stocked guest pantry area. *Directions:* Take I-95 to Route 295 North (Exit 44). Follow Route 195 to Exit 28, Coastal Route 1 Bath/Brunswick until Rockland. At the first traffic light, turn left onto Broadway. After next traffic light, proceed to the fourth road, turn right on Talbot Ave.

BERRY MANOR INN
Innkeepers: Cheryl Michaelsen & Michael LaPosta
81 Talbot Ave
P.O. Box 1117
Rockland, ME 04841, USA
Tel: (207) 596-7696, Fax: (207) 596-9958
Toll Free: (800) 774-5692
12 Rooms, Double: $115–$380
Open: all year, Credit cards: all major
Select Registry

I first learned of Waterford when my dear friend Helen decided to return to her family ties in Maine. When I think of Waterford I think of an idyllic, classic New England town with its white steepled church on a grassy knoll. The Waterford Inne, a bed and breakfast with eight guestrooms, provides a terrific place to stay. The inn is a 19th-century farmhouse on a country lane amidst 25 acres of fields and woods—just viewing it tells you that this is another of those homes that now serves guests as it once did the original family. The guestrooms are uniquely decorated, mixing the warmth of antique furnishings with contemporary comforts in their modern bathrooms. The simple but elegant common rooms echo the decor of the bedrooms, with antiques and art, barn-board, brass, pewter, and primitives. With advance notice the innkeepers will provide a special dinner but there are also numerous restaurants nearby. Skiing and other winter sports are available in the area and in the summer there are many musical events, while antiquing is fun year round. *Directions:* Leave the Maine Turnpike (I-95) at exit 63, following Route 26 north for about 28 miles to Norway where you pick up Route 118 west. Drive 9 miles to Route 37, turn left, and travel half a mile to Chadbourne Road. Turn right and the inn is half-a-mile up the hill.

WATERFORD INNE
Innkeeper: Barbara Vanderzanden
P.O. Box 149
Waterford, ME 04088, USA
Tel & Fax: (207) 583-4037
8 Rooms, Double: $110–$200
Restaurant: dinner for guests, public by reservation
Open: all year, Credit cards: AX
Select Registry

At the end of a long country road, the Squire Tarbox Inn, a farmhouse dating from 1763 to 1825, listed on the National Register of Historic Places, exudes the peace and quiet of the countryside surrounding it. This rambling colonial farm affords a lovely spot to settle and to enjoy the splendor of being in the country. Sure, you can walk the path that leads to the water's edge and do some boating but I'd settle in with a good book in front of a wood-burning fire and let time slide by. The common rooms and the cozy dining rooms all have fireplaces. Guests can enjoy the mouth-watering meals created by the Swiss owner and chef. The dinner menu, with an emphasis on local produce, is an exciting culinary adventure. Bedrooms, generally king, are made up with featherbeds and most have fireplaces. For those who do want to venture out, there are harbors and beaches nearby, plenty of antiquing, shopping at discount stores, countryside excursions, and several fascinating museums with a variety of different themes. The inn's 11 bedrooms are simply, but very comfortably, decorated. *Directions:* From the south, take I-95 to I-295 to Rte 1, traveling north through Brunswick. Seven miles north of Bath Bridge, turn right on Rte 144. From the north, take south on Rte 1 through Wiscasset to Rte 144. Once on Rte 144 travel for 8½ miles—the inn is on the right.

❄ ☕ ✈ 💳 🐕 @ W P ⦿ 🚫 ⚓ 🚶 🐎 🦆 ⚓

SQUIRE TARBOX INN
Innkeepers: Mario & Veronica De Pietro
1181 Main Road
Westport Island
Westport, ME 04578, USA
Tel: (207) 882-7693, Fax: (207) 882-7107
Toll Free: (800) 818-0626
11 Rooms, Double: $115–$199
Open: Apr to Jan, Credit cards: all major
Select Registry

Once you cross into Maine life, seems different: first there's the smell of the sea air; then there are views down picturesque inlets of open water and the rise and fall of the ocean tides. Next you see the signs for lobster and the lobster boats—and you realize that you are in a place where the people, the food, and the scenery are unique. At the Dockside Guest Quarters, whose lawns and gardens sweep down to the water's edge, you are immediately captured by the setting on the water and the fishing boats bobbing up and down. The bedrooms and suites, which are located in several buildings, are comfortably decorated, but it's the views that capture your eye and demand your attention. I stayed in one of the suites with a nicely furnished living room, bedroom, and a full bath. Your visit will be enhanced by your hosts, the Lustys, who encourage you to take advantage of all the coast-oriented activities such as boating, fishing, beach walking, and biking. Nearby you find whale watching, lobstering, golf, tennis, summer theater, lots of antiquing, lighthouses, and outlet stores for the avid shopper. Lunch and dinner are served in the inn's restaurant where you can dine on the porch overlooking the harbor and all of its activities, while breakfast is served in the Maine House. *Directions:* From I-95 take exit 7. Turn south on Route 1. Turn left onto Route 1A, continuing on through York Village. Turn right on Route 103 then left immediately after crossing the York River onto Harris Island Road

DOCKSIDE GUEST QUARTERS
Innkeeper: The Lusty Family
22 Harris Island Road
York, ME 03909, USA
Tel: (207) 363-2868, Fax: (207) 363-1977
Toll Free: (888) 860-7428
19 Rooms, Double: $130–$235, 6 Suites: $205–$298
Minimum Stay Required: weekends Jul & Aug
Restaurant: closed Mon
Closed: Jan to Apr, Credit cards: MC, VS
Select Registry

Massachusetts
Places to Stay

Barnstable is one of those wonderfully quaint villages found on the north shore of Cape Cod and Ashley Manor is an inn worthy of a visit. Dating back to 1699, the inn sits back from the road in 2 acres of landscaped gardens surrounded by high hedges. Ashley Manor reveals its age with its wide-board flooring, large open-hearth fireplaces, and hand-glazed wainscoting. This inn is both elegant and warm, with beautiful decor and furnishings that include Oriental rugs, antiques, and handsome country furniture. Relax in the comfortable parlor and library or enjoy the privacy of your lovely room, which is equipped with everything you need for a pampered stay—imported chocolates and the finest soaps, shampoos, and lotions. All but one has a cozy fireplace and the suites offer the additional luxury of large whirlpool tubs. Breakfast is served in the parlor, the formal dining room, or in good weather on the terrace. If you have any spare time, you can play tennis. *Directions:* From Boston take Route 3 south to Sagamore Bridge onto Cape Cod, then follow Route 6 to exit 6. Turn immediately left onto Route 132 north to Route 6A and go about 3 miles through Barnstable Village to the traffic light. The inn is 6/10 mile down on the left.

ASHLEY MANOR
Innkeepers: Patricia Martin & Vince Toreno
3660 Olde Kings Hwy at Main St., Rte 6A
P.O. Box 856
Barnstable, MA 02630, USA
Tel: (508) 362-8044, Toll Free: (888) 535-2246
6 Rooms, Double: $145–$235
Open: all year, Credit cards: all major

In a perfect location just off Boston Common on Charles Street, site of many antique shops, restaurants, and boutiques, you find the new Beacon Hill Hotel & Bistro, a very sophisticated small hotel with the feel of a bed and breakfast. The bedrooms, reached via an elevator are small, but have all the amenities that a traveler might expect including a flat-screen TV mounted on the wall. Nine of the rooms have queen beds, two have doubles, one has twin beds, and on the top floor there is an in-room suite. The color palette of the bedrooms' decor is soft and soothing, with tones of taupe accented by off-white trim and black accessories. Satellite TV is available, including the movie channels, and there are telephones with dual lines and a data port for Internet access. Most of the rooms do not have seating areas but there is a small and comfortable sitting area for guests on the second floor. The hotel is air-conditioned and there is parking available for guests—a very nice feature in downtown Boston. The trendy but comfortable adjoining bistro-restaurant, which has received much acclaim, provides room service and the hotel offers all the concierge services one could want for maximizing a stay in the Boston area. *Directions:* From Storrow Drive take the Government Center exit. At the end of the off ramp proceed through two stoplights, leaving the CVS Pharmacy on your left, onto Charles Street. The hotel is on the left on the corner of Chestnut and Charles Streets.

❄ ☕ ⚒ 🏧 ☎ 🛗 @ W P ⍔ 🖼 ⚿ ⚓ ⚓ 🎿 ⛷ 🚶

BEACON HILL HOTEL & BISTRO
Innkeepers: Peter & Cecilia Rait
25 Charles Street
Boston, MA 02114, USA
Tel: (617) 723-7575, Fax: (617) 723-7525
Toll Free: (888) 959-2442
13 Rooms, Double: $245–$405
Open: all year, Credit cards: all major

The Charles Street Inn is beautifully located on the flat of Beacon Hill, the historic district where colonial merchants first built their homes, within walking distance of all you may want to explore in downtown Boston. The inn's guestrooms—two per floor—offer 21st-century comforts while retaining a 19th-century elegance. Each one is uniquely decorated in period colors, fabrics, and furnishings and named for a famous Boston Victorian. Front rooms with queen beds offer views of Charles Street, with its tempting restaurants and unique shops, while rooms at the back are larger and quieter, overlooking the very private area of Mount Vernon Square, and most feature king beds. Each room has a sitting area where you may enjoy your deluxe breakfast and relax in style. The rooms' superb amenities include working marble fireplaces, air conditioning, extra-large whirlpool spa tubs, robes, slippers, in-room mini-fridge, coffee pots and tea kettles, complete set of dishes, wireless and high-speed internet access, cable TV, DVD, VCR, and Bose AM/FM/CD systems. Baths have granite counters, white tile finishes, and cherry-wood cabinets. *Directions:* From I-90 (Mass Pike) take the Cambridge Storrow Drive exit, following Storrow Drive to the Government Center/Kendall Square exit, then turn right off the exit onto Charles Street.

CHARLES STREET INN
Innkeepers: Louise Venden & Sally Deane
94 Charles Street
Boston, MA 02114-4643, USA
Tel: (617) 314-8900, Fax: (617) 371-0009
Toll Free: (877) 772-8900
9 Rooms, Double: $250–$575
Open: all year, Credit cards: all major
Select Registry

One of the many pleasures of visiting Boston is that you can walk to almost everything you'd like to see. The best location is the Clarendon Square Inn, as its doors open onto all of Boston's restaurants, galleries, and shopping. This historic property, with its traditional exterior, has been transformed into an elegant urban retreat. Guest suites are spacious with ornamental fireplaces and limestone bathrooms. High-count cotton sheets, down pillows, and Aveda bath amenities will pamper you. There is a sundeck on the roof, complete with a hot-tub overlooking Boston's skyline. The inn's parlor has 11-foot high ceilings with period detail and a grand piano. The garden suite's modern furniture, subtle textures, and calming colors stimulate, but also relax. The window seat in the bay room, furnished in Empire style and decorated in deep sensuous colors, invites you to curl up with a book or perhaps a glass of wine. Such is the style and experience you will have at an inn whose owners have traveled widely, capturing and translating the finest elements to make your stay memorable and your return guaranteed. *Directions:* From Mass Pike Route 90, take exit 22 for Copley Square, keep right on the off-ramp to Copley. Take first right onto Dartmouth Street. At 2nd light take right onto Warren Avenue. West Brookline St is the 2nd left and the inn the 5th house.

CLARENDON SQUARE INN
Owner: Stephen Gross
Innkeeper: Karen Cigala
198 West Brookline Street
Boston, MA 02118, USA
Tel: (617) 536-2229
3 Rooms, Double: $195–$495
Open: all year, Credit cards: all major

Elegant is the word that sums up every aspect of one of Boston's loveliest hotels. In a great location next to the State House, within a few minutes' walk of all the historical buildings and the Freedom Trail, with Boston Common just across the way, and with every creature comfort offered by the hotel's staff, there is no better place to spend the night. Sophisticated in every sense, Fifteen Beacon welcomes you into its front lobby where the concierge and the reception desk staff make you instantly feel like a treasured returning guest. The muted palette of colors used throughout is warm and inviting, contemporary in feel, and totally relaxing. In your bedroom the sitting areas, the fireplace, the wall coverings, the carpet, the artwork, and the crispness of the bed and its linens all contribute to the ambiance of this special experience. In one room, a spotlight focused attention on the simple beauty of a tall glass cylinder filled with apples. The elegant bathrooms provide every amenity in a very contemporary setting. A delightful place to relax is the roof deck with herb garden, where you can drink in lovely views while nibbling on something delicious brought to you by room service. *Directions:* From Storrow Drive take the Government Center exit. Go straight through the traffic light on Cambridge Street for ¾ mile to Park Street, turn right and drive to the end. At the light turn right on Beacon Street for 1½ blocks to the inn on the left.

❄ ⚡ 💳 ☎ ♿ 🍴 @ W P ‖ 🛋 ⚓ ♿ ⚓ 🎯 🕯

FIFTEEN BEACON
Innkeeper: Amy Finsilver
15 Beacon Street
Boston, MA 02108, USA
Tel: (617) 670-1500, Fax: (617) 670-2525
Toll Free: (877) 982-3226
60 Rooms, Double: $395–$2500*
*Breakfast not included: $40
Open: all year, Credit cards: all major

In the heart of Boston's Back Bay on Exeter Street stands The Lenox, recently renovated by the Saunders family into a very chic place for you to stay while you are visiting the many attractions of Boston. It is located in the heart of Boylston and Newbury Streets' shopping and art galleries, which could keep you busy for days. Copley Place and the Prudential Center are a few steps from the hotel. The hotel features 212 guestrooms, each with private bathroom. Since the hotel was recently refurbished, the rooms are especially attractive. One of the rooms I visited had a corner fireplace, wonderfully comfortable seating, and two queen beds. It was decorated in tones of taupe and had flowered drapes, which pulled across the windows in the evening. This is a full-service hotel offering amenities such as concierge and valet, voice mail, in-room fax machines, wireless internet, phones with modem ports, laundry service, and conference facilities. Azure is the formal dining room (where breakfast is also served) but there is also a pub, Solas, serving lighter food in a casual setting and the City Bar, serving food and drink in an engaging ambiance. Room service is also available. The hotel has the bonus of an on-site exercise room. *Directions:* Take I-93 into Boston, exiting at the signs to Copley Square. Turn right at Beacon Street for four blocks and then take a left on Exeter Street. The Lenox is four blocks down on the right.

❄ ⚡ 💳 ☎ 🛗 🍽 @ W P ¶ ⚓ ♿ ⚓ 🧍 🚶

THE LENOX
Owner: Saunders Hotel Group
61 Exeter Street
Boston, MA 02116, USA
Tel: (617) 536-5300, Fax: (617) 236-0351
Toll Free: (800) 225-7676
214 Rooms, 4 Suites & 12 Junior Suites
Double: $295–$3500*
*Breakfast not included: $15–$25
Open: all year, Credit cards: all major

As you drive along Cape Cod's north shore route you're instantly attracted to the Brewster By The Sea Inn and Spa with its neat and tidy appearance. Brewster is but one of several little villages that are charming with their historical homes and ambiance. You enter into the inn's large gathering room decorated in an English-country motif, with a fireplace at one end and a lovely sitting area at the other end of this expansive space with its cathedral ceiling. A full gourmet breakfast is served in this area during cooler months and in the summer on the deck, which leads out to the heated pool and spa. While the beach is just a short distance away, the pool area is so attractive it might be tempting to stay right at the inn. In the afternoon the owners serve tea to guests returning from a day of exploring. In terms of accommodation guests can choose between the four rooms in the Olde Farmhouse with its original wood floors, fireplaces and canopy beds and the four spacious, contemporary rooms in the New Orchard House, built in 1998. Named for the furniture from Milan used in the decor, The Refugio Suite (translated to Refuge) is spectacular with a large, king-size bedroom, private patio and a living room and kitchenette. Regardless of location, all the guestrooms are attractively decorated. *Directions:* From Boston, take Rte 3 south to Bourne Bridge to Rte 6 to exit 9b (Rte 134). Turn right onto Rte 134 for about 3 miles to Rte 6A, then turn right onto 6A for about 2 miles.

❄ ☕ 🚲 💳 ☎ @ W P ✿ ≈ ⚓ 🎿 🏃 🐎 ⛵ 🍴

BREWSTER BY THE SEA, EUROPEAN INN & SPA
Innkeepers: Donna & Byron Cain
716 Main Street
Brewster, MA 02631, USA
Tel: (508) 896-3910, Fax: (508) 896-4232
Toll Free: (800) 892-3910
8 Rooms, Double: $125–$275
2 Suites: $155–$325
Open: all year, Credit cards: all major

Sea captains' homes fill the landscape in this lovely Cape Cod town. The Captain Freeman Inn was home to one of those merchants whose wealth came from the rich clipper trade in the late 1800s and a picture of his ship, the Kingfisher, hangs in the entry hall. Elegant architectural details are everywhere in this building—ornate plaster moldings, wood floors in intricate patterns, a commanding center staircase, and a parlor with marble fireplace and floor-to-ceiling windows. There are traditional and luxury guestrooms, all wonderful and all air-conditioned. The luxury rooms have queen canopy beds, fireplaces, and spa tubs in the bathrooms. Among the traditional rooms it is hard to choose a favorite between the cozy bedroom with dark paneling, queen bed, and hand-sewn canopy and the queen bedroom with the pine four-poster and lace canopy. Some rooms can accommodate an extra person. An elegant wraparound porch is a perfect spot to rock away the hours with iced tea or lemonade. The inn has its own swimming pool. A short walk from the inn will bring you to the local beach. The Captain Freeman Inn has winter weekend cooking classes. *Directions:* Leave Route 6 at exit 10, taking Route 124 towards Brewster. At the end of Route 124, go right on Route 6A, then left on Breakwater to the first driveway on the left.

CAPTAIN FREEMAN INN
Innkeepers: Donna & Peter Amadeo
15 Breakwater Road
Brewster, MA 02631, USA
Tel: (508) 896-7481, Fax: (508) 896-5618
Toll Free: (800) 843-4664
12 Rooms, Double: $150–$250
Minimum Stay Required: 2 nights from Jul to Sep
Open: all year, Credit cards: MC, VS
Select Registry

Like so many of the homes along the north shore of Cape Cod, this 1780s home once belonged to a sea captain. It has now been restored to become an inn offering seven bedrooms, all with private bathrooms, although four of the room's bathrooms are located across the hall from the room—plan to use one of the inn's robes and you'll be all set. The bedrooms are attractively decorated in simple Cape-Cod style with comfortable, homelike furnishings. Whether you choose to relax in your bedroom or in the inn's living room, this is an inn that has the ambiance of home, a sentiment reinforced by the innkeeper, whose gracious welcome will make you feel like a friend rather than a guest. In the morning a full breakfast is served either in the keeping room or outside on the deck with its surrounding gardens. The inn is air-conditioned for comfort in the warm summer months. Brewster has good restaurants, antique shops, and places to browse around, and is a pleasant town for walking. Here you are within an easy drive of the Cape Cod National Seashore where Atlantic Ocean beaches beckon you to stroll along their edge. Using the inn as the place for a good night's rest, you can enjoy bird watching, nature walks, wildlife preserves, boating, swimming, bicycling, golf, tennis, and horseback riding. *Directions:* From Boston, take Route 3 south to Sagamore Bridge to Route 6 to exit 9B. Follow Route 134 north then at Route 6A turn right for 3 miles to the inn on the left.

ISAIAH CLARK HOUSE
Innkeepers: Steve & Philomena
1187 Main Street
Brewster, MA 02631, USA
Tel: (508) 896-2223, Fax: (508) 896-2138
Toll Free: (800) 822-4001
7 Rooms, Double: $99–$179
Minimum Stay Required: 3 nights on weekends & holidays
Open: Apr 24 to Nov 15, Credit cards: all major

Situated on the outskirts of Cambridge and Boston, close to Harvard Square and conveniently located near the subway, A Cambridge House has 15 bedrooms, each with private bath and all elegantly furnished with premier fabrics and charming decor. While the rooms are not large, they provide everything the visitor might want, and most especially that cozy feeling of home. The four-poster beds have down comforters and each room has comfortable seating, a telephone, wireless internet access and color TV. Free wireless internet is available in the lounge. Many of the rooms have fireplaces. The flowered or patterned wallpapers are exquisite and in some rooms the matching fabric has been used on the bed canopy. A continental breakfast is served in either of two equally beautiful living rooms. Coffee and tea are served all day. The inn provides complimentary parking on the inn property. Public transportation is the key to getting around Boston and Cambridge: it's easy and convenient and you'll be glad to leave your car while you explore the endless array of things to do in the Boston area. Logan Airport is about 20 minutes from the inn. *Directions:* The inn may be reached by car, taxi, subway or bus and has very detailed directions, which are given to every guest. Please contact the hotel directly for written directions.

A CAMBRIDGE HOUSE INN
Innkeepers: Hong & Arnold Roquerre
2218 Massachusetts Avenue
Cambridge, MA 02140-1836, USA
Tel: (617) 491-6300, Fax: (617) 868-2848
Toll Free: (800) 232-9989
15 Rooms, Double: $129–$249
Open: all year, Credit cards: all major

Captain Hiram Harding, a well know sea captain in the 1800s, built this home in 1839, and the inn's very individual rooms are named after his family and the ships he sailed. This inn is an elegant compound with its guestrooms clustered around a handsome Greek Revival home. The common areas are attractively furnished with antiques and the dining-room sun porch is surrounded by floor-to-ceiling windows giving views into the delightful gardens. Breakfast is served here with sterling silver and fine china on linen-covered tables. Each bedroom is individually decorated and many will remind you of the cozy feeling of colonial times with their beamed ceilings, fireplaces, and queen or king beds with antique bedposts. Many rooms have original random-width pine floors, adding to the decor's charm. All rooms have private baths, a few have spa tubs, and several have private decks. I loved my room with its dark paneling, massive king bed, and a fireplace with two comfortable wing chairs. The Clarissa and Lydia Harding suites are examples of the owners' passion to offer the best of accommodations. Among the many amenities you'll find a new fitness center with exercise room and outdoor heated pool. *Directions:* Leave Rte 6 at exit 11 south, taking Rte 137 to Rte 28. Turn left; drive about 3 miles to the rotary. Follow the rotary around to the left (still on Rte 28) toward Orleans. The inn is ½ mile along on the left.

❄ ☕ ✄ 🖼 ☎ 🚹 🏋 @ W P 🚭 ♣ ≈ 🎿 🖼 ⛷ 🚣 🏌 🐾 ⚓

CAPTAIN'S HOUSE INN
Innkeepers: Jill & James Meyer
369-377 Old Harbor Road
Chatham, MA 02633, USA
Tel: (508) 945-0127, Fax: (508) 945-0866
Toll Free: (800) 315-0728
12 Rooms, Double: $185–$350
4 Suites: $185–$475
Open: all year, Credit cards: all major
Select Registry

The historic town of Concord is one of those very special New England towns that draw the visitor in to share their past and to experience their welcoming charm. Here you find a quaint village with interesting shops, lovely old homes lining the streets, a magnificent white Unitarian church set back on the green, and on the far edge of the green a landmark inn—Concord's Colonial Inn, built in 1716 as a family residence. It became an inn in 1889, providing cozy bars with fireplaces, a choice of dining rooms, and comfortably decorated guestrooms. Several wings have been added to the original structure, giving 56 guestrooms in the various buildings, including the Cottage and Rebecca's Guest House. The inn reflects all the busyness of a hotel that can accommodate up to 80 for a meeting or six private room functions, but there are many places where the guest can find a quiet place to sit and enjoy the very special warmth that comes from a house that has lived so long. The bedrooms have all the amenities expected by the business traveler: concierge, voice mail, fax, wireless high speed internet access, cable TV/DVD, and laundry service. Suites with kitchenettes are perfect for extended stays. *Directions:* Concord is easily reached by taking Route 2 from downtown Boston or from the I-95/Route 128. Signs on Route 2 lead you into Concord and the inn sits at the far end of the village green.

❄ ✎ 🖮 ☎ 🛗 @ W P 🍴 🚭 🖼 ✎ ⛷ 🚶 🏃 🐎 ⛷ ⚓ ❦

CONCORD'S COLONIAL INN
Owner: Jurgen Demisch
48 Monument Square
Concord, MA 01742, USA
Tel: (978) 369-9200, Fax: (978) 371-1533
Toll Free: (800) 370-9200
56 Rooms, Double: $129–$279*
7 Suites: $279–$359*
*Breakfast not included: $10–$20
Open: all year, Credit cards: all major

The town of Concord is steeped in the history of the founding of the American Colonies and in the battles with Britain that led to independence. Set amongst trees and gardens, the Hawthorne Inn, built in 1870 and situated on land that once belonged to Ralph Waldo Emerson, the Alcotts, and Nathaniel Hawthorne, is within easy walking distance of many of the town's points of historical interest. The bedrooms are named after famous people or places associated with this area—for example, Emerson, Alcott, Walden, and Sleepy Hollow—and the books in the rooms continue the theme. Flowered wallpapers, queen canopy beds, and hand-sewn quilts make the bedrooms very comfortable. They are not large but they provide all you'll want after a day of touring the history-filled countryside. Children are welcomed and if yours are interested in history, it would be hard to think of a better place to stay. The owners are art aficionados and have hung the walls with an eclectic collection of contemporary art. Continental breakfast, the only meal served, offers fresh fruit, juice, home-baked breads, and either a selection of teas or the inn's own blend of coffee. The innkeepers have prepared a week's program of things for you to do while visiting the area—follow their suggestions for a memorable and educational vacation. *Directions:* Take exit 30 (Route 2A west) from Routes 128 and 95. Bear right at the fork toward Concord for 1.2 miles. The inn is across from Hawthorne's home.

HAWTHORNE INN
Innkeepers: Gregory Burch & Marilyn Mudry
462 Lexington Road
Concord, MA 01742, USA
Tel: (978) 369-5610, Fax: (978) 287-4949
7 Rooms, Double: $155–$315
Open: all year, Credit cards: all major
Select Registry

Visiting historic Deerfield is dropping into the heart of a 330-year-old New England village, with historic homes lining its wide Main Street. Fourteen of the village's old houses hold more than 20,000 objects—furniture, silver, glass, ceramics, and textiles—made or used in America between 1650 and 1850. The classic 1884 Deerfield Inn is the centerpiece of this village and its 23 guestrooms are all named after people associated with the village's history. Horatio Alger, room 141, has pastel window draperies inspired by a book on period valances. The wallpaper picks up the floral, romantic theme and the mahogany king-sized sleigh bed has an inviting patchwork quilt across the foot. Many of the bedrooms have the vibrant paintwork typical of the Federal period in New England, while others are reminiscent of the English settlers that first made Deerfield their home. The Everett House room has a delicate English window treatment and sunny wallpaper in greens and warm yellows, with cheerful throw pillows on the four-poster bed. All rooms have private baths, telephones, flat screen TVs, and individual climate controls and many have antique four-posters. The award-winning restaurant serves American cuisine, the terrace café provides light meals, and the tavern offers local and international brews. *Directions:* Going north on I-91 take exit 24, exit 25 going south. Deerfield Village is just off Routes 5 and 10 north.

❄ ☕ ✍ 💳 ☎ 🛗 W P 🍴 🖼 ♿ 🏃 👫

DEERFIELD INN
Innkeepers: Jane Howard & Karl Sabo
81 Old Main Street
Deerfield, MA 01342-0305, USA
Tel: (413) 774-5587, Fax: (413) 775-7221
Toll Free: (800) 926-3865
24 Rooms, Double: $160–$240
Closed: Christmas, Credit cards: all major
Select Registry

The Isaiah Hall Bed & Breakfast Inn sits on a street running parallel to Route 6A, which gives it the simple advantage of being away from the hustle and bustle of the principal tourist route along the north shore of Cape Cod. This farmhouse was built in 1857 by Isaiah Hall, whose grandfather cultivated the first cranberry bogs for which the Cape is so deservedly famous. There are twelve guestrooms in the main house and the adjoining carriage house. A recently added two bedroom, two bath suite is lovely and ideal for families. The attractively furnished, air-conditioned rooms, with double, queen, and king beds, are equipped with TV/DVDs, wireless internet access, clock-radios, hairdryers, and bathrobes. One suite has a king four-poster pine bed, a sitting room with a pullout sofa, a refrigerator, and a balcony overlooking the gardens at the rear of the inn. A great breakfast awaits you in the dining room at one of two tables (the 12-foot cherry table is wonderful and gives you the chance to meet fellow guests) as well as tea and something delicious in the late afternoon. For relaxing, there's a porch with rockers and a comfortable parlor. It's only a short stroll to the sandy beach, and the street on which the inn is located just begs for you to walk along its length and admire the neighboring homes. *Directions:* From Boston, take I-93 to Rte 3 to Rte 6 (Bourne Bridge) to exit 8. Turn left for 1.2 miles to Rte 6A, right for 3.4 miles to Hope Lane, left onto Hope Lane. Turn right on Whig Street.

ISAIAH HALL BED & BREAKFAST INN
Innkeepers: Jerry & Judy Neal
152 Whig Street
P.O. Box 1007
Dennis, MA 02638, USA
Tel: (508) 385-9928, Toll Free: (800) 736-0160
12 Rooms, Double: $140–$190
3 Suites: $215–$405
Minimum Stay Required: In summer
Open: all year, Credit cards: all major

Founded in 1620, Duxbury is a quaint New England town and the Powder Point Bed & Breakfast is located in an exclusive residential district that populates a peninsula with easy access to bike trails and beaches. After converting a wing of their home to accommodate their children, Richard and Linda decided to offer their charming guestrooms to more than just their extended family. With its own separate entrance, guests enjoy a lovely living room, back sun porch and expanse of lawn and garden. Just off the living room, the Rose Room has a queen four-poster bed, fireplace, and a sitting area vestibule with a desk for writing postcards. There's a cozy floral comforter inviting you to take an afternoon nap and a full bathroom. Climb the stair to the Blue and Green rooms that share a bath—ideal for family or friends traveling together. The Blue Room has a queen bed, a bureaued closet and the bath with a tub/shower combination. The Green Room has dark walnut twin beds which may be converted into a king, a fireplace and two wing chairs. Refreshments are offered afternoons and breakfast is an elegant buffet—described by the innkeepers as "an expanded continental with an European flair." Richard and Linda encourage guests to settle in and use the accommodation as their home, to come and go as they like. *Directions:* From Boston, take Rte 93 south to Rte 3 to exit 11, take Rte 14 east to the town of Duxbury. Turn left on Powder Point Ave.

❄ ☕ 💳 ☎ @ W P 🚭 🖼 ⚓ 🚶 ⚓

POWDER POINT BED & BREAKFAST
Innkeepers: Richard & Linda Quigley
182 Powder Point Avenue
Duxbury, MA 02332, USA
Tel: (781) 934-7727, Fax: (781) 934-2773
Toll Free: (866) 934-7727
3 Rooms, Double: $195–$335
Open: all year, Credit cards: all major

Halfway along the length of Cape Cod an "elbow" marks the start of the unspoiled, unhurried, and absolutely beautiful Outer Cape. With 40 miles of National Seashore, this is a very special place, with none of the tourist activities usually associated with the Cape. There, on a street of colonial homes, you'll find The Whalewalk Inn, an 1830s whaling master's home that has been meticulously restored to provide 16 beautifully decorated and spacious guestrooms, each with private bath, in the main house and the recently built carriage house. The rooms are wonderful with a sophisticated country decor using individual palettes of colors. I loved the king-sized bedroom with its own private entrance, fireplace, and bathroom with whirlpool tub and steam shower. Innkeepers Elaine and Kevin are always on a quest for new art objects to go in each room and equally passionate about food, offering memorable gourmet breakfasts. After a day at the beach, riding the Rail Trail, kayaking, shopping or museum hopping, visit The Spa, designed for your comfort and catering to your preferences with a full range of services including sauna, hot tub, indoor pool, and exercise equipment. When the sun goes down the inn glows with lights and candles in its windows. Inside, the experience is romantic and rejuvenating. *Directions:* Take Route 6 to the Orleans rotary, then the Rock Harbor exit off the rotary. Turn left on Rock Harbor Road and right on Bridge Road.

❄ ☕ ⚙ 💳 🍴 @ W ⵂ P 🚫 ❧ ≈ 🖼 ♿ ⚓ 🎿 👫 🐎 ⚘ 🍷

THE WHALEWALK INN & SPA
Innkeepers: Elaine & Kevin Conlin
220 Bridge Road
Eastham, MA 02642, USA
Tel: (508) 255-0617, Fax: (508) 240-0017
Toll Free: (800) 440-1281
16 Rooms, Double: $220–$420
5 Suites: $310–$420, 1 Cottage: $310 daily
Minimum Stay Required: 2 nights
Open: Apr to Jan 1, Credit cards: AX, MC, VS
Select Registry

Just down from the white steepled church in the quaint, enchanting port town of Harwich sits the delightful Dunscroft-By-The-Sea. This two-story, wood-shingled, shuttered house is charming and beautifully decorated. To the left of the entry is a gorgeous living room with cream-colored sofas in front of a cozy brick fire near the enclosed garden porch. In the elegant dining room guests enjoy a bountiful breakfast around one large table. The inn offers eight bedrooms in the main house and one in the garden cottage which also has a living room, fireplace, and kitchen. All the rooms in the main house are lovely. I was impressed by the personalized welcome note in each room, to Robert and Elizabeth in room 1, a lovely front corner room; to Scarlett and Rhett in room 2, a larger room with king canopy bed, Jacuzzi tub, and views over the side garden; to Cleo and Anthony in room 3, a pretty front corner room; to Sonny and Cher in number 4 with Jacuzzi tub; and to Edward and Wallis in room 5 with handsome king canopy bed and corner windows overlooking the back garden. A rose theme pervades the inn, from the mailbox to the handsome wallpapers decorating many rooms. *Directions:* From Boston follow Route 3 to Cape Cod then Route 6 in the direction of "Hyannis to Provincetown." Take exit 10, Route 124 south to Route 28. Turn left on 28 and then go ¾ mile to Pilgrim Road, alongside the white church at the town center.

❄ ☕ ▣ 🛗 @ W P ⚲ ⚓ 🎿 👫 🐎 ⛷ 🛶

ALYCE'S DUNSCROFT-BY-THE-SEA   **Cover painting**
Innkeeper: Alyce R. Mundy
24 Pilgrim Road
Harwich Port, MA 02646, USA
Tel: (508) 432-0810, Toll Free: (800) 432-4345
8 Rooms, Double: $155–$395
1 Cottage: $255–$475 daily
Closed: Dec to Jan, Credit cards: MC, VS

Nestled on the vast protected acreage of the Crane Estate, this handsome inn looks out over salt marshes and sand dunes to the distant Atlantic. The inn enjoys a lovely entry off a wraparound porch, warmed by a welcoming fire. Off the entry to one side is the guest parlor and in the oldest part of the house is the inn's beautiful dining room whose bright, fresh decor of blues, creams, and whites is a perfect complement at breakfast to the morning light. With the exception of one room off the lobby, guestrooms, all unique in decor, are found at the top of the handsome staircase. On the first floor are two of the inn's most dramatic rooms with stunning views of the marsh and ocean. Cornelius, whose subtle decor of soft beiges and whites was selected so as not to compete with the view out of one entire wall of windows, and the very pretty and inviting Miné with its wood-burning fireplace, sweet floral decor, and windows that look up to the wooded hillside. A full breakfast is included in the rate. *Directions:* On Route 128 North, exit 15 and turn left on School St. Follow it for three miles. Bear right onto Route 133 west until crossing the Ipswich town line. Turn right at the sign for Castle Hill onto Northgate Rd. At the road's end, bear right onto Argilla and travel 1.9 miles to the inn.

❄ 🖻 ⚡ 🚬 ☎ 🏨 @ W P ⑅ ♿ ⚓ 🎿 🚶 ⚓

INN AT CASTLE HILL
Innkeeper: Bob Chok
280 Argilla Road
Ipswich, MA 01938, USA
Tel: (978) 412-2555, Fax: (978) 412-2556
10 Rooms, Double: $115–$385
Open: Apr to Dec, Credit cards: all major

Built in the 1920s as a summer home for a New York physician, Applegate is now a commanding country inn with a four-column façade set among perennial gardens, towering pine trees, and rolling lawns. A particularly gracious front hall has a lovely carved staircase leading up to the second floor. In addition to the living room, there is a TV room with a VCR and a video library for the use of guests. The bedrooms and cottage are furnished with reproduction antiques and provide all the amenities one would expect as a guest in a gracious home of this period. Room 1 has a four-poster king bed and a sofa in the sitting area, which has a fireplace; the bathroom contains a large steam shower. Room 3 has a French-style sleigh bed, a fireplace, and views out to the lawns and pine trees. Two new luxury suites with balconies and fireplaces offer a choice of a soaking tub or whirlpool tub for two. The Carriage House Cottage, with two bedrooms sharing one bath, a full kitchen, living room, dining room, and deck, would be ideal for a family or for two couples traveling together. The Carriage House also contains two luxury suites with large Jacuzzis and gas fireplaces. Amenities include a pool, bicycles, and 6 acres of grounds. A full gourmet breakfast is served in the candlelit dining room and wine and cheese are served in the evening. *Directions:* Take the Massachusetts Turnpike to exit 2 to Route 20 to the first stop sign. Continue on to the inn on the left.

❄ ☕ 🍴 ♨ 💳 ☎ @ W P 🚭 ≋ 🎿 🖼 ⛷ 🏊 🚶 🏇 ⛷ 🚴 🍷

APPLEGATE INN
Innkeepers: Len & Gloria Friedman
279 West Park Street
Lee, MA 01238, USA
Tel: (413) 243-4451, Fax: (413) 243-9832
Toll Free: (800) 691-9012
5 Rooms, Double: $195–$275
5 Suites: $270–$395
1 Cottage: $270–$375 daily
Open: all year, Credit cards: all major
Select Registry

Devonfield is a gracious, large country home set on a 32 acre pastoral meadow shaded by birch trees, with the rolling tapestry of the Berkshire Hills beyond. This 200 year old historic estate has been graciously updated and is filled with fine antiques. It is sophisticated, yet, comfortable and inviting. There are ten beautifully appointed guestrooms (six large bedrooms, three suites, and a guest cottage), each with furniture and amenities chosen for your comfort. This Federal style of architecture lends itself to a graciousness not often found in inns of other architectural construction, and here you really feel like a guest in a country home. Stay several nights here in the coziness of your own bedroom with wood-burning fireplace or in the large living room and enjoy all that this area has to offer, or make use of the heated pool, the tennis court, and the bicycles available to guests. In winter bring along your cross-country skis and cross the meadows in the brisk country air. This inn is known for its breakfasts, which are as luxurious as the inn itself. In the afternoon there's a cup of tea to be enjoyed in front of the fire or outdoors on the patio. There are Jacuzzis and TVs and in the Penthouse Suite and the Wilhelmina Cottage there are kitchenettes. Guests are treated to brandy, chocolates, and a special brand of hospitality from Devonfield's innkeepers. *Directions:* From Stockbridge, drive north from Main Street on Rte 7 for 8/10 mile to Lee Rd, which becomes Stockbridge Rd.

❄ ☕ 🏌 ☕ 💳 📷 🐕 🍴 @ W Y P 🚭 🏊 🚶 🖼 ♿ ⛱ 🎿 🏃 🐎 ⛷ ⚓ 🍷

DEVONFIELD INN
Innkeepers: Ronnie & Bruce Singer
85 Stockbridge Road
Lee, MA 01238, USA
Tel: (413) 243-3298, Fax: (413) 243-1360
Toll Free: (800) 664-0880
10 Rooms, Double: $160–$375
5 Suites, 1 Cottage: $275–$375
Minimum Stay Required: 2 nights weekends in Jul & Aug
Open: all year, Credit cards: all major
Select Registry

Blantyre, a Tudor-style mansion built in 1902, is set on a hill on 115 acres of spectacular Berkshire countryside. Replicating a grand Scottish manor, Blantyre is indeed a step back into a place and time of elegance and gracious living, bringing to the visitor a world of serene European ambiance, calm, courtesy, charm, and cuisine. From the main hall with its immense fireplace and massive, ornate furniture, a sweeping oak staircase leads you up to eight of the bedrooms. I love the grandeur of The Paterson Suite with its king mahogany four-poster bed sitting beneath exquisite flower prints, large sitting area with fireplace, and two bathrooms. Additional guestrooms are found in the carriage house and cottages. In the carriage house, Wyndhurst has a king four-poster bed and French windows opening onto the expansive lawns. One of the cottages, The Ice House, has been converted to a magnificent suite of rooms and a separate guestroom on the lower level. Several rooms have fireplaces and all provide every luxurious amenity. The conservatory is the setting for breakfast and lunch. Dinner is served in the formal dining room of the main house. Exclusive for guests, the Potting Shed offers intimate spa services and in winter the tennis courts convert to an ice-skating rink complete with a Snow Concierge and a nearby warming hut is popular with guests who have taken advantage of the extensive snowshoeing trails. *Directions:* Leave I-90 at exit 2 in Lee; take Rte 20 west 3 miles.

BLANTYRE
Innkeeper: Ann Fitzpatrick Brown
16 Blantyre Road
P.O. Box 995, Lenox, MA 01240, USA
Tel: (413) 637-3556, Fax: (413) 637-4282
11 Rooms, Double: $550–$950*, 8 Suites: $750–$1300*
4 Cottages: $950–$1800* daily
*Service: 20%
Minimum Stay Required: on weekends
Open: all year, Credit cards: all major
Relais & Châteaux

The Brook Farm Inn has an ideal Berkshires location, within walking distance of Lenox center and Tanglewood. The main building, born a gracious Victorian home, has 12 guestrooms. The newer carriage house has 3 luxury accommodations with private entrances and decks overlooking the garden. Guests of the carriage house also enjoy amenities such as whirlpool tubs. The serene setting of the inn is of a wooded glen, with an acre of award-winning gardens, surrounding a heated in-ground pool. Upon entering you are enveloped in warm hospitality and comfortable elegance. The library, at the center of the inn, has high ceilings, antique furniture and a window seat begging you to curl up and read. There is also a wood-burning fireplace where tea and fresh scones are served each afternoon. A full breakfast is also included. On the second floor of the main building, room number 2 is richly furnished with a mahogany antique dresser, queen canopy bed, fireplace, velvet-covered wing chairs and drapes and a large bathroom. Rooms are also available with king and twin beds. A guest pantry thoughtfully provides ice, refrigerators, hot water tap and hot beverage supplies. *Directions:* Take the Massachusetts Turnpike east or west to exit 2 to Route 20 west and turn left on Route 183. At the monument in the center of Lenox go left downhill on old Stockbridge Road. Make the first right on Hawthorne Street.

❄ 🍴 🛷 💳 ☎ @ W P 🚭 ≋ ♿ ⚓ 🏃 🏃 🐎 🏂

BROOK FARM INN
Innkeepers: Phil & Linda Halpern
15 Hawthorne Street
Lenox, MA 01240, USA
Tel: (413) 637-3013, Fax: (413) 637-4751
Toll Free: (800) 285-7638
15 Rooms, Double: $145–$425
1 Suite: $325–$425
Minimum Stay Required: holidays & often in summer
Open: all year, Credit cards: all major
Select Registry

Gateways, a majestic inn that fronts Walker Street at the heart of Lenox, was once the summer mansion of Harley Procter of Procter and Gamble. Today, guests bask in the present owners' warmth of welcome and sense of humor (Fabrizio brings his own touch of Italian charm), which create a comfortable balance of elegance and hospitality. Just off the entry you find a lovely bedroom, The Berkshire, converted from what was once Mr. Procter's study, and the dining room, a very elegant room with a dark-rust wall and gorgeous high moldings contrasting in white. The menu, created by Rosemary the chef, is considered one of the best in Lenox and the wine list is marvelous. Climb the absolutely gorgeous wide staircase as its wide platform and gorgeous banister wind up to guestrooms. We selected what was Mr. Procter's own bedroom, a large front-corner room whose bath enjoys a claw-foot tub designed especially to accommodate his exceptional height. The next-door room is bright and sunny and decorated in cheery yellows. Room 4, formerly Mrs. Procter's apartment, is the only suite—a large living room was once her bedchamber and her porch is now the bedroom, enclosed by a bounty of windows framed in yards of rich, gorgeous fabric. *Directions:* Traveling Route 7 north, turn left at the second traffic light in Lenox onto Route 7A (Kemble Street). Continue to the stop sign and turn left—Gateways is immediately on your right.

❄ ☕ 🎿 💳 ☎ @ W P 🍴 🚭 ✚ 🚶 🖼 ⚲ 🎿 👫 🐎 ⛷

GATEWAYS INN & RESTAURANT
Innkeepers: Fabrizio & Rosemary Chiariello
51 Walker Street
Lenox, MA 01240, USA
Tel: (413) 637-2532, Fax: (413) 637-1432
Toll Free: (888) 492-9466
11 Rooms, Double: $120–$345, 1 Suite: $230–$515
Minimum Stay Required: 3 nights Weekends in summer
Restaurant: closed on Mon
Open: all year, Credit cards: all major
Select Registry

Marblehead is one of the great sailing capitals of the world today as it was in centuries past when tall-masted schooners carried the products of a new nation to and from Europe and the Far East. 17th- and 18th-century homes crowd the narrow, winding streets of one of the most popular places to visit on the New England coast. Within this historic district is an elegantly decorated inn that will make you feel as though you have stepped back in time while enjoying all the amenities of the 21st century. I loved the flowered wallpapers used in the front hallway, in the dining room, and in the parlors. Guestrooms have king and queen beds, some with canopies, most have fireplaces, some have decks or patios, some have double Jacuzzis, but all provide a cozy ambiance and fine furnishings. Enjoy the stunning view from the rooftop walk from which you can see the famous Marblehead light. Surprisingly in a town where houses crowd the streets, there is a lovely garden and a heated swimming pool. This is a formal inn but one of such comfort that you will instantly feel the warm welcome of the inn's staff and become yet another of its centuries of houseguests. Breakfast is served in the large dining room at a lovely long mahogany table. Guests can now enjoy the inhouse pub. *Directions:* From Boston take Rte 1A north to Rte 129 east to Marblehead. Take the first right after the Caldwell Banker office: the inn is 1/8 mile on the right.

HARBOR LIGHT INN
Innkeepers: Suzanne & Peter Conway
58 Washington Street
Marblehead, MA 01945, USA
Tel: (781) 631-2186, Fax: (781) 631-2216
19 Rooms, Double: $165–$365
1 Suite: $295–$365
Minimum Stay Required: Weekends in season
Open: all year, Credit cards: all major
Select Registry

Take an interesting Greek Revival home within walking distance of everything in town; add major refurbishments; mix traditional decor with modern; hire an artist to faux paint; plan cozy common rooms, a living room with views of the garden, and lovely dining rooms; throw in a fitness center and add an eclectic collection of art—and you have created a fabulous sanctuary on Martha's Vineyard: the Hob Knob Hotel. Of course, the guestrooms provide every amenity you could possibly wish for. One of my favorite rooms is tucked up under the eaves with a painted four-poster bed, painted bedside tables and bureau, and chairs with English chintz fabrics. Enjoy a wonderful breakfast, afternoon tea with freshly baked goodies, and a frosty pitcher of lemonade on the beautiful wraparound porch, and then, if you've caught that bass on the hotel's charter boat, the kitchen will grill it for you and friends at a private dinner party. The hotel's staff suggest activities to keep you busy—fishing, walking the beaches, visiting galleries, kayaking—or will direct you to a chair by the fire in the living room. The hotel also has a wonderful fitness center, spa and massage services. *Directions:* You reach the island of Martha's Vineyard by plane from New York or Boston or by car ferry from Woods Hole or seasonally by passenger ferry from Hyannis or New Bedford.

※ ☕ ♨ ☕ 💳 ☎ 🏋 @ W ♈ P 🌺 🖼 🗝 ⚓ 🎣 🚶 🏇 ⛵

HOB KNOB
General Manager: Mark Venette
128 Main Street
P.O. Box 239
Martha's Vineyard—Edgartown, MA 02539, USA
Tel: (508) 627-9510, Fax: (508) 627-4560
Toll Free: (800) 696-2723
17 Rooms, Double: $175–$620
1 Suite: $300–$620
Minimum Stay Required
Open: all year, Credit cards: all major

Up island, away from the bustling towns on Martha's Vineyard, is a charming inn and restaurant on its own secluded 6-acres—the Beach Plum Inn. Sitting on top of a hill with views of the sea and down to the harbor where fishermen come and go, it has a special charm all of its own. The inn exudes a traditional feel in its island architecture and comfortable furnishings and yet its dining room, with windows to the lawns, gardens, and the sea, and mirror to reflect all that's happening, is very contemporary. The restaurant, specializing in fresh fish and prime meats accompanied by local produce, has the reputation as one of the best places to eat on the island. Bring your own wine, though, as the town is "dry" and you cannot buy alcohol here. The greeting is warm and welcoming at the Beach Plum Inn and the rooms are very comfortable. Mine had a queen bed, a bureau, a writing desk, and windows all around so that the freshness of the countryside was mine to enjoy. The bathroom was large and had a two-person spa tub (and shower). There are also cottages with their own decks. For recreation you'll find beaches for walking and swimming, golf, fishing, croquet, horseback riding, hiking, and more. *Directions:* Travel by plane or ferry to the island of Martha's Vineyard, then by taxi or rental car on the Edgartown-Vineyard Haven Road to Beetlebung Corner. Follow signs to Menemsha to a triangle then bear left to the inn on right.

BEACH PLUM INN AND RESTAURANT
Owners: Sarah & Bob Nixon
Manager: Brian Smith
50 Beach Plum Lane
P.O. Box 38
Martha's Vineyard—Menemsha, MA 02552, USA
Tel: (508) 645-9454, Fax: (508) 645-2801
5 Rooms & 6 Cottages: $215–$450
Open: May 1 to Oct 30, Credit cards: all major

The Mansion House, originally built in 1794 was completely recreated in 2003. The opportunities for building anew have been handsomely captured, providing many rewards for the lucky traveler as guest. Conveniences and amenities are top priority. Among the new rooms are suites with sitting rooms and separate bedrooms, some with private balconies. All are wonderful for those coming to enjoy this property, especially for its extensive spa services. There's so much within the new walls that leaving will require a fair amount of effort. The restaurant Zephrus, Seafood & Grill, highly rated by Zagat, serves delicious meals to accommodate guest time and preference. Guests who forget that this is a dry town (no alcohol) may have deliveries made from a neighboring town. A gourmet buffet breakfast is served in the restaurant or on the porch. Many guests use the hand painted room trays to bring breakfast up to the spectacular roof deck cupola where you can look down onto the harbor or gaze at the neighboring houses and church steeples. Under the building, there is a 75-foot indoor pool, mineral spring pool, and adjoining spa facility. A health club, with sauna and steambath, has trainers to guide you through exercise programs including yoga, aerobics, and conditioning. This inn is almost a town unto itself, with all that it offers, including boutiques to tantalize its browsers. *Directions:* Take the ferry to Vineyard Haven and just walk up the street to the Mansion House.

※ ■ ✄ ▭ ☎ ♨ ✗ @ W Υ P ¶ ✿ ≈ ▨ ⌂ ⅄ ⚓ 🏌 🏃 🐎 🚤

MANSION HOUSE
Innkeepers: Sherman & Susan Goldstein
Main Street
P.O. Box 428
Martha's Vineyard—Vineyard Haven, MA 02568, USA
Tel: (508) 693-2200, Fax: (508) 693-4095
Toll Free: (800) 332-4112
40 Rooms, Double: $99–$538
Open: all year, Credit cards: AX, MC, VS

The owners of the Thorncroft Inn have devoted over 30 years to caring for guests here and have created an environment and a service level that are hard to beat. However, rather than resting on their laurels, they have continued to refine their service and to create new ways to make the guest experience even better. Thought has been given to every detail in the guestrooms, which are wonderful. The twelve rooms and one suite are in two restored buildings furnished with antiques and there's also a separate cottage. Ten of the bedrooms have wood-burning fireplaces and canopied beds. I stayed in a second-floor room that provided me with every comfort in the world, including coffee delivered to my room and breakfast-in-bed. In the inn itself there are two common rooms and two dining areas for breakfast, each with tables intimately set for two. On the morning I was there, the breakfast of quiche and an array of fresh fruits was so well presented and so colorful that it reminded me of a Gauguin painting. There are lovely paths through the woods and I felt that somehow they, too, had been designed to add to my relaxation. *Directions:* Take the Steamship Authority ferry from Woods Hole. Turn right at the first stop sign and next right onto Main Street. The inn is 1 mile along on the left.

※ ➧ ✂ ▭ ☎ @ W P ▣ ⚘ ⚒ ⚓ ☂ ⚘ 🚶 🏇 ⚓

THORNCROFT INN
Innkeepers: Lynn & Karl Buder
460 Main Street
P.O. Box 1022
Martha's Vineyard—Vineyard Haven, MA 02568, USA
Tel: (508) 693-3333, Fax: (508) 693-5419
Toll Free: (800) 332-1236
14 Rooms, 1 Cottage, Double: $195–$495
Minimum Stay Required: Holidays & high season
Open: all year, Credit cards: all major
Select Registry

The stately 1838 Greek Revival family home of whaling-ship captain Uriah Russell has been transformed into a very elegant inn in the town of Nantucket on the very charming island of Nantucket. Common rooms and bedrooms are furnished with a mix of authentic and reproduction antiques that give the inn a great deal of charm and warmth. Bedrooms have handmade four-poster beds with canopies, goose-down comforters with flower-print covers, Oriental carpets, and marble bathrooms. Each of the very attractively and elegantly furnished rooms has a private bath, air conditioning, TV, and telephone with data port. I particularly loved room 7 at the back of the building, which overlooks the garden. Breakfast, consisting of freshly squeezed orange juice, fresh fruit, hot and cold cereals, and homemade baked goods, is served in the dining room or on that lovely garden terrace where you can enjoy the bubbling fountain. I loved the commercial espresso machine from which you can choose a cappuccino, café latte, or an espresso. One of the many wonderful things about Nantucket is that it is an easy walk from the ferry docks to almost everything there is to do and every place there is to stay. *Directions:* From the steamship ferry landing walk up Broad Street, turn left on Center Street, then second right onto Hussey Street. From the Hy-Line landing walk up Main Street, turn right on Center Street, then third left onto Hussey Street.

PINEAPPLE INN
Innkeeper: Christopher Karlson
10 Hussey Street
Nantucket Island—Nantucket, MA 02554, USA
Tel: (508) 228-9992, Fax: (508) 325-6051
12 Rooms, Double: $110–$375
Open: end-Apr to beg-Dec, Credit cards: all major

There is a magic to being on the island of Nantucket and in the heart of its principal town. Stay here in a warm and cozy post-and-beam guesthouse with innkeepers who make you feel like family and it's difficult to imagine life much better. Seven Sea Street, newly built in traditional style, is appointed with early-American furnishings combined with all the modern conveniences. The guestrooms have queen beds with fishnet canopies, TVs, telephones, small refrigerators, and all those other amenities including air conditioning that make your stay so pleasant. I stayed in a simply but comfortably furnished small suite with a separate living room. Puddy, the inn cat, made it quite evident that he intended to spend the night in my room—cats do know cat people! There's a relaxing common room with a pot-bellied stove and a dining room with a long table on which breakfast is served. A Continental breakfast is available in your room if you don't feel like socializing in the morning. There's a hot tub for which you can sign up for that extra bit of relaxation. It's just a few blocks' walk from the inn to the ferry and to Main Street with all its fabulous architecture—don't miss the Three Bricks mansions built by a merchant for his three sons, and the upscale shops and galleries. *Directions:* By air from Boston, New York, and Providence. By ferry from Woods Hole, New Bedford, and Hyannis—the inn is three minutes from the dock.

❄ ☕ ⚓ 💳 ☎ ♨ @ W ♈ P 🚫 ✿ 🖼 ⚓ 🎿 🏃 🐎 ⛵

SEVEN SEA STREET
Innkeepers: Mary & Matthew Parker
7 Sea Street
Nantucket Island—Nantucket, MA 02554, USA
Tel: (508) 228-3577, Fax: (508) 228-3578
Toll Free: (800) 651-9262
13 Rooms, Double: $99–$319
2 Suites: $159–$419
Minimum Stay Required: Weekends in season
Open: all year, Credit cards: all major
Select Registry

Set just off Main Street in the charming town of Nantucket is the Union Street Inn, dating back to about 1770. From there you can walk to all the town's historic homes, shops, and galleries, so you'll only need transportation to visit the more distant villages like Siasconset and Wauwinet (bikers might welcome the challenge). This is an exceptional, attractively decorated inn whose bedrooms have queen and king beds, often four-posters, and fireplaces. Room 3 on the first floor could well be my favorite with its red curtains and bed drapes and the two wing chairs in front of the fireplace. Across the hall, room 1 has a queen bed and green and white toile decorating the walls and bed. Upstairs, room 14 with its soft patterned wallpaper has a queen pencil-post bed and views out of its windows to neighboring trees and an ivy-covered hillside. Rooms have cable TV, Frette linens, duvets, bathrobes, and air conditioning. A full, cooked breakfast is served either in the dining room, on the terrace, or in your own room, and "goodies" are offered in the afternoon. The inn provides a walking tour through some of the old cobblestone streets to many of the town's charming homes, churches, and scenic sights. Numerous restaurants are close by: menus and suggestions are available from the innkeepers. *Directions:* Take the ferry to the island, walk five minutes to the inn from the ferry dock, or fly to the island and take a cab or rent a car.

❄ ☕ 🚲 💳 👬 @ W P 🚭 🖼 ⚓ 🎿 🏃 🏄 🍴

UNION STREET INN
Innkeepers: Ken & Deborah Withrow
7 Union Street
Nantucket Island—Nantucket, MA 02554, USA
Tel: (508) 228-9222, Fax: (508) 325-0848
Toll Free: (888) 517-0707
11 Rooms, Double: $160–$495
1 Suite: $255–$595
Open: Apr to Oct, Credit cards: all major
Select Registry

The White Elephant is simply a special place. It stretches beside a harbor on the charming island of Nantucket and offers a high level of accommodation and attentive personal service in a relaxed atmosphere. Almost everything you could want is available to you. This is what the White Elephant is all about, and it meets and exceeds its goals of ensuring the guest a treasured visit that will be remembered only as being too short. From the greeting by the doormen to that of the front desk staff, your visit here will be one of a series of highlights as the staff effortlessly anticipates your desires. Rooms are extraordinarily comfortable—mine had a sitting room with a fireplace and doors opening to a small deck overlooking that magnetic view of a working harbor. The White Elephant is only a few blocks from all of Nantucket town's shops, galleries, and restaurants. When you tire of all this charm, you can return to the inn and stretch out in the sun with the libation of your choice and a good book, and let the world go by. The Brant Point Grill will provide you with breakfast and at the end of the day, after a cocktail or a glass of wine in the attractive bar, a dinner where you will enjoy every taste. Amenities at the inn include an exercise room, a library, jitney service to the beaches, transportation to the ferry back to reality, and a business center. *Directions:* There is a complimentary shuttle service from the steamship ferry dock, just a few minutes away.

WHITE ELEPHANT
Owner: The Karp Family, Innkeeper: Bettina Landt
50 Easton Street, P.O. Box 2580
Nantucket Island—Nantucket, MA 02584, USA
Tel: (508) 228-2500, Fax: (508) 325-1195
Toll Free: (800) 445-6574
23 Rooms, Double: $275–$775*, 30 Suites: $335–$1400*
11 Cottages: $335–$1400* daily
1 Loft: $2000–$3000* daily
*Breakfast not included
Open: Apr to Dec, Credit cards: all major

This delightful inn sits on a bluff overlooking the ocean in the island's most charming and quaint village away from all the hustle and bustle of the town of Nantucket. Climbing roses, often growing up and over the roof, festoon the weathered shingled cottages that line the streets of Siasconset, creating an old-fashioned look. The Summer House accommodations consist of a group of cottages with a common lawn and Adirondack chairs fronting a path to the inn's attractive restaurant. The cottages are decorated with hand-painted floral designs echoing the charm of the gardens surrounding the inn. English country pine antiques, white eyelet sheets, comforters, terry bathrobes, and comfortable seating are some of the amenities of the cottages. Some also have fireplaces and spa tubs. The inn serves a Continental breakfast each morning on the wide veranda of the building in which dinner is served in the evenings. This restaurant has the feel of island charm—it has a cozy bar at one end, with tall stools for intimate conversation, and then an expansive room with tables where guests enjoy dinner with flickering candles, fresh flowers, and music from the piano bar. Down the bluff there is a pool surrounded by loungers for sunning, a Beachside Bistro for lunches and dinners—and the sandy beach just begging for your visit. *Directions:* By road or bike path, 8 miles from the town of Nantucket to Siasconset to Ocean Avenue to the inn.

❄ ▪🍵 CREDIT ☎ 👫 @ W ⍟ P ⑪ 🚭 ≋ 🖼 🐾

SUMMER HOUSE COTTAGE
Innkeeper: Danielle de Benedictis
Manager: Susan Manolis
17 Ocean Avenue
Box 880
Nantucket Island—Siasconset, MA 02564, USA
Tel: (508) 257-4577, Fax: (508) 257-4590
17 Cottages: $275–$2000
Open: end-Apr to Nov, Credit cards: all major

"It takes a bit of extra effort to get yourself to most very special places." So says the brochure for The Wauwinet, and it's true. This inn is located on a spit of land jutting into the sea, a ten-minute drive from the town of Nantucket, with a wildlife refuge north of the inn providing many more miles of wonderfully wild isolation. Comprised of a cluster of cottages and the main house with 26 bedrooms, the inn is furnished with tasteful and comfortable seating areas, queen or king beds, and full bathrooms. I found it almost impossible to choose a favorite because the rooms are cozy and individually decorated with original country antiques, and have very attractive artwork and views to the bay or the garden. The ambiance is most definitely sophisticated and yet very comfortable. The Wauwinet's restaurant, TOPPER'S, is fabulous in its setting, décor, food and service—and its 20,000 bottles of wine. Seafood is always a specialty but there's a full menu for your enjoyment. Paths lead to beaches on either the Atlantic or Nantucket Bay and the grounds have flower gardens with climbing roses, hydrangea and an expanse of lawn overlooking the ocean—all enclosed by sand dunes and yet opened by paths leading to sparkling waters. Keep busy with sailing, tennis, biking, walking, sea fishing, and bird watching—or settle in for a decadent day of pampering at their exclusive Spa by the Sea. *Directions:* Travel by ferry from Hyannis or by air from major northeast coast cities.

❄ ☕ 🚲 ☕ CREDIT 📷 ♿ @ W P 🍽 🚭 ☘ 🏃 🖼 ♿ ⚓ 🚶 🏃 ⛵ 🎷

THE WAUWINET
Owner: The Karp Family, Innkeeper: Eric Landt
Wauwinet Road, P.O. Box 2580
Nantucket Island—Wauwinet, MA 02584, USA
Tel: (508) 228-0145, Fax: (508) 228-6712
Toll Free: (800) 426-8718
26 Rooms, Double: $300–$1100
4 Cottages: $600–$1200 daily
Dinner: $65–$85
Open: May to Oct, Credit cards: all major
Relais & Châteaux

Six 1890s row houses, once the homes of mill workers in North Adams, have been renovated into a new hotel with 47 rooms and suites. Uniquely conceived and executed, these buildings have been combined and now have two long porches (with rocking chairs of course)—hence the name of the hotel. In the building where the reception and office are located there are two common rooms, one a living room with a fireplace and the other a den and a dining room where the expanded Continental breakfast is served. The rooms are individually decorated in a contemporary style, yet use lamps and other accessories from the 1940s and 1950s. The feeling of the rooms is definitely contemporary, with amenities presented in elegant but minimally designed containers—tissue, for example, is housed in a stainless-steel box. Guests have complimentary access to the Business Nook (equipped with a computer with DSL and printer) as well as the sauna, fitness room, outdoor hot tub and year-round lap pool. Extended-stay units with kitchenettes are also available. The Porches Inn is located across the street from the Massachusetts Museum of Contemporary Art, the largest contemporary art museum in the country. *Directions:* Take Route 7 to Williamstown to Route 2 east. Go left onto Brown Street to River Street, and right at River Street.

❄ ☕ 🏋 💳 🍴 @ W Ⓨ P 🚭 ❀ ≈ 🖼 ♿ 🎿 👣 🎿 ⛷ ⚓

THE PORCHES INN
Innkeeper: Sarah Goodwin
231 River Street
North Adams, MA 01247, USA
Tel: (413) 664-0400, Fax: (413) 664-0401
47 Rooms, Double: $180–$355
21 Suites: $180–$505
Open: all year, Credit cards: all major

One couldn't ask for a more idyllic setting. The soft yellow, shuttered, two-story house on the corner, opposite the waterfront walk of Plymouth, will catch your eye. I couldn't help but think that from the vantage point of the wrap-around porch, this would be the place to plant oneself to watch the town's patriotic fourth of July parade. Lucky for the traveler, Roger and Brenda have converted the charming home to offer overnight accommodation. There are three guestrooms with very different offerings. The coziest in size, but with spectacular water views, is the Mayflower Suite in the front of the home at the top of the entry stairs. The four-poster, queen-sized bed is positioned to enjoy unobstructed views through the front corner windows, with a sofa tucked in the narrow passage set opposite an expanse of window. Choose the Governor Bradford Suite and you will enjoy three rooms: a back bedroom with angled water views, a cozy living room with water views, and a kitchen that opens onto an expanse of back deck with a separate outside entrance off the deck's stairway. Entered from off the front porch is another queen-bedded room that enjoys its own private sun porch. To start their day, guests can enjoy coffee, tea and coffee cake on the front porch overlooking the harbor. A voucher for a scrumptious hot breakfast is offered for the neighboring Harbor Cafe. *Directions:* From Boston take Rte 3 South toward Cape Cod. Take Exit 6A in Plymouth; travel east on Rte 44 E to the waterfront.

🛏 🚵 @ W ⚓ 🛆

BY THE SEA B & B
Innkeepers: Roger & Brenda Silvieus
22 Winslow Street
Plymouth, MA 02360, USA
Tel: (508) 830-9643, Toll Free: (800) 593-9688
3 Rooms, Double: $150–$190
Minimum Stay Required: 2 nights
Open: Apr 1 to Dec 31, Credit cards: none

Crowne Pointe, within walking distance of the heart of Provincetown, offers spacious, lovely guestrooms in a complex of neighboring buildings. Enter into the office and your first impression is one of elegance, which pervades the inn, then your hearts are won by the smells wafting from the open kitchen. A lavish, hot breakfast buffet is set in the charming small dining room and in the evenings guests gather in the public areas for wine and hors d'oeuvres. Bedrooms are handsome, with walls painted in rich colors of rusts, greens, maroons, and golds to complement the elegance of furnishings, fabrics, art, and rugs. Many rooms have fireplaces, intimate decks, Jacuzzis, and kitchenettes, and all rooms enjoy TVs, VCRs, telephones with voice mail, wet bars, and nightly turn-down service. My favorite guestrooms were those in the main house, which are decorated with the owners' personal furniture. The Crowne Pointe room, with its beautiful clock and gorgeous hand-carved headboard dating from 1830, is a favorite. Luxury apartments and efficiencies are also available. Guests delight in the full-service Shui Spa with full steam room and sauna, meditation garden, and mineral bath. Guests also enjoy the fine dining restaurant. *Directions:* From Route 6, take the third Provincetown exit, turning left on Shank Painer Road. Continue to Bradford Street and turn right—the inn is on the left. Or leave your car behind and take the hotel's complimentary transportation from the airport or ferry.

❄ ☕ ⚓ 💳 ☎ ⛓ W Ⴤ P ⅋ ❦ ≋ 🖼 ⚓ 🕴 🚶 ⚓

CROWNE POINTE HISTORIC INN & SPA
Innkeepers: Ken, Tom & David
82 Bradford Street
Provincetown, MA 02657, USA
Tel: (508) 487-6767, Fax: (508) 487-5554
Toll Free: (877) 276-9631
40 Rooms, Double: $99–$627
Open: all year, Credit cards: MC, VS
Select Registry

The Inn at Richmond is set in the countryside just to the west of Lenox and Tanglewood in 27 lovely acres of gardens, lawns, and fields with cottages and barns (and a wonderful "allee" of maples leading to the barn). Staying here is like being a guest on a sophisticated farm, with horses grazing in paddocks surrounded by white fences, which contrast sharply with the bright-green grass. A new owner, Carl Dunham is making every effort to share his passion for the business and home and strives to make your stay enjoyable. Each queen or king bedroom is air-conditioned and has a private bathroom, telephone, and cable TV. The Chanticleer Suite, in colors of yellow, cranberry, and hunter green, has a cherry pencil-post queen bed. The Federal Suite has a mahogany king four-poster bed, fireplace, bath with shower and claw-foot tub, and a sitting room with a sofa bed and cable TV/VCR. The cottages are special, with their own entrances and private decks, fireplaces, and whirlpool tubs. I'd stay in one of these if I could linger for more than one night—a necessity if you are going to be able to enjoy all that there is to do. Breakfasts are delectable—I enjoyed a medley of fresh fruits, cheese, a smoked-salmon frittata with asparagus, potatoes, onions, and dill, and buckets of great coffee. *Directions:* From Boston take the Mass. Turnpike (I-90) to exit 1 to Route 102/41 through West Stockbridge and continue on Route 41 for 6 miles to the inn on the left.

❋ ➠ ✧ 📷 ☎ 🏨 @ W P ✿ 🖼 ⚓ ⚓ 🚴 🏇 ⛷ 🎿 🌿

THE INN AT RICHMOND
Innkeepers: Pam Knisley & Carl M. Dunham
802 State Road
Richmond, MA 01254, USA
Tel: (413) 698-2566, Fax: (413) 698-2100
Toll Free: (888) 968-4748
6 Rooms, Double: $160–$360
3 Cottages: $200–$380 daily
Open: all year, Credit cards: MC, VS
Select Registry

This handsome white clapboard inn (which once welcomed Ralph Waldo Emerson into its peace and comfort) enjoys a wonderful location looking out to sea on the outskirts of picturesque Rockport. The lovely entry hallway leads to a spacious grand salon painted in a soft yellow, which beautifully complements the handsome, rich, wide-plank floors. The dining room (which also hosts wedding receptions), dressed in striking reds and blues, leads through French doors into a porch set with more tables—the blue-water views are magnificent. We saw rooms ranging from the small Emerson Room at the top of the stairs with its white iron bed and small bath with tub shower to room 305 with its inviting iron king bed with views, spa tub built into the old closet, and separate toilet and shower. Room 303 is small and pretty in a rose and cream print and has views of the water. Some of the top-floor rooms have low ceilings but the bonus of small balconies and all rooms have cable TV. A large pool is set dramatically in the back garden, looking out to the sea. *Directions:* In Gloucester follow Route 128 through two traffic circles and turn left onto Route 127 north at the traffic light. Continue about 4 miles. Stay on Route 127 (it takes a sharp left at Rockport's Five Corners), follow signs to Pigeon Cove, and continue for 2 miles, turning right onto Phillips Avenue at the Emerson Inn sign.

EMERSON INN BY THE SEA
Innkeepers: Bruce & Michele Coates
1 Cathedral Avenue, Rockport, MA 01966, USA
Tel: (978) 546-6321, Fax: (978) 546-7043
Toll Free: (800) 964-5550
36 Rooms, Double: $99–$399, 2 Suites: $139–$399
2 Cottages: $1500–$4000 weekly
Minimum Stay Required: Weekends May to Nov
Restaurant: dinner only, reservations required
Open: all year, Credit cards: all major
Select Registry

Perched on the ledges above the ocean about an hour north of Boston airport sits the Yankee Clipper Inn, its two buildings housing the guest accommodations (which include three suites), nicely separated from one another by landscaping and by the rolling terrain. Most of the rooms have views of the ocean through large picture windows, with comfortable chairs positioned for watching the ever-changing scenery of the seashore. Bedrooms are comfortably furnished with queen, king, or full beds, and all have private baths; several have been recently updated with marble tile. Seven rooms have jetted tubs. The owners have been updating the decor of the rooms, making them even more desirable as places to unwind for several days. In the Quarterdeck house new bathrooms have been installed in four rooms, some with jetted tubs. A swimming pool is available on the property and nearby you find tennis, golf, hiking, fishing, biking, and summer theater. Rockport is a charming village with galleries, antique shops, and restaurants as well as a large community of artists who spend the summer there. This would be a great stopover for anyone headed for Maine and the upper New England coast. *Directions:* Take Route 128 north to Cape Ann through Gloucester. Turn left on Route 127 for about 3 miles to Rockport's Five Corners and a sign for Pigeon Cove, where the road makes a sharp left. Turn left and continue for 1-2/10 miles to the inn.

YANKEE CLIPPER INN
Innkeepers: Randy & Cathy Marks
127 Granite Street
P.O. Box 2399
Rockport, MA 01966, USA
Tel: (978) 546-3407, Fax: (978) 546-9730
Toll Free: (800) 545-3699
16 Rooms, Double: $199–$389
Open: all year, Credit cards: all major

Travelers are drawn to Salem for many reasons: the haunting tales of witches, the House of Seven Gables made famous in the writings of Nathaniel Hawthorne, the incredible Peabody-Essex Museum, the Maritime National Historic Site and Pickering Wharf. The Hawthorne Hotel, just across from Salem Common and within walking distance of all historic sites, is a handsome brick building. Just off the entry is the award-winning Nathaniel Restaurant. The grand and spacious lobby has comfortable and intimate seating arrangements. Off the lobby is the charming Tavern, which serves casual fare at fireside tables, from 11 am to 11 pm. Guestrooms are all similar, with reproduction furniture in style with the period of the hotel, but vary in size and amenities. The six suites are all corner rooms with a separate bedroom and a sitting room equipped with sofa bed. A National Historic building, this is a nice hotel with a good location. *Directions:* From I-95 or US1 to Route 28 north, take exit 26 east, Lowell Street, to Peabody. Proceed through Peabody center, turn onto Bridge Street (Route 107 north), then drive just over a mile to Winter Street (Route 1A south). Turn right and follow Route 1A around Salem Common. From Logan Airport, follow Route 1A north for 15 miles—the Hawthorne is on the right.

HAWTHORNE HOTEL
Innkeeper: Juli Lederhaus
On the Common
Salem, MA 01970, USA
Tel: (978) 744-4080, Fax: (978) 745-9842
Toll Free: (800) 729-7829
89 Rooms, Double: $109–$249*
6 Suites: $209–$349*
*Breakfast not included: $10–$15
Open: all year, Credit cards: all major

Take an old abbey, its next-door parish house, and an adjoining home, add them together, and what you have is a wonderfully innovative inn and restaurant. Name the eight bedrooms in the Drew House after members of the family, the six bedrooms in The Abbey after the days of the week, Monday through Saturday, and add on the eight rooms in the Village Inn and you have a delightful complex for your individual enjoyment or for a family wedding, a reunion, or a gathering of friends. The restaurant setting is the old abbey church and the owner has cleverly preserved its old structure while making the restaurant and bar (the old confessional, obviously) into something fun and different. During the summer, wine-tastings are held weekly. The rooms in each of the three buildings include queen and king beds. On the third floor of the Village Inn there are perfect family accommodations with a queen bed and a separate room with twin beds. Both the Drew House and the Village Inn have common rooms where you can relax or meet up with friends. Recently renovated, the former Meeting House and Doll Museum now offers luxurious guestrooms (sentimentally named for historic dolls) and public areas. A Continental breakfast buffet is served to all guests in The Abbey. *Directions:* From Boston take I-93 south to the Sagamore Bridge, to Rte 6 east, to exit 2 to Sandwich, then take Rte 6A to Jarves St. Turn left to the inn.

BELFRY INNE & BISTRO
Innkeeper: Christopher Wilson
8 Jarves Street
P.O. Box 2211
Sandwich, MA 02563, USA
Tel: (508) 888-8550, Fax: (508) 888-3922
25 Rooms, Double: $179–$315
Open: all year, Credit cards: all major

In the center of the lovely town of Sandwich, one of the gateways to Cape Cod, sits the Dan'l Webster Inn. The inn, the oldest in the country, occupies the site of a tavern built before the American Revolution and named for its most famous resident. This is a full-service inn with a cozy tavern, an informal dining room with a large fireplace, and a formal dining room with a glass wall looking onto an enclosed courtyard and garden. These are especially attractive spots where you can enjoy both the ambiance and the food. In the tavern the food focuses on tasty appetizers, a variety of salads, burgers, sandwiches, and, in the evening, a number of entrees. If you prefer a more gourmet meal, head for the restaurant where the emphasis is on fresh seafood, with plenty of additional choices for meat lovers. All guestrooms are attractively appointed with period furniture including canopy or four-poster beds, highboy dressers, desks, and overstuffed chairs. I enjoyed a lovely, newer room with a fireplace, canopy bed, luxurious spa tub, and heated marble floor in the bathroom. For breakfast you will receive a voucher towards the purchase of your choice off the à la carte menu. In addition to the inn's outdoor swimming pool, amenities include a full-service spa for men and women featuring 100% organic products. *Directions:* From Boston take Route 3 south to Route 6 then take exit 2. Turn left on Route 130 for 2 miles, going right at the fork—the inn is on the left.

❄ ✂ 💳 ☎ ♨ @ W P ⑪ 🚭 ❀ ≈ 🖼 ✂ ♿ ⚓ 🚶 🏃 ⛷

DAN'L WEBSTER INN & SPA
Innkeeper: The Catania Family
149 Main Street
Sandwich, MA 02563, USA
Tel: (508) 888-3622, Fax: (508) 888-5156
Toll Free: (800) 444-3566
48 Rooms, Double: $129–$379*
*Breakfast not included: à la carte menu
Open: all year, Credit cards: all major
Select Registry

The Isaiah Jones Homestead, built in 1849, has many wonderful antiques of the sort that you would love to have in your own home. However, my envy of those antiques extends beyond the furniture, for I would love to install the graceful curved staircase leading from the front hall to the bedrooms in my home in California. The gathering room has an 11-foot ceiling and crown molding reminiscent of the Victorian era in which the home was built. Toast your toes by the fireplace and relax with a cup of tea nestled by the window. Breakfasts, served by candlelight at the mahogany dining table, are welcoming with the early-morning aroma of freshly baked breads and delicious entrees. All the bedrooms have queen or king size beds, either a fireplace or glass-front stove, and four have whirlpool tubs. The Weeks room has a king bed, sitting room, and a bathroom with a two-person spa. The inn has a living room that welcomes you and a breakfast room that is filled with morning sunshine. There's a small porch where you can sit and rock while reading a good book. The location is ideal for walking into the center of the village of Sandwich, to the Glass Museum, the antique shops, and to the restaurants. Being just 3 miles east of the Sagamore Bridge, Sandwich is a great spot for an extended stay at the start or the end of your trip to Cape Cod. *Directions:* Leave Rte 6 at exit 2, turning left on Rte 130 to center of Sandwich. Turn right on Main St. by the white church; the inn is on left, 2/10 mile.

ISAIAH JONES HOMESTEAD
Innkeepers: Don & Katherine Sanderson
165 Main Street
Sandwich, MA 02563, USA
Tel: (508) 888-9115, Fax: (508) 888-9648
Toll Free: (800) 526-1625
7 Rooms, Double: $165–$300
Minimum Stay Required: Weekends Jun to Nov
Open: all year, Credit cards: all major
Select Registry

As you are meandering along the coast of the "elbow" of Cape Cod, you find yourself enjoying the beauty and the scenery of Pleasant Bay. Here on a high hill overlooking the bay is "A Little Inn." The history of the inn dates back to 1798 and some believe that it was a stop for slaves traveling along the "underground railroad." The inn has nine beautifully appointed bedrooms. Four bedrooms are located in the Main House; three charming Bay rooms over look the garden with a view of the bay and the Carriage House has two lovely rooms with sitting areas. A European breakfast buffet is served overlooking the bay or garden. The inn has its own dock for those who wish to arrive by boat, swim or just sit and enjoy the sunrise. Next door to the inn is a cranberry bog, the scene of much activity as the berries ripen and are gathered for harvest. The quaint villages of Chatham and Orleans are close by with all their restaurants, shops, galleries, and activities. Nauset and Skaket beaches are within easy reach. There are also many scenic trails along the shoreline. *Directions:* From Boston take I-93 to Route 3 south to Sagamore Bridge to exit 11 (Brewster and Chatham). Turn left on Route 137 then left again onto Pleasant Bay Road. Continue straight at the stop sign at Route 39 then go left on Route 28 for ¾ mile to the inn on the left.

A LITTLE INN ON PLEASANT BAY
Innkeepers: Sandra & Bernd Zeller, Pamela Adam
654 South Orleans Road
P.O. Box 190
South Orleans, MA 02662, USA
Tel: (508) 255-0780, Fax: (508) 632-2400
Toll Free: (888) 332-3351
9 Rooms, Double: $215–$300
Open: mid-Apr to Dec, Credit cards: all major

The Inn at Stockbridge is a large Georgian-style building, constructed in 1906, situated down a driveway winding through a 12-acre estate. You arrive at a columned porch and on the other side of the front door is a very large, welcoming hall flanked by the dining room on one side and the gracious living room on the other. The living room, where wine is served in the afternoon, is comfortably furnished and reading by the fire here is a real pleasure. The inn's guestrooms are in the main house, the cottage house, and the recently built barn. Always a favorite, Blagdon, the original master bedroom, decorated in soft shades of yellow, has a spacious sitting area in front of the fireplace and a lovely four-poster canopy king bed. The four spacious deluxe barn suites—Shakespeare, Wharton, Rockwell, and Shaker—all enjoy gas fireplaces, whirlpool tubs, and private decks, and each is decorated appropriately for its name. The inn prides itself on its breakfasts, formal affairs by candlelight, and Len loves to share his breakfast recipes with guests. The inn is close to so many things to do that you'll have trouble deciding between the antiquing, the music festivals, the Norman Rockwell Museum, and a variety of sports. *Directions:* Take the Massachusetts Turnpike to exit 2, drive west on Route 102 to Route 7 north, then go 1-2/10 miles to the inn on the right. From New York take the Taconic Parkway to Route 23 east and Route 7 north past Stockbridge for 1-2/10 miles.

❄ ☕ ✄ ☕ 💳 ☎ ♨ ♟ @ W P 🚭 ✿ ≈ 🖼 💧 🏌 🚶 ⛷

INN AT STOCKBRIDGE
Innkeepers: Alice & Len Schiller
Route 7N
P.O. Box 618
Stockbridge, MA 01262, USA
Tel: (413) 298-3337, Fax: (413) 298-3406
Toll Free: (888) 466-7865
16 Rooms, Double: $156–$375
Minimum Stay Required: 3 nights in summer & holidays
Open: all year, Credit cards: all major
Select Registry

The Red Lion Inn dates back to 1773 when it was a small tavern where coaches stopped on their journey between Boston and Albany. Today this inn is an institution: visitors come to experience the setting, the history, the collections, the food, and the ambiance established by generations of hospitality. The owners take pride in maintaining the antique charm and authenticity of the inn. The floors tilt, the walls are not square, and the furnishings look as if they have been there forever. There are 108 guestrooms, 95 with private baths, all offering the amenities of a quality hostelry. Rooms have antique beds (be sure to specify your choice of queen or twins when you make your reservation), flowered wallpapers, white bedspreads, comfortable seating, and good lighting. Some rooms in the main building, my favorites, look out to the Main Street, while others look out to the several buildings that also house guests. Stockbridge and the Berkshires are rich in festivals of the performing arts—Tanglewood is close by—and fine-art and antique galleries. There is easy access to a wealth of sports and the inn has a pool. Stockbridge is New England at its best, especially in the fall with its glorious foliage in full color. *Directions:* Take I-90 to exit 2 at Lee, then Route 102 west to Main Street, Stockbridge. The inn is on the left.

THE RED LION INN
Owner: The Fitzpatrick Family
Innkeeper: Bruce Finn
30 Main Street
Stockbridge, MA 01262, USA
Tel: (413) 298-5545, Fax: (413) 298-5130
108 Rooms, Double: $125–$460*
*Breakfast not included: $15–$20
Open: all year, Credit cards: all major

Sturbridge's location at the intersection of the Massachusetts Turnpike (I-90) and I-84 (between Connecticut and Massachusetts) gives it a perfect position for travelers coming and going through New England. The Publick House Historic Inn offers a selection of places to stay: the Publick House, the Chamberlain House, and the Country Lodge. Rooms at inns are more our cup of tea but if you do stay at the lodge you'll find attractive motel-like rooms with private balconies. The Chamberlain House features six gracious suites. At the Publick House Historic Inn the simply but comfortably furnished rooms (all non-smoking) are part of a building dating back to 1771—this inn has served as a tavern and pub since pre-Revolutionary days. In this building you find two different dining rooms: The Tap Room and Ebenezer's Tavern. The Dining Room, where I can attest to the deliciousness of the fabulous lobster pie or the turkey dinner, is also where breakfast is served. For a different ambiance but with the same menu for lunch or dinner you might want to settle in Ebenezer's Tavern. Historic Sturbridge Village is just a few minutes' drive away. *Directions:* Located on the green and common in Sturbridge. After leaving I-84 or I-90, follow the signs to Route 131.

PUBLICK HOUSE HISTORIC INN
Innkeeper: Michael Glick
Route 131
Sturbridge, MA 01566, USA
Tel: (508) 347-3313, Fax: (508) 347-5073
Toll Free: (800) 782-5425
115 Rooms, Double: $79–$139*
9 Suites: $150–$250*
*Breakfast not included: $6
Open: all year, Credit cards: all major

Longfellow's Wayside Inn, located on 106 acres not far west of Boston, has been open since 1716 and consequently is one of America's oldest operating inns. Preserving its heritage is the successful result of the owner's love of this inn. The original old bar room with its large fireplace, beamed ceiling, and Windsor chairs offers a cozy and welcoming spot for relaxing. The inn is perhaps best known as a restaurant and there are several comfortable dining rooms in various parts of the building. The ten guestrooms are cozy, comfortably furnished, and large enough for a sitting area and private bathroom with tub and shower. A full breakfast is served. As a National Historic Site, the inn provides a self-guided walking tour which not only takes you through the rooms of the inn with their individual history but also to the various buildings on the grounds, which include a working grist mill where the whole-wheat flour and cornmeal used in the bakery is ground. The Redstone School house of Mary Had a Little Lamb fame was moved to this site years ago and can be toured in seasonable weather. Also on the grounds you find the Martha-Mary Chapel, built in 1940 by Henry Ford in memory of his mother and mother-in-law and now a popular venue for weddings. The inn is now completely handicap accessible. *Directions:* Just west of Boston, between Boston and Worcester off Route 20. 11 miles west of Route 128 and 7 miles east of Route 495. Follow signs to the inn.

❄ ☕ 🛴 CREDIT ☎ ♨ W ║ ♠ ♿ 🚶 👫 ⛷

LONGFELLOW'S WAYSIDE INN
Innkeeper: John J. Cowden, Jr.
Wayside Inn Road
Sudbury, MA 01776, USA
Tel: (978) 443-1776, Fax: (978) 443-9630
Toll Free: (800) 339-1776
10 Rooms, Double: $125–$175
Closed: Christmas & Jul 4, Credit cards: all major
Select Registry

New Hampshire
Places to Stay

The Glynn House Inn is located in the heart of New Hampshire's lakes & mountains and provides the perfect base for recreation, romance and relaxation. The Inn is a meticulously restored Victorian situated on a tree-lined street in a residential section of Ashland. Skillful redecoration has taken this lovely property to a new plateau. The sitting room, dining room and extensive porches are places to relax. There are 13 spacious guest rooms, which are tastefully decorated with period furnishings, queen size beds, private baths, romantic fireplaces, luxurious bathrobes, Afghan blankets, central air, LCD TV's and DVD players. Eight of the rooms are deluxe suites that also offer bubbling double whirlpool baths, and game boxes. Guests receive a sumptuous gourmet breakfast, which is served at separate tables in the graciously inviting dining room. Afternoon tea and refreshments are provided daily in the adjoining sitting room. Wine and hors d'oeuvres are offered each evening. The surrounding area is a recreation paradise. Guests can enjoy the entire range of winter and summer sports. Traveling the back country roads allows visitors to savor the delights of New Hampshire's delightful lakes and enchanting mountains. The inn is non-smoking. Four deluxe suites are pet friendly with convenient access to the gardens. *Directions:* Take I-93 to exit 24 to Ashland. Turn left on Highland Street to the inn.

GLYNN HOUSE INN
Innkeepers: Pamela, Ingrid & Glenn Heidenreich
59 Highland Street
Ashland, NH 03217, USA
Tel: (603) 968-3775, Toll Free: (866) 686-4362
13 Rooms, Double: $149–$299
8 Suites: $209–$299
Open: all year, Credit cards: MC, VS
Select Registry

Just ten minutes from the southern outskirts of Manchester and conveniently located the same distance from the airport, the Bedford Village Inn is a complex of yellow buildings sitting above the main road to the city. Now surrounded by urban sprawl, the inn dates back to the time when Bedford was a farming community and the core of the complex is the original barn and Federal-style farmhouse built in 1810. Although the complex appears quite large, the inn has just 14 deluxe guest suites—eight luxury suites, four executive suites with separate sitting areas, two two-bedroom annex suites and the new, luxurious Woodbury Cottage. All the rooms are appointed with marble baths, Jacuzzi tubs, four-poster beds, good lighting, and lots of amenities such as fine towels and soaps. The former milking room is now a comfortable sitting room for guests, with sofas set in front of a large fireplace. The barn also boasts an enormous room that is host to weddings and large functions. The inn's acclaimed restaurant is actually eight individually decorated, intimate dining rooms. We chose to dine in the Tavern Bar, which offered simpler, reasonably priced but still excellent fare. *Directions:* Take Rte 93 to Rte 293 to Rte 101 west. Follow Rte 101 to the first set of lights (intersection of Rtes 101 and 114), make a left turn, continuing on Rte 101 west. Go through the next set of traffic lights. The next right-hand turn is Village Inn Lane that takes you to the inn.

BEDFORD VILLAGE INN
Innkeepers: Jack & Andrea Carnevale
2 Olde Bedford Way
Bedford, NH 03110, USA
Tel: (603) 472-2001, Fax: (603) 472-2769
Toll Free: (800) 852-1166
14 Rooms, Double: $235–$275
6 Suites: $350–$650
1 Cottage: $750 daily
Open: all year, Credit cards: all major

Adair sits on top of a hill in a stunning, 200-acre country estate encompassing rock walls, ponds, and gardens, with lovely views of the White Mountains. Its main house, painted white, is a great example of the architecture of the 1920s and is furnished elegantly with period antiques, fine reproductions, and original art. The entrance hallway is large and the dining and living rooms flow from each side. The guestrooms are lovely and many have fireplaces. The Kinsman is a large suite with a king sleigh bed, floor-to-ceiling windows, and a door leading to a private balcony. It also has a fireplace with comfortable reading chairs and a large two-person whirlpool tub. The Waterford room offers a cherry-wood queen bed, a corner fireplace with sitting area, and a bathroom with a two-person soaking tub. On the lower level you can relax in the Tap Room with its regulation pool table and in several comfortable sitting areas. In the afternoon when you return from the day's activities, tea is served with scrumptious cakes or cookies and, in season, dinner is available Thursday through Monday in the lovely dining room. If you stay here you'll want to save some time for a stroll on the many trails surrounding the inn. *Directions:* Leave I-93 at exit 40 onto Route 302 east, turn sharp left at the Adair sign, and follow signs to the inn. From the east, take Route 302 west for about 3 miles past Bethlehem, and turn right at the sign to the inn.

❄ ☕ ⚗ 💳 @ W P ¶ 🚭 ⚐ 🏃 👫 🎿

ADAIR COUNTRY INN & RESTAURANT
Innkeepers: Ilia & Brad Chapman
80 Guider Lane
Bethlehem, NH 03574, USA
Tel: (603) 444-2600, Fax: (603) 444-4823
Toll Free: (888) 444-2600
9 Rooms, Double: $195–$295, 1 Suite: $325–$375
Minimum Stay Required: Fall Foliage & holidays
Restaurant: Thu to Mon in season
Open: all year, Credit cards: all major
Select Registry

Originally a 1787 New Hampshire farm, Chesterfield Inn today offers 15 guest accommodations in a variety of rooms that boast fireplaces, balconies, and full bathrooms with whirlpool tubs. Guestrooms put privacy and comfort first: they are spacious and traditionally decorated, and have individually controlled heating and air conditioning, telephones, TVs, and refrigerators. I looked at a room with flowered wallpaper, two wing chairs, and a king bed on top of which was a cozy quilt for napping. There were views out onto the lawn and the gardens surrounding the inn. The dining room serves dinner six nights a week and food preparation emphasizes fresh ingredients in unique flavor combinations. The seafood served at the inn comes from Boston, herbs from the garden, and other produce from local farms, all making for a delicious dinner. The parlor, dining room, and terrace are ideal settings for functions as intimate as a family gathering or as large as a wedding. This inn is located right off the major north-south interstate and is ideally situated for an extended stay in the area or a stopover when coming or going. *Directions:* Take I-91 to exit 3, following Route 9 east for 2 miles. Turn left onto Cross Road to the inn.

❄ ☕ 🎿 💳 ☎ 🐕 🏨 @ W Ⓨ P 🍽 🖼 ⛓ ♿ 🏃 👫 ⛷

CHESTERFIELD INN
Innkeepers: Judy & Phil Hueber
Route 9
P.O. Box 155
Chesterfield, NH 03443, USA
Tel: (603) 256-3211, Fax: (603) 256-6131
Toll Free: (800) 355-5515
15 Rooms, Double: $175–$345, 2 Suites: $275–$300
Restaurant: dinner only, Mon to Sat
Closed: Dec 24 and 25, Credit cards: all major
Select Registry

The Three Chimneys Inn, constructed in 1649 with an addition about a hundred years later, is perfectly located for those visiting the University of New Hampshire. Full of New England charm, beamed ceilings, dark and warmly inviting paneling, four-poster beds, and large armoires are found throughout and are just what you would expect in such a setting. Many of the beds have Edwardian drapes and a few rooms have spa tubs for two. Bedrooms have telephones, TVs, data ports, wireless internet, air conditioning, hairdryers, and makeup mirrors, some have working fireplaces, and Oriental carpets are used throughout. Breakfast is served in one of the two dining rooms to guests only, but lunch and dinner are available to the public as well. The frost Sawyer Tavern with its hand-hewn beams and granite walls surrounding the 1649 cooking-hearth fireplace is cozy and welcoming. Windsor chairs provide comfortable seating at tables in several adjoining dining rooms where wide floorboards add to the charm. There is a more formal dining room on the first floor, and in the summer the Conservatory Terrace provides outdoor dining. This inn has the facilities to host conferences and is popular for weddings. *Directions:* Take I-95 north to exit 4 (Spaulding Turnpike/Route 16). Take exit 6W (Durham/Concord), turn left at the bottom of the ramp and travel 1 mile to the light. Go left at the light. The inn is on the hill above Durham Town Hall.

❋ ◧ ⚞ ⊟ ☎ @ W P � ⊘ 🖼 ⚑ ⚓ ⚐ 🏃 👫 🐎 🚵 ⚘

THREE CHIMNEYS INN
Innkeeper: Karen Meyer
17 Newmarket Road
Durham, NH 03824, USA
Tel: (603) 868-7800, Fax: (603) 868-2964
Toll Free: (888) 399-9777
23 Rooms, Double: $129–$239
1 Suite: $179–$239
Open: all year, Credit cards: all major

The historic Inn at Crotched Mountain dates back 175 years and has lots of charm with warm paneling, big fireplaces, and comfortable furniture. From the inn the views look out to the swimming pool and tennis courts and then in the distance to the Piscatagoug Valley—one of those splendid vistas that varies as the light of the morning changes into brilliant sunshine and then late in the day as the shadows creep across the distant hills. Most of the cozy bedrooms have views over the distant mountain range, all have comfortable chairs or a loveseat for reading. The inn is a great place to stay if you enjoy walking and in the winter months you can get your exercise with cross-country or downhill skiing. From this location you have access to many local antique and craft shops. If you are as fond of English Cockers as I am, then you can be sure that your welcome will be a friendly one as the family has two in residence: Frances and Rover. The Inn at Crotched Mountain is open seasonally, so be sure to note their open dates when you plan your trip in this part of New Hampshire. Light fare is served in the Winslow Tavern on Saturday nights. *Directions:* Take I-93 north to Route 101, driving west to Route 114 then north to Goffstown. Take Route 13 southwest to New Boston, Route 136 west to Francestown, then Route 47 north for 2½ miles. Turn left onto Mountain Road after 1 mile.

INN AT CROTCHED MOUNTAIN
Innkeepers: Rose & John Perry
534 Mountain Road
Francestown, NH 03043, USA
Tel: (603) 588-6840, Fax: (603) 588-6623
13 Rooms, Double: $85–$150
Restaurant: open Sat
Closed: 1st 3 weeks of Nov, Apr, Credit cards: none
Select Registry

The Hancock Inn has been around since 1789, the first year of George Washington's presidency, and stands on a quarter-mile stretch of Hancock's Main Street where every house is listed in the National Register of Historic Places. Wide pine floorboards, paneling on the walls, cozy fireplaces, an old tavern pub, and an excellent restaurant ensure you of a comfortable and pleasurable stay. Without any doubt, the bedroom with the most history in this guide is the one in this inn with walls beautifully hand-painted by the renowned itinerant painter, inventor, and writer, Rufus Porter. There are fourteen other guestrooms, all with private baths and eight with fireplaces. Handmade quilts, cable TV, telephone, and air conditioning are de rigueur. The tavern is a great place to meet other guests, have a drink, and play a game of checkers. The inn's restaurant, which has been awarded many honors, presents hearty American fare with a large serving of New England, like cranberry pot roast, Nantucket seafood chowder, and roasted duckling with rosemary-mint brown sauce. In the area you can go antiquing, pick apples, go for a hike, or cut your own Christmas tree. *Directions:* From New York take I-91 to Brattleboro then Route 9 to Keene to Route 123. Turn right to the inn.

HANCOCK INN
Innkeepers: Robert Short & Laurie Ware
33 Main Street
P.O. Box 96
Hancock, NH 03449, USA
Tel: (603) 525-3318, Toll Free: (800) 525-1789
12 Rooms, Double: $125–$260
2 Suites: $180–$290
Minimum Stay Required: 2 nights in Summer & Fall
Open: all year, Credit cards: all major
Select Registry

The Notchland Inn gives you the chance to get away from it all and yet be within a few miles of lots of activities. Built in the 1860s, this granite mansion is located on 100 acres of the White Mountain National Forest, sitting atop a knoll at the base of one mountain and looking across at two others. The inn has the air of a wonderful old summer home, a feeling that permeates every room. There are seven rooms, six suites, and three cottages, each with a wood-burning fireplace. Carter is a large two-room suite with the fireplace in the bedroom, a queen bed made of cherry with an arched headboard, and handmade stained glass hanging in two windows. There are a sofa and a rocker in the sitting room and a two-person spa tub in the bathroom. Doors open to a large deck with great views. On the second floor of the former one-room schoolhouse is the Dixville Suite, another two-room suite where you can lie in the country-French queen bed and look across the sitting room to the fireplace or to the view from the window. In the bath there's a large corner soaking tub. The inn's living room is especially fine, designed by Gustav Stickley, a founder of the Arts and Craft movement, and has lovely furniture of that style. The inn serves a five-course dinner five days a week in a romantic dining room overlooking the gardens and the pond. *Directions:* Take I-93 north to exit 35 to Route 3 north for 10 miles to Route 302. Turn right on Route 302 for 17½ miles to the inn.

❄ 🍵 ⚗ 🍜 💳 🐕 🏨 @ W P 🍴 🚯 🔔 ⚓ 🍽 🏇 ⛷

NOTCHLAND INN
Innkeepers: Les Schoof & Ed Butler
2 Morey Road
Hart's Location, NH 03812, USA
Tel: (603) 374-6131, Fax: (603) 374-6168
Toll Free: (800) 866-6131
8 Rooms, Double: $199–$265
5 Suites & 3 Cottages: $280–$335
Minimum Stay Required: Weekends
Restaurant: dinner Wed to Sun
Open: all year, Credit cards: MC, VS, Select Registry

This is an intimate country inn that has been renovated and decorated with a sincere intent to preserve the integrity of the architecture and the history of the property. The entry to this charming, white-clapboard, two-story New England inn is cozy and opposite the reception desk is a bar tucked into a hallway niche. At the back, overlooking the gardens and antique barns, you find the dining rooms where breakfast and dinner are served. Beyond the dining room is an elegant formal parlor made cozy by a wood-burning fireplace. Also located on the first floor are two guestrooms, one with a queen bed warmed by one of the inn's true working fireplaces. At the top of the stairs is one of the larger rooms, number three, decorated in blue and cranberry with wing chairs in front of a fireplace and king bed. There are ten rooms in the main house, varying in price according to size and amenities, and four in the Carriage House with two person Jacuzzi tubs. Amenities offered include an outdoor swimming pool, wedding and conferencing facilities. *Directions:* 17 miles west of Concord off Routes 202/9. Take Route 114 south to the blinking light and village center. Turn right and the inn is ½ mile along on the right.

COLBY HILL INN
Innkeepers: Cyndi & Mason Cobb
33 The Oaks Street
P.O. Box 779
Henniker, NH 03242, USA
Tel: (603) 428-3281, Fax: (603) 428-9218
Toll Free: (800) 531-0330
14 Rooms, Double: $140–$279
Open: all year, Credit cards: all major
Select Registry

Who hasn't heard of Golden Pond and who wouldn't be delighted to stay at this inn perched on Shepard Hill among ancient pines with a 65-mile panoramic view of Squam Lake and the surrounding mountains? Impressive and enchanting at the same time, with beamed ceilings, fireplaces, moldings, and large, gracious rooms, the house will delight you with its architectural details. The bedrooms are elegant and well appointed. The Buckingham Room's old-world charm made it the master bedroom, with a king four-poster with canopy, striking black-and-ivory decor, and double French doors leading to a private deck from which there are views of the lake and the foothills. The Sandwich Room, decorated with the work of local craftsman highlights the New Hampshire theme from the state flower, lilac in the wall-covering to the botanical lamps boasting New Hampshire wildflowers. During the warmer months you can enjoy a poolside lunch beside the heated pool which overlooks the breathtakingly picturesque Squam Range. Dining in the elegant dining room with its acclaimed cuisine or in our casual M Bistro is another of the pleasures of staying here, while in the afternoon you can enjoy a formal English tea. Tennis, swimming, croquet, and badminton are available within the 14 acres of the estate. *Directions:* Take I-93 to exit 24, go south on Route 3 for 4-7/10 miles then turn right at the inn sign.

MANOR ON GOLDEN POND
Innkeepers: Mary Ellen & Brian Shields
Route 3, P.O. Box T
Holderness, NH 03245, USA
Tel: (603) 968-3348, Fax: (603) 968-2116
Toll Free: (800) 545-2141
24 Rooms, Double: $210–$475
2 Suites: $410–$475
Carriage house & cottages (open seasonally)
Open: all year, Credit cards: all major
Select Registry

Tucked away on a side loop of Route 16 between Jackson and North Conway, there are several inns where skiers love to stay. It's easy to understand why skiers and non-skiers alike would love the New England Inn for its variety of lodging choices: rooms in the inn, cottages, log cabins, cottage suites, and the new adults-only lodge across the street with its spectacular log-cabin construction. Many of the accommodations have Jacuzzi spa tubs for two, most have fireplaces, and many have an extra bed. Rooms in the inn are traditionally decorated; all are comfortable, but the cottages and the lodge are guests' favorites. The new lodge is quite special, with a natural wildlife decor achieved with beams, antler chandeliers, and mounted animal trophies in the grand, high-ceilinged entrance hall. The king-bedded Bear Room upstairs has a two-person Jacuzzi tub in one corner of the extra-comfortable living room along with a gas fireplace and TV/VCR set into a fieldstone surround. The Tuckerman Tavern has a full bar and serves an extensive dinner menu. There are several living rooms for relaxing before and after dinner, but it would probably be hard not to steal away to one's room. The inn has a seasonal outdoor swimming pool and children's wading pool. Children are welcome in the family cottage suites. *Directions:* Take Route 16 north to North Conway to Route 16A, Intervale Resort Loop. The inn is about a mile on the right.

NEW ENGLAND INN
Innkeepers: Larry, Dianne, Lance & Jessica Merrill
Route 16A
P.O. Box 100
Intervale (North Conway), NH 03845, USA
Tel: (603) 356-5541, Fax: (603) 356-2191
Toll Free: (800) 826-3466
31 Rooms, Double: $69–$250
3 Cottages, 6 Cabins
Open: all year, Credit cards: all major

The design concepts of Stanford White have inspired Jim and Ibby Cooper in their rebuilding of the Inn at Thorn Hill after a disastrous fire destroyed all of it in late 2002. They have taken the opportunity to maintain the essence and character of this marvelous inn while adding the facilities most desired by guests today. The inn has been enlarged to 25 rooms, including four suites. Each room has a gas fireplace, private bath, wireless internet access, TV/DVD, and spa tubs for two. Some rooms have steam showers or showers for two; some have views of the mountains with their ever-changing patterns of sun and shadow. The inn's award-winning dining room now offers fine dining in an enlarged room with French doors leading to a wraparound porch, a private dining room seating 20, a downstairs dining room for 40, and a lounge serving more casual meals. The lounge has been configured in a new turret-like space, which also creates a uniquely designed area on the second floor. An elevator has been installed, permitting handicap access to bedrooms on the second and third floors. The inn still has three cottages and a carriage house for guests, all decorated in French country style. Attractive packages for spa, golfing, skiing, and other outdoor activities are offered. *Directions:* From Boston take I-95 north to the Spaulding Turnpike then Route 16 north to Jackson. Follow signs to the inn.

INN AT THORN HILL AND SPA
Innkeepers: Ibby & Jim Cooper
Thorn Hill Road, P.O. Box A, Jackson, NH 03846, USA
Tel: (603) 383-4242, Fax: (603) 383-8062
Toll Free: (800) 289-8990
25 Rooms, Double: $169–$440
4 Suites & 3 Cottages: $299–$440
Minimum Stay Required: Weekends & Fall Foliage
Restaurant: closed Tue & Wed in Apr & beg-May
Open: all year, Credit cards: all major
Select Registry

Located away from the bustling commercial areas of North Conway, the acclaimed Buttonwood Inn sits on a hill amidst 6 acres of fields and forest—yet it's just minutes to the ski areas and to town. This inn was originally an 1820s farmhouse and the owners have retained that country atmosphere with antiques, quilts, and period stenciling. There are ten well-appointed bedrooms, each with private bath. My favorite was a room painted in a shade of cream that had a pencil-post four-poster queen bed, wonderful wide-board floors, scattered area rugs, a sofa, gas fireplace, spa tub for two, cable TV, DVD and telephone. Breakfasts are special here. Guests have no trouble finding a good restaurant for dinner in North Conway or Jackson. When you're not out exploring the surrounding area, you can swim in the inn's heated pool, relax in the outdoor hot tub, enjoy the award-winning gardens, and hike or cross-country ski nearby. North Conway offers seven major ski resorts, more than 200 tax-free shops and outlets, over 50 restaurants, golf, tubing, kayaking, canoeing, fishing, ice-skating, snowshoeing, and sleigh rides. *Directions:* From Boston take I-95 to the Spaulding Turnpike to Route 16 north to North Conway. In the village turn right on Kearsarge Street for 1½ miles to the stop sign. Cross the intersection and drive up the hill to the inn.

BUTTONWOOD INN
Innkeepers: Paula & Bill Petrone
64 Mount Surprise Road
P.O. Box 1817
North Conway, NH 03860-1817, USA
Tel: (603) 356-2625, Fax: (603) 356-3140
Toll Free: (800) 258 2625
10 Rooms, Double: $99–$299, 1 Suite: $190–$340
Minimum Stay Required: Weekends, Holidays, Fall Foliage
Open: all year, Credit cards: AX, MC, VS
Select Registry

Home Hill is a gorgeous country-house estate on the banks of the Connecticut River. To reach the inn, we traveled up a beautiful tree-lined drive blanketed in snow and could only imagine how lovely it would be with autumn's brilliant foliage or with sunlight filtering through summer's thick greenery. Home Hill Inn is spectacular and I was captivated from the moment we stepped inside. The inn has a wonderful European ambiance with warm Provençal colors washing the interior walls, walls dressed in gorgeous papers, beautiful fabrics selected for the bed spreads and armchairs. The main house accommodates the intimate dining rooms and a few guestrooms. I loved all these rooms but most especially St. Gaudens, one of the coziest—a charming corner room with lots of light that filters over the beautiful rich rose and tans that decorate the rooms. The Carriage House offers six guestrooms, while the pool house provides guest quarters in summer only. Under the artful and incredible direction of chef, Paula Snow, the restaurant is excellent and the setting is memorable. Home Hill's dining room features dramatic floor-to-ceiling French doors, a décor awash in country reds and yellows and elegant furnishings accented by custom-designed chandeliers—an inviting atmosphere for unforgettable dining *Directions:* From West Lebanon, head south on 12A, travel 3 miles, then turn right onto River Rd. The inn is 3-3/10 miles farther on the left.

❄ ☕ 🎿 ♨ CREDIT ☎ 🏨 🍸 @ P 🍴 🚭 ≈ 🎿 🚶 🎿 🎿

HOME HILL INN
Innkeeper: Paula Snow
703 River Road
Plainfield, NH 03781, USA
Tel: (603) 675-6165, Fax: (603) 675-5220
11 Rooms, Double: $160–$250
1 Suite: $200–$250
Open: all year, Credit cards: all major

Rhode Island
Places to Stay

Block Island, described by the Nature Conservancy as one of the last 12 great places in the Western Hemisphere, can be reached by ferry or plane from Connecticut, Rhode Island, or Long Island. There is nothing like an island with its magical feeling of being a place apart—in this unspoiled spot you really feel you have stepped back in time. The 1661 Inn and Hotel Manisses, with fifty-seven guestrooms in seven buildings, offers a range of delightful accommodations. Rooms are individually decorated, with various combinations of whirlpool tubs, decks, ocean views, and wood-burning fireplaces. Some rooms accommodate three or more persons, very convenient for families. There are wide porches for sitting and gazing at the ocean with its ever-changing activity and light. Breakfast (at The 1661 Inn) includes several hot entrees. Dinner, showcasing local seafood, is enjoyed at the Hotel Manisses, where you find fine dining in a casual atmosphere. On this island there is much or little to do—strolling along wide sandy beaches, bicycling, hiking, horseback riding, shopping, boating, fishing, bird watching, kayaking, and visiting historical lighthouses—or relaxing at the hotel with a good book. *Directions:* By ferry: from Point Judith (year round) and Montauk, NY. By air: from Westerly and Providence or by charter. Contact the inn for schedules.

THE 1661 INN & HOTEL MANISSES
Innkeepers: Justin Abrams, Rita & Steve Draper
1 Spring Street
P.O. Box 1
Block Island, RI 02807, USA
Tel: (401) 466-2421, Fax: (401) 466-3162
Toll Free: (800) 626-4773
65 Rooms, Double: $160–$420
Restaurant: dinner daily in season
Open: all year, Credit cards: MC, VS

Cliffside, Adele Turner, and the Abigail Stoneman Inn are all inns owned by Winthrop Baker. Each is a gem of décor and specializes in attention to guests' needs, comfort, and service. Rooms are sumptuously decorated with lush fabrics, beds are covered with exquisite comforters, and wallpapers tastefully chosen. All have individually controlled air conditioning. The Abigail Stoneman Inn is unique, not for the number of rooms (only five), but in the number of amenities offered—including a choice of 20 different pillows. Guests choose from 30 complimentary premium soaps, gels, and bath oils; which are then delivered on a tray to their room. There is also a Bottled Water Menu of 24 international favorites from which to choose, in a room devoted to their display with information provided to assist in the selection. Each room or suite has a two-person spa tub, at least one fireplace, high ceilings, and tall windows. The two level suite at the top of the building has a circular staircase that leads you to a library sitting room with a fireplace and comfortable wing chairs. All three inns offer high English tea in the afternoons, 45 varieties in all (with all the pomp and substance one would expect to find in England), and upon your return from dinner, a selection of sweets. *Directions:* Route 95 to exit 38 to Route 138 E to Newport Bridges. Take Scenic Newport exit to right off ramp onto America Cup Blvd, to Bellevue Ave through light to Touro Street to inn.

❄ ☕ 🛎 💳 ☎ @ W P 🚭 ✿ 🖼 ⚓ 🧍 👫 🐎 💧 🏌

ABIGAIL STONEMAN INN
Owner: Winthrop Baker
Innkeeper: Wendy Knox
102 Touro Street
Newport, RI 02840, USA
Tel: (401) 847-1811, Fax: (401) 848-5850
Toll Free: (800) 845-1811
5 Rooms, Double: $425–$725
Open: all year, Credit cards: all major

The Adele Turner, Cliffside, and Abigail Stoneman inns comprise the Legendary Inns of Newport. The Adele Turner Inn is the one located nearest to the heart of Newport's collection of shops, restaurants, and tourist activity. Its 13 rooms are luxuriously decorated; each is a pure pleasure to stay in for their attention to detail and the comfort. Each bed makes a statement with its high posts and formal presentation. There are fireplaces, spa tubs, beautifully appointed fabrics on the beds, striking wallpapers, and comfortable seating, including window seats to curl onto with a good book. Like its sister properties, the Adele Turner serves an elegant English tea in the afternoon, but the daily winetasting events are an exclusive Adele delight. The staff sommelier pairs fine wines with artisan cheeses for a unique taste experience. Exceeding even the culinary delights, which include a full breakfast served in the dining room, is the sense of care that has gone into the preparation for your visit. This is Newport—the Newport that derives its reputation from the days of the Mansions and the Cliff Walk along the ocean. This is a place to visit, absorb and return to again-and-again. *Directions:* Take route 95 N to exit 3B, then Route 138 E over Newport Bridges to Scenic Newport. Exit to America Cup Blvd to end. Go left on Memorial Blvd, and then make a second left on Bellevue Ave. Take another left onto Pelham Street, the inn is on the left.

❄ ☞ ✄ ▦ ☎ @ W P ⊘ ▣ ⚓ 🏋 🏃 🏇 ⚓ ❦

ADELE TURNER INN
Owner: Winthrop Baker
Innkeeper: Kevin Conley
93 Pelham Street
Newport, RI 02840, USA
Tel: (401) 847-1811, Fax: (401) 848-5850
Toll Free: (800) 845-1811
13 Rooms, Double: $125–$525
Open: all year, Credit cards: all major
Select Registry

With its superb oceanside location on 40 gorgeous acres at the west end of Newport's world-renowned Ocean Drive, the Castle Hill Inn & Resort offers guests romance, seclusion, and beauty. This Victorian mansion has been elegantly restored, with guestrooms in the main building, the private Harbor Houses, and a Swiss-style chalet. The renovated Beach House rooms with their breathtaking views, king beds, fireplaces, and beautifully equipped bathrooms are situated on a private white-sand beach. In the main house bedrooms are decorated with Victorian furniture, while the other guestrooms are decorated in an elegant seaside style. All are comfortable and inviting. Castle Hill's dining room has lovely views out to sea and the sunset; and any meal here, including a decadent afternoon tea at the top of the stairs in front of a fire, is an experience not to miss. The two-story Turret Suite, with 360-degree views, a sensational cupola, soaking tub, steam shower, fireplace, and every possible luxury, is extraordinary. Newport is such a small, intimate town and the mansions are so amazingly large that a visit here garners a near-perfect ten. *Directions:* From New York City take I-95 to Route 138 east. Take the first exit off the Newport Bridge and turn right at the second light. Turn right on Americas Cup then at the fifth light turn right on Thames to Wellington and then right on Ocean Drive for 3 miles. The inn is on the right.

❄ ☕ ⚡ 💳 ☎ 🛗 @ W Y P ⑪ ⚓ ♿ ⚓ 🚣 🏃 🚶 🐎 ⛴ ⛳

CASTLE HILL INN & RESORT
Innkeeper: Nathalie M. Ward
590 Ocean Drive
Newport, RI 02840, USA
Tel: (401) 849-3800, Fax: (401) 849-3838
Toll Free: (888) 466-1355
32 Rooms, Double: $395–$1250
3 Suites: $595–$1650
Open: all year, Credit cards: all major
Relais & Châteaux

For about 40 years the legendary artist Beatrice Turner lived a sheltered life in this fabulous Victorian manor house, and in that time created a vast number of paintings of herself—over 100 of her works are on display in the inn. There is a feeling of grandeur in all the 16 rooms and suites with their fireplaces, private baths, air conditioning, telephones, and cable TV. The unusual Tower Suite features a Victorian cupola tower and octagonal cathedral ceiling, Queen Eastlake bed, fireplace, and bay window with its own seat for gazing out at the world below. There's morning coffee room service, a full gourmet breakfast, and an afternoon Victorian tea that's way beyond sensational. The inn is decorated with fine period antiques and the fabrics used on the upholstered pieces are luxurious. Bathrooms are elegantly supplied with everything you desire. Add to all the above warm hospitality, good company, genial innkeepers, and fine food; and you will enjoy a stay you'll long remember. The inn is perfectly located a five-minute walk from the beach on a quiet, tree-lined street, a half block from the Cliff Walk, Newport's renowned seaside walking trail in front of its even more legendary mansions which are open for touring. This inn has it all. *Directions:* From New York City take I-95 north to exit 3 in Rhode Island for Route 138 east into Newport. From Boston take I-93 south to Route 24 south then Route 138 south. The inn is on the corner of Cliff and Seaview.

CLIFFSIDE INN
Innkeeper: Winthrop Baker
Innkeeper: Lynzie Golden
2 Seaview Avenue
Newport, RI 02840, USA
Tel: (401) 847-1811, Fax: (401) 848-5850
Toll Free: (800) 845-1811
16 Rooms, Double: $150–$595
Open: all year, Credit cards: all major
Select Registry

You'll be totally enchanted by the best of accommodations, hospitality, and gorgeous decor in the inn owned by Dennis Blair and Grant Edmondson in the heart of Newport. Located on magical Bellevue Avenue, this inn has it all. It will capture your heart and demand a return visit. All nine guestrooms are decorated differently but in high style, great use of color, sumptuous fabrics, and a sense of drama—enhancing your experience in this city of lavish, extraordinary old homes. The two-room, two-level Chesterfield Suite, designed to pamper, is decorated in warm, lush tones of reds and gold, warm woods, a canopy four-poster king bed, fireplace, two-person spa tub, and marble walk-in steam shower. The "Carrie in Paris" suite with a magnificent French Regency bed, fireplace, spa tub and two-person "rain" shower is striking in its color palette of gold, yellows, periwinkle blues, and crimson reds. Silk curtains flow in the breeze overlooking the elegant Bellevue Avenue neighborhood. A formal dining room is the setting for a full "not to be missed" breakfast, fortifying you for the day's activities. In the afternoon, there's an English tea in winter and cooling refreshments in warmer seasons. *Directions:* From north, take Route 138 south to Newport beaches. Go through the second light and at the next major intersection turn right on Bellevue Ave. From west, follow route 138 east over Narragansett Bay to scenic 238 through the harbor front left on Bellevue Ave.

HYDRANGEA HOUSE INN
Innkeepers: Dennis Blair & Grant Edmondson
16 Bellevue Avenue
Newport, RI 02840, USA
Tel: (800) 945-4667, Fax: (401) 846-6602
3 Rooms, Double: $265–$295
7 Suites: $385–$475
Minimum Stay Required: 2 or 3 nights depending on season
Open: all year, Credit cards: all major
Select Registry

Home to Brown University, Providence is a charming city and it is quickly becoming one of Rhode Island's treasures. Three rivers weave a course through the heart of town and segment the key districts: the lovely residential and university quarter, the business, convention center and mall, and the seat of government. Tucked just on the other side of the I-95 from the State House, the Christopher Dodge House is a convenient base from which to explore Providence and rooms are competitively priced. One of three neighboring buildings converted to offer travelers lodging referred to as the State House Inns, this is most definitely our favorite of the group, as the architecture of this three story, brick, 1858 Italianate manor affords lofty, eleven foot ceilings and spacious accommodation. A lovely banistered main stairway (as well as back stair) winds up to the guestrooms which are attractively decorated with early American reproductions. Each guestroom enjoys a private, marble tiled bathroom, many boast a gas fireplace or stove and room furnishings include a comfortable reading chair, desk and comfortable bed. With exposed brick walls and tall windows that frame the backyard greenery, the dining room is a restful spot to enjoy the breakfast buffet. *Directions:* From I-95 northbound, take exit 23. At light at end of ramp go straight onto State St. Take first right onto Smith St; pass the State House; take 3rd left onto Holden St to the corner of West Park St.

CHRISTOPHER DODGE HOUSE
Owners/Innkeepers: Ken & Phyllis Parker
Owners/Innkeepers: Frank & Monica Hopton
11 West Park Street
Providence, RI 02908, USA
Tel: (401) 351-6111, Fax: (401) 351-4261
14 Rooms, Double: $119–$250
Open: all year, Credit cards: all major

Actually located on a quiet country road in Seekonk, MA, yet only a ten-minute drive from downtown Providence, we reference the location of this inn in Rhode Island. The Jacob Hill Farm Bed and Breakfast Inn was built in 1722 and was once known as the Jacob Hill Hunt Club where the legendary Vanderbilts hung their hats. Today this property has been transformed into an inn, with guestrooms providing every comfort. The recipient of numerous awards for its decor and hospitality, all the rooms are individually decorated. Most of the rooms have fireplaces and some of the private bathrooms have Jacuzzi tubs. Four new, luxurious rooms have been added in the barn and as well as a Billiard room with Plasma Home Theater. There is air conditioning for the summer months if the usual breeze here on top of the hill isn't blowing. On the property you find a pool and tennis court and there are plenty of places to sit and look out over the valley below. The owners take great pride in every detail of this inn that they have created and their breakfasts are no exception—a great start to the day's activities. *Directions:* From Providence take Rte 195 east and leave at Massachusetts Exit 1, turning left at the light (Route 114A). After about a mile bear right at the fork (blinking light). At next light, turn right on Route 44, then after 1 mile turn left on Jacob Street. The inn is on the left at the top of the hill.

HISTORIC JACOB HILL FARM B&B INN
Innkeepers: Eleonora & Bill Rezek
P.O. Box 41326
Providence, RI 02940, USA
Tel: (508) 336-9165, Toll Free: (888) 336-9165
12 Rooms, Double: $199–$459
Open: all year, Credit cards: all major
Select Registry

This part of Rhode Island is an overlooked stretch of coast with beautiful beaches just made for walking and squiggling your toes in the sand. On the shore road, just a short distance from these beaches, is The Villa, an inn of eight guestrooms where you can enjoy the gardens and the pool as much as the inn's interiors. The inn's living room is comfortably furnished and there is an adjoining dining area where guests have breakfast if they do not want to eat poolside or in their rooms. Guests select from a varied and changing menu the night before. Two of the bedrooms are located in a separate building looking down at the gardens and the pool. All guestrooms have a two person Jacuzzi. A hot tub provides the perfect evening relaxation if you like to stare at the stars from a steaming, relaxing cauldron of bubbles. The Villa is located in an area close to the quaint historic village of Watch Hill with its many shops and harbor activity. One of the remaining carousels in the country is found here and it provides a great opportunity to relive your youth. From here you can take excursions to Mystic Seaport, Newport, and Block Island. Barbara and Michael are gracious innkeepers and assure a memorable stay. *Directions:* From Boston take I-95 to the Westerly area, exiting at Route 1A to the inn on the right. Watch for house numbers as the inn is not easily visible.

❄ ☕ ✵ CREDIT ☎ ♨ @ W Y P ≈ ⚓ 🎿 👣

THE VILLA
Innkeepers: Barbara & Michael Cardiff
190 Shore Road
Westerly, RI 02891, USA
Tel: (401) 596-1054, Fax: (401) 596-6268
Toll Free: (800) 722-9240
8 Rooms, Double: $150–$320
Open: all year, Credit cards: all major

Vermont
Places to Stay

A little-traveled two-lane road leads you to one of the most captivating country inns you'll ever stay in. Set on a knoll overlooking the Adirondack Mountains, 15 minutes from the town of Middlebury, Whitford House is surrounded by rich farmland. Inside the inn, in addition to the extraordinarily delightful innkeepers, there's a heart of a home you'll never forget. You'll love its comfortable living rooms, the charming dining room, the open kitchen, and the use of old barn wood for walls, cabinets, and bookcases, which adds to the country appeal. There are four bedrooms, three in the main house and one in a guest cottage, furnished with queen and king beds. In the guesthouse there is a queen sofa bed in the living room as well a king bed in the bedroom that can be converted into twins. There's a brick patio outside the cottage, making a perfect place for you and your friends to watch the sun set over the Adirondacks. A full breakfast is served and when the menu calls for maple syrup, you'll know it came from the maple trees near the property. This is an inn you'll always remember and want to return to as often as possible. *Directions:* From Boston, take I-93 to I-89 to exit 3 in Vermont near Bethel. Follow Route 107 to Route 100 north to Route 125 to Middlebury to Route 22A. Refer to a local map for detailed directions to the inn.

WHITFORD HOUSE
Innkeepers: Bruce & Barbara Carson
912 Grandey Road
Addison (near Middlebury), VT 05491, USA
Tel: (802) 758-2704, Fax: (802) 329-2154
Toll Free: (800) 746-2704
3 Rooms, Double: $125–$175
1 Cottage: $250–$275 daily
Open: all year, Credit cards: MC, VS

Built in 1820 as a stagecoach stop by Major Edward Simons, the historic Rowell's Inn sits right up front on a small country road and waits to greet you as a guest. In 1910 the inn changed hands and the elegant tin ceilings, cherry and maple dining-room floors, central heating, and indoor plumbing were added. This is not a fancy inn, but rather one in which you will be very comfortable for a night's rest as you visit this portion of Vermont. Bedrooms have private bathrooms and are nicely furnished. The Miss Caitlin Room has a brass queen bed with canopy, blue flowered wallpaper, wonderful wide-plank floors, a wood-burning fireplace, and a bathroom with a tub and hand-held showerhead. The Miss Juliette Room has both a double and a twin bed. On the third floor the F. A. Rowell Suite has a double bed, a trundle bed, a claw-foot tub, and a towel warmer (for me one of life's nicest amenities). The Major Simons Suite has a king bed and a ceiling fan. As one would expect, there's a dark, wonderfully atmospheric tavern room—it's easy to imagine the gatherings there almost 200 years ago. This room contains a most incredible wood-burning stove—I'd like to have brought it home. The inn's restaurant serves breakfast and a four-course dinner with a single entree. Note that there are no telephones or TVs in the rooms. *Directions:* On Route 11 connecting Route 7 and I-91. The inn is 7 miles west of Chester and 7 miles east of Londonderry.

❄ ☕ 🚲 💳 ♨ W P 🍴 🚶 👥 🎿

ROWELL'S INN
Innkeepers: Michael Brengolini & Susan McNulty
1834 Simonsville Road
Route 11
Andover, VT 05143, USA
Tel: (802) 875-3658, Fax: (802) 875-3680
Toll Free: (800) 728-0842
7 Rooms, Double: $90–$175
Restaurant: dinner weekends only
Open: all year, Credit cards: all major

West Mountain Inn sits way up on a hill with glorious views down the long winding driveway to the valley below. There are 150 acres on which to roam, with wildflowers, a bird sanctuary, alpacas, hiking trails, and the Battenkill River where you might want to try your fishing skills. Accommodation in the main house is in twelve bedrooms and three suites. The Booker T. Washington room has original butternut paneling, your choice of either king or twin beds, and views of neighboring mountains and pastures. The Rockwell Kent suite has a native-butternut cathedral ceiling in the king-sized bedroom and a spacious living room with fireplace. There are three townhouses at the historic mill, which may be rented with or without meals. Each of these has a living room with satellite TV, kitchen, master bedroom, and a cozy guestroom. The restaurant serves hearty country breakfasts and elegant five-course dinners and à la carte dining are offered seven days a week. Whether it's winter or summer or the peak time of foliage when all of New England comes ablaze, this inn is a great place to be. *Directions:* Leave Route 7 north at exit 3, turning left at the end of the ramp. Take the access road to the end and turn right on Route 7A into Arlington. Drive 1 mile then turn left on Route 313 for ½ mile, go left on River Road, over the green bridge, and into the inn's driveway on the left.

❄ ☕ 🧺 💳 🛗 @ W P 🍴 ♿ ⚓ 🚶 🧗 🏇 ⛴

WEST MOUNTAIN INN
Innkeeper: The Carlson Family
River Road
Arlington, VT 05250, USA
Tel: (802) 375-6516, Fax: (802) 375-6553
13 Rooms, Double: $175–$280
7 Suites: $215–$340
3 Townhouses
Open: all year, Credit cards: all major
Select Registry

You really must stay at the Maple Leaf Inn to appreciate all the thoughtful touches that Nancy and Mike lavish on their guests, from the surprise gift on your bedside pillow to the lovely stenciling unique to each guestroom (all king-sized). Although newly built, this beautiful three-story, gray-and-white inn with wraparound porch has a traditional feel and incorporates a few signature antique pieces. On the first floor you find an inviting library, a lovely sitting room, and an attractive dining room with oak tables set in front of the fireplace with beautiful botanical prints on the walls. Also on this floor is a beautiful L-shaped guestroom with a high cathedral ceiling. Second-floor rooms are decorated and themed by season. We settled into Autumn Woods with its bed set against the wall to maximize the angle of the fireplace, windows on three sides, and decadent bathroom with Jacuzzi tub. Winter Haven, the most expensive room, with a true two-person Jacuzzi, is a feminine room in creams and whites with a precious winter village scene stenciled above the windows, mantle, and door. On the top floor Sweet Dreams has a lovely four-poster bed, a double rocker to dream in, and stenciling with glow-in-the-dark stars. Breakfast, served in the dining room, is a gourmet bounty. *Directions:* From Woodstock turn off Route 4 in town onto Route 12 north. Travel 9 miles to the Maple Leaf Inn located on the right side, ¼ mile before the Barnard General Store.

MAPLE LEAF INN
Innkeepers: Nancy & Mike Boyle
P.O. Box 273
5890 Vermont Route 12
Barnard (near Woodstock), VT 05031, USA
Tel: (802) 234-5342, Fax: (802) 234-6456
Toll Free: (800) 516-2753
7 Rooms, Double: $160–$290, 1 Suite: $250–$280
Minimum Stay Required: 2 nights Weekends in season
Open: all year, Credit cards: all major
Select Registry

Absolute perfection—your own farmhouse home in Vermont on 300 acres with country charm, urban sophistication, ingenious decoration, and every amenity in the world—at a price, but unique. In the evening guests come together for cocktails, wine, and lively conversation in the Barn Room, a large but warmly gracious room with fireplace and groupings of comfortable sofas and chairs. The dining room has vaulted ceilings with yet another blazing fire. There is no menu, but you will be dazzled by the chef's imaginative creations using the very freshest and finest ingredients. Meals leave your senses satiated and you are ready to linger over a brandy in the pub. There are four guestrooms in the main house and several cottages connected by winding roads (but otherwise serenely separate) each with its own style of decor and each in its own setting. I loved the Meadow Cottage, a Moroccan fantasy inside a Vermont clapboard structure—it's nothing short of a desert king's traveling palace. There's wonderful tile, a cozy sitting area in front of the fire, and a majestic bedchamber with hand-wrought bronze columns supporting a tented ceiling. The bathroom echoes this decor with its large tub, shower, and plush amenities. The inn also has a fitness room, spa, guest entertainment center, and everything else you might want. *Directions:* Please contact the hotel for directions.

❄ ☕ 💳 ☎ ⛓ 🎿 @ W Ⴤ P 🍴 🚭 ✿ 🏕 🖼 🐾 ⛷ 🎿 🐎 🎿

TWIN FARMS
Manager: Michael Beardsley
P. O. Box 115, Barnard, VT 05031, USA
Tel: (802) 234-9999, Fax: (802) 234-9990
Toll Free: (800) 894-6327
*20 Rooms, Double: $1300–$3100**
*10 Suites: $1300–$1900**
10 Cottages: $2000–$3000 daily*
**Includes all meals, *Service: 18%*
Minimum Stay Required: Weekends & Holidays
Closed: Apr, Credit cards: all major

The Lilac Inn is nestled in the Champlain Valley, surrounded by the Green Mountains and the Adirondacks, on the prettiest street in the region, in the small historic town of Brandon, chartered in 1746. Built in 1909 as a summer cottage for Albert Farr; the Greek Revival style home, with five-arched façade, rivaled the finest homes in Brandon. The inn's nine guestrooms have been discreetly modernized so as not to distract from the historic character of the home. Each room is unique and filled with treasures from over thirty years of collecting. There are two dining rooms, the casual tavern and the more formal West Garden Room, whose menu focuses on creative use of Vermont produce and has won numerous awards for the inn. Built around a cobblestone courtyard, embraced by two acres of landscaped grounds with cascading ponds and Vermont stonewalls, the inn's lovely setting and excellent reception facilities make it a popular choice for weddings. Brandon is situated near the major ski mountains and near Lakes Champlain and Dunmore, with rivers and streams creating great opportunities for fishing, swimming, and boating. Other attractions nearby include golfing and all the activities of the college town of Middlebury. Shelburne Museum is within an easy day's visit. *Directions:* From the north or south follow Route 7 to Brandon then take Route 73 east to the inn.

LILAC INN
Innkeepers: Shelly & Doug Sawyer
53 Park Street
Brandon, VT 05733, USA
Tel: (802) 247-5463, Fax: (802) 247-5499
Toll Free: (800) 221-0720
9 Rooms, Double: $130–$330
Minimum Stay Required: 2 nights on weekends
Restaurant: open seasonally
Open: all year, Credit cards: AX, MC, VS

Think casual, think relaxed, think of a place where you can put your feet up, read a book, and be totally natural and without pretense. Think October Country Inn! In this quaint, ten-bedroom inn, a 19th-century farmhouse, you'll find sincere hospitality and delicious food. This is the kind of inn where they will put an extra bed in the room for that third person traveling with you. Some of the upstairs bedrooms are under the eaves but they're quite spacious enough for a good night's rest. Rooms have flowered wallpapers and a variety of brass, iron, and wooden headboards. Be sure to save some time to sit by the fire in the living room: a table behind the sofa had so many games on it, I couldn't figure out which I'd play first. This inn is noted for its food and its reputation has spread far and wide, although breakfast and dinner are offered only to resident guests. There's a swimming pool on the grounds, gardens for walking in, and plenty of diversions nearby —skiing, golf, cycling, summer theatre, and antiquing, to name just a few. One of the guests wrote in the inn's guest book, "I think I'll stay forever and send for my family. Maybe…" *Directions:* From Woodstock drive 8 miles west on Route 4 to the junction with Route 100A. Continue on Route 4 for 200 yards, take the first right (opposite Long Trail Brewery) then right again to the inn.

OCTOBER COUNTRY INN
Innkeepers: Edie & Chuck Janisse
362 Upper Road
P.O. Box 66
Bridgewater Corners, VT 05035, USA
Tel: (802) 672-3412, Fax: (802) 672-1163
Toll Free: (800) 648-8421
10 Rooms, Double: $165–$195
Restaurant: dinner for guests only, by reservation
Open: all year, Credit cards: MC, VS
Select Registry

Frank Dudley constructed this Victorian mansion in 1881 and today it continues to provide the warmth, welcome, and service that were present in that earlier era. Lang House's eleven bedrooms, each with private bath, are decorated in the style of the mansion as it once was. They are large and comfortable, with space for you to unpack and spread out, and space for you to read, either in bed or in a comfortable chair with a good reading light. My room, the Hayward, had a queen bed with fishnet canopy, good reading lights, an armoire for my clothes, and a comfortable chair in which to curl up for a nap. The innkeepers serve a delicious breakfast with a choice of entrée: the gingerbread waffles were new to me and were very tasty with Vermont (of course!) maple syrup. From the inn you can walk to town, to the shops, and to the several educational institutions that are found here in Burlington. Because the town is located on Lake Champlain there is a lot of activity along the edge of the shore. Ferries cross the lake to New York State, saving you lots of driving time and giving you a nice break in a day of driving. Just south is the Shelburne Museum, a "must" for all ages. *Directions:* From I-89 take exit 14W, Route 2, which turns into Main Street. As you come down the hill, the inn is on your right just before the traffic light.

LANG HOUSE
Innkeeper: Kim Borsarage
360 Main Street
Burlington, VT 05401, USA
Tel: (802) 652-2500, Fax: (802) 651-8717
Toll Free: (877) 919-9799
11 Rooms, Double: $145–$225
Minimum Stay Required: 2 nights weekends, Jun to Nov
Open: all year, Credit cards: all major
Select Registry

When a historic home in what was a city's grandest neighborhood is made into an inn welcoming guests from near and far, everyone wins. Such is the case with the Willard Street Inn, a stately Georgian/Queen Anne Revival-style mansion built in 1881 in the hill section of Burlington with views out to Lake Champlain. This is a home of high ceilings, richly ornate woodwork, and grand staircases. Bedrooms are very large and while they all begin with their Victorian heritage, they are all completed with uniquely appointed decor and private bathrooms. Victorian Cabernet is, as you would expect, warm and inviting; Nantucket with its carved, four-poster king bed is elegantly spacious; and the sitting area in the turret of the Tower Room offers views of the lake will spoil you without a doubt. The Woodhouse Suite, named for the original owner, has a loveseat facing a gas stove and a tiled, two-person shower. Breakfast, served in the solarium, features Vermont products, seasonal items from the gardens, and a delightful dash of the unexpected. Enjoy a cup of afternoon tea in the English round garden, or stroll the 1.5 acres of lawn and gardens. From the inn you can walk to Burlington's universities, the waterfront, the Church Street Marketplace, shops and restaurants. *Directions:* From Boston, take I-89 north to exit 14W to Route 2 west to South Willard Street (Route 7 south). Turn left two blocks to the inn on the right.

❄ ☕ ✂ 💳 ☎ @ W P ⚓ 🎿 👣 ⛷ 🚵 🏌

WILLARD STREET INN
Innkeepers: Larry & Katie Davis
Manager: Carrie Davis
349 South Willard Street
Burlington, VT 05401, USA
Tel: (802) 651-8710, Fax: (802) 651-8714
Toll Free: (800) 577-8712
12 Rooms, Double: $140–$240
2 Suites: $220–$240
Open: all year, Credit cards: all major
Select Registry

There are two things in Vermont that are just about perfect: one is the charming town of Dorset—quintessential New England—and the second is the hospitality of Linda and Jim, the owners and innkeepers of this wonderful property, Barrows House. This is a historic inn of nine buildings scattered about on eleven acres with exceptional gardens just a few blocks to the Dorset Playhouse. The inn has a swimming pool, tennis courts, lawn games, bicycles, cross-country ski equipment, and a sauna. Guestrooms are complete with every amenity. Halstead House, located up the hill in the woods, offers the most remote accommodation. The suite here has a small bedroom with a queen bed, handmade quilt, and braided rugs on the floor, and the bathroom features a two-person whirlpool tub. In the sitting room there's a loveseat in front of the wood-burning fireplace, TV/VCR, small fridge, and a bar sink. There's also a small patio for summer relaxation. The Stable Suite #2 in the old hay loft has wide floorboards, window seats in the bedroom, bathroom, and sitting room, cathedral ceilings, a gas fireplace, old barn beams, a king canopy bed, and a TV/VCR in the sitting room. The restaurant serves breakfast and dinner every day. By the way, this is a great family inn where well-behaved guests of all ages are always welcome. *Directions:* Located on Route 30, about 6½ miles north of the center of Manchester, just a block short of the Dorset town green.

❄ ☕ ⚒ 💳 📷 🐕 🛎 @ W P 🍴 🚭 ≈ 🏃 🖼 ⚘ ♿ 🏌 🚶 🐎 🎿 ⚓

BARROWS HOUSE
Innkeepers: Linda & Jim McGinnis
3156 Route 30, P.O. Box 98
Dorset, VT 05251-0098, USA
Tel: (802) 867-4455, Fax: (802) 867-0132
Toll Free: (800) 639-1620
18 Rooms, Double: $135–$200*
10 Suites: $180–$255*, 3 Cottages*
*Service: 10%
Open: all year, Credit cards: all major
Select Registry

The Blueberry Hill Inn invites you into their special, tranquil world in the Green Mountain National Forest, a world of quiet, fresh air, lovely food, and luxurious accommodations. In the original part of the inn, built in 1813, there are four bedrooms. There are also accommodations in three greenhouse rooms, four pondside rooms, and a cottage decorated with colonial furnishings—primarily antiques and antique quilts. The inn is a recreation destination, with skiing and hiking being the biggest attractions. Just a few minutes away is Lake Dunmore where you can swim and windsurf and boat. However, I could just as easily be perfectly content with doing nothing but read, relax, and take a walk into this pristine world. There is a spring-fed pond for swimming and a wood-fired sauna. The inn has great trekking and trail guides for its guests. The cooking is gourmet here and meals are a real treat, with flowers from the inn's gardens decorating the plates of food. What a great visual feast this makes the dining experience! For over 30 years the inn has been baking cookies and putting them in the cookie jar for guests and non-guests alike. Now cookies are available by mail to those who wish to order a memory of a time spent at Blueberry Hill Inn. *Directions:* Off Route 73 east of Brandon, follow Forest Road #32. Off Route 125, 1 mile east of Ripton, follow Forest Road #32 for 6 miles to the inn.

BLUEBERRY HILL INN
Innkeeper: Tony Clark
1307 Goshen-Ripton Road
Goshen, VT 05733, USA
Tel: (802) 247-6735, Fax: (802) 247-3983
Toll Free: (800) 448-0707
12 Rooms, Double: $280–$360*
1 Cottage
*Service: 15%
*Includes breakfast & dinner
Open: all year, Credit cards: all major

The Old Tavern at Grafton makes one of those architectural statements that you never forget—its façade is both wide and tall and it has an appealing porch that just beckons you to sit and relax. Guestrooms are found in the main tavern and two cottages and there are also four guesthouses, most with full kitchens, which can each accommodate up to eight people. I saw several of the rooms, which have flowered wallpapers and private baths with all the amenities, and are traditionally decorated in a comfortable style. The attractive dining room is traditional in its decor, with a lovely sideboard and tables set for two, four, or six and there is café serving lunch and light suppers. Your room rate includes a full country breakfast and afternoon tea. What's especially charming about this inn is its tavern pub, a short walk down the hall from the main building. Its two stories exude New England charm with old barn-board walls, hand-hewn timbered beams, and lots of cozy seating in front of the large wood-burning fireplace. The Old Tavern has its own stables so you can make arrangements to bring your horse—you could both have a great vacation in this New England town! The inn offers discounts to senior citizens and repeat guests. *Directions:* Take exit 5 off I-91. Grafton is located at the intersection of Routes 35 and 121.

OLD TAVERN
Innkeeper: Kevin O'Donnell
Main Street
P.O. Box 9
Grafton, VT 05146, USA
Tel: (802) 843-2231, Fax: (802) 843-2245
Toll Free: (800) 843-1801
46 Rooms, Double: $160–$420
4 Guesthouses: $675–$950
Closed: mid-Mar to May, Credit cards: all major

Three Mountain Inn has all you'll want for as long a time as you can be a guest. This romantic 1790s country inn on the main street of the little town of Jamaica, just under the shadow of the Green Mountains, is ideally located for access to skiing, but also great for Fall foliage, not far from shopping, and perfect for wandering. The living room with its large fireplace is warm and welcoming and the dining rooms are simply but tastefully furnished—what's complex is the tasty food that comes from the kitchen. The traditionally furnished bedrooms all have private baths and telephones. I stayed in Jamaica, a suite whose living room had a gas fireplace, a sofa and two wing chairs for reading, and Colonial-print wallpaper. The bedroom, painted pale, creamy yellow, had tables with good reading lights on either side of the four-poster queen bed. The Arlington, just down the hall, was furnished with a queen bed, an armoire, a sofa, and a wing chair, and had pale-cream-painted walls; an added luxury was a two-person spa tub. Even though this is a sleepy mountain town, I'd probably choose one of the back rooms to be sure of a night's rest that is as refreshing as the style and welcome of the innkeepers. *Directions:* From Brattleboro take I-91 to exit 2 and go north on Route 30. From Manchester take Route 30 south.

❄ ☕ ☄ 💳 ☎ 🏠 @ W P ⊪ ≈ 🏃 🏇 🚴 ⛷ 🎿

THREE MOUNTAIN INN
Innkeepers: Jennifer & Ed Dorta-Duque
Route 30
P.O. Box 180
Jamaica, VT 05343, USA
Tel: (802) 874-4140, Fax: (802) 874-4745
Toll Free: (800) 532-9399
15 Rooms, Double: $165–$360
1 Cottage
Open: all year, Credit cards: all major
Select Registry

Afternoon tea was being served as I arrived at Rabbit Hill Inn—just what I had been thinking I would like. This was just one example of the way the innkeepers and staff here seem to anticipate your every need—they have honed the art of personal service to absolute perfection, with many thoughtful touches like transforming your bedroom with candlelight and soft music when you return to it after dinner. There are nineteen rooms and suites with private bathrooms in two historic buildings—most have fireplaces and many have whirlpools tubs, but all are individual and special. I stayed on the second floor of the main building in the Canopy Chamber, a corner room with views of the White Mountains and the inn's gardens. The queen bed was waiting to share with me a perfect night's rest, the gas fireplace had a chaise lounge in front of it with pillows to make me comfortable, and on the bed was a note from the staff asking if there was anything else I might want. The room also had a desk, a Boston rocker, and access to a lovely porch. The inn's dining room serves delectable, award-winning, multi-course dinners. Rabbit Hill's 15 acres provide you with lawn games, a swimming pond, trails for hiking and skiing, fishing, and canoeing. *Directions:* From I-91, take exit 19 to I-93 south. Leave at exit 1, turning right onto Route 18 south for 7 miles to the inn. From I-93 north, take exit 44, turning left onto Route 18 north. Drive 2 miles to the inn.

❄ ☕ 🚗 💳 ♿ @ W P 🍴 ♿ 🚶 🐎 ⛷ 🍷

RABBIT HILL INN
Innkeepers: Leslie & Brian Mulcahy
Route 18
Lower Waterford, VT 05848, USA
Tel: (802) 748-5168, Fax: (802) 748-8342
Toll Free: (800) 762-8669
19 Rooms, Double: $199–$400
Minimum Stay Required: Weekends & Holidays
Closed: beg-Apr, beg-Nov & Dec 24-25
Credit cards: all major
Select Registry

The Andrie Rose Inn is found on a quiet side street in the town of Ludlow in four buildings, and since each building has a small number of rooms, you never feel as if you are a guest in a large establishment. With 17 rooms you can expect and receive various sizes of rooms with queen, king, or double beds. There are also suites and accommodations ideal for families with kitchens, laundry facilities and even gas grills on the decks. The Manchester can sleep up to ten while the Weston and Woodstock suites can accommodate as many as twelve guests. Here and there in some of the rooms are spa tubs, steam showers, and fireplaces. The inn's website provides details on its varying accommodations and is a great way to find just what you want. On Friday and Saturday evenings the inn serves dinner by reservation. In the main lodge there is a welcoming living room with a fireplace, which is a great place to meet other guests and relax either before or after dinner at the inn or in one of the town's restaurants. There is also a separate TV room with a large screen. Walk to the town's shops, drive to the nearby Okemo mountain, enjoy the surrounding countryside—all are within easy reach of the Andrie Rose Inn. They just added an outdoor hot tub. *Directions:* From New York, take I-91 north to exit 6 in Vermont then follow Route 103 north to Ludlow. Turn left on Depot Street and right on Pleasant Street to the inn.

❄ ☕ 🚲 💳 ☎ 🐾 @ W ⟊ P 🍴 🏃 ⛺ ⛵ 🎿 🏇 🚶 🐎 🛷

ANDRIE ROSE INN
Innkeepers: Michael & Irene Maston
13 Pleasant Street
Ludlow, VT 05149, USA
Tel: (802) 228-4846, Fax: (802) 228-7910
Toll Free: (800) 223-4846
17 Rooms, Double: $110–$330
2 Condos: $325 daily
Restaurant: dinner Fri & Sat with reservation by noon
Closed: Apr, Credit cards: all major

The Governor's Inn was built in 1890 as the private residence of Vermont Governor William Stickney in Ludlow's village. This lovely late Victorian country home has been converted to an inn with exceptional attention to detail by your hosts, Jim and Cathy Kubec, who pamper their guests and provide genuine hospitality. The inn welcomes guests into eight tastefully decorated and furnished guestrooms, all with a private bath and most with a gas fireplace. One of my favorites, Jessica's Room, has a king bed, gas fireplace, cable TV, two-person water massage tub, large skylight, and views of the village and mountains. The common rooms offer guests a chance to sit and chat within the inn's architectural and interior period details or relax near the slate fireplace in the parlor. Food is the focus of much attention at the inn. In addition to a full breakfast on antique china in the morning, tea with sweets in the afternoon, and a fixed-price gourmet dinner available for groups of six or more; upon request Cathy will prepare a "Vermont Country Picnic" which includes a bountiful gourmet lunch with picnic basket and accessories. The Governor's Inn also offers a series of cooking and innkeeping seminars throughout the year. The inn is located near the village green, less than a mile from the Okemo Mountain. *Directions:* Take I-95 to I-91 to Exit 6 to Route 103 North to Ludlow.

THE GOVERNOR'S INN
Innkeepers: Jim & Cathy Kubec
86 Main Street
Ludlow, VT 05149, USA
Tel: (802) 228-8830, Fax: (802) 228-2961
Toll Free: (800) 468-3766
7 Rooms, Double: $159–$269, 1 Suite: $249–$304
Minimum Stay Required: Holidays & some Weekends
Closed: two weeks in Apr, two weeks in Nov, Dec 23-26
Credit cards: all major
Select Registry

Perched on a hill with sweeping views of the valley below and the Green Mountains, the Inn at Ormsby Hill is a restored 1764 manor house listed on the Register of Historic Places. Attention to detail is everywhere, from the decor of the common rooms and the bedchambers, to the dining room where Chris is the master of her trade. Simply scrumptious breakfasts are served in the attractively decorated conservatory with its views out to the surrounding mountains. The living room made me feel completely at home—I could either curl up by the fire or simply relax in the luxurious surroundings. The ten guestrooms have canopied beds, fireplaces, flat screen televisions, endless amenities, spa tubs for two and a few even have two-person steam saunas. All the rooms are great, but one of my favorites, The Frances Suite, enjoys a large sitting room, bedroom, his and her bathrooms, two fireplaces and a private deck with a fabulous mountain view. There's a porch out back with old wicker furniture and a painted board floor, perfect for a second cup of breakfast coffee and a peaceful reverie. Innkeepers Chris and Ted are pros and I am sure that staying with them in the Manchester area will make for memories that will bring you back often. *Directions:* In Manchester Center, at the junction of Routes 11, 30, and 7A, take historic Route 7A south. The inn is approximately 3 miles along on the left.

INN AT ORMSBY HILL
Innkeepers: Chris & Ted Sprague
1842 Main Street
Manchester, VT 05255, USA
Tel: (802) 362-1163, Fax: (802) 362-5176
Toll Free: (800) 670-2841
8 Rooms, Double: $205–$410
2 Suites: $330–$535
Open: all year, Credit cards: all major
Select Registry

The Red Clover Inn is a retreat away from the cares of the world. This inn truly feels like a private home. The beamed-ceilinged keeping room is most inviting with its fireside sofas and wonderful leather wingbacks. Guestrooms, all air-conditioned, with private bathrooms, king or queen beds, and lovely mountain views, are in two buildings—seven in the farmhouse and seven newer rooms in the carriage house. The three newest rooms are especially deluxe and extremely spacious, with king beds, whirlpool tubs from which you can see the gas fireplace, and beamed ceilings. Carriage house rooms have TVs and some have VCR/DVDs. Thursday through Sunday, guests are invited to enjoy an elegant candlelit dinner featuring a menu sumptuous in content and presentation. The inn is conveniently located near the major ski areas of central Vermont. In the summer hiking and horseback riding are popular. Less strenuous activities include antiquing and attending concerts and plays. Note: As this edition goes to press we have learned that the inn is closed for renovation but will reopen for the 2008/2009 winter season. *Directions:* Five miles west of Killington, turn left from Route 4 onto Woodward Road and drive ½ mile to the inn on the left. Five miles east of Rutland, turn right from Route 4 onto Woodward Road and drive half a mile to the inn on the left.

❄ ☕ ✄ ♨ 💳 🐕 🛗 @ W P 🍴 🚭 🖼 🎿 🏃 🐎 🎿 ⚓

RED CLOVER INN
Innkeepers: Bill & Tricia Treen Pedersen
7 Woodward Road
Mendon (Killington), VT 05701, USA
Tel: (802) 775-2290, Fax: (802) 773-0594
Toll Free: (800) 752-0571
14 Rooms, Double: $150–$295
Open: all year, Credit cards: all major

Newfane is a "must-visit" beautiful New England town and has been one of my favorites for 40 years or so. The historic green and all the houses that surround the county courthouse stand as they have since the 1840s and behind the courthouse you find the Four Columns Inn. The inn is a popular base for sightseeing in this area, and if you'd like to visit during foliage time (generally the first half of October), you'll need to make reservations as much as a year ahead. There are 15 guestrooms with private baths, showers, free wireless internet and free telephone service. Most rooms have fireplaces, spa tubs, cable television and DVD players. The inn has an extensive DVD library for guest use. My personal favorite was room 12, with its king pencil-post cherry-wood bed and a fireplace open on one side to the bedroom and on the other to the bathroom. There's an attractive sitting area with two comfortable chairs, a painted armoire, and views of woods. The inn's restaurant produces impeccable, creative cuisine blending New American, Asian, and French traditions into taste sensations (once again, reservations are needed well in advance, even for houseguests). Presentations are so spectacular that it's hard to decide whether dinner looks better or tastes better. *Directions:* Leave I-91 at exit 2 and turn left onto Western Ave for half a mile then turn left onto Cedar Street. At the third stop sign turn left onto Route 30 north for 11 miles. The inn is on Newfane Green behind courthouse.

FOUR COLUMNS INN
Innkeepers: Debbie & Bruce Pfander
P.O. Box 278
Newfane, VT 05345, USA
Tel: (802) 365-7713, Fax: (802) 365-0022
Toll Free: (800) 787-6633
15 Rooms, Double: $175–$400
Open: all year, Credit cards: all major
Select Registry

Aptly named, this inn is located right on Route 7 in the middle of Shelburne where you can walk to shops and restaurants or drive a short distance to the Shelburne Museum. It's an 1886 Queen Anne Victorian with front doors made out of tiger oak. There are two common rooms for guests to relax in, complete with fireplace, scrolled woodwork, and comfortable armchairs. The inn's nine very comfortable bedrooms, several of which can be made into twins, are divided between the main house and the carriage barn. I stayed in the Fletcher Room with a queen bed, a chair to relax in by the window, a skylight, and a full private bath with tub and shower. Though the rooms may be decorated in Victorian style, they lack nothing for the comfort of the guest: air conditioning, TVs, free WiFi, and telephones are standard. A great American breakfast is served in the mornings from 8 to 10:00am so you can partake at your pleasure. In the afternoon after a day of busy activity, return to the inn for a cup of tea and a cookie—just enough to tide you over till you walk to one of the neighboring restaurants. Hospitality is high on the list of reasons to stay at this inn and the innkeeper makes sure that you are more than welcome. The inn is on the main street and double glazing makes the rooms quieter, but you're still aware that you are in town. *Directions:* From Boston, take I-93 to I-89 to exit 13 to Route 7 south. Drive about 4½ miles to the inn on the left.

❄ ☕ ✂ 💳 ☎ 🐕 @ W P 🖼 ⚓ 🏃 👫 🎿 ⚓ 🚣

HEART OF THE VILLAGE INN
Innkeepers: Geoff & Maureen Conrad
5347 Shelburne Road
Shelburne, VT 05482-0953, USA
Tel: (802) 985-2800, Fax: (802) 985-2870
Toll Free: (877) 808-1834
8 Rooms, Double: $150–$230
1 Suite: $250–$270
Minimum Stay Required: 2 nights Weekends May to Nov
Open: all year, Credit cards: all major
Select Registry

It would be hard to imagine a more spectacular setting than that of the Inn at Shelburne Farms, which sits in a 1,400-acre estate overlooking Lake Champlain and the Adirondack Mountains. The grounds are a creation of Frederick Law Olmsted, the architect who designed New York's Central Park. The estate is owned by a nonprofit organization devoted to preserving, maintaining and adapting its historic buildings and landscape for teaching and demonstrating the stewardship of natural and agricultural resources. The dramatic, 60-room Queen Anne mansion has 24 guestrooms, 17 with private bathrooms, which are individual in their decor and vary dramatically in price. The most popular rooms are on the second floor, facing the lake and decorated with fine antiques. Of those, the W. Seward Webb bedroom has William Morris wallpaper and a massive double bed, while the handsome Empire Room has furnishings, drapes, and wall coverings of the Empire period. Tucked under the eaves of the third floor overlooking the garden are the least expensive rooms. Afternoon tea is served daily for guests. Apart from touring Shelburne Farms itself, also plan to visit the Shelburne Museum with its 37 historic buildings housing exhibits from 300 years of life in America. *Directions:* Leave I-89 at Vermont exit 13 onto Route 7 south for 5 miles as far as the light in the center of Shelburne. Turn right onto Harbor Road to the first stop sign and go left into Shelburne Farms.

INN AT SHELBURNE FARMS
Innkeeper: Karen Polihronakis
1611 Harbor Road
Shelburne, VT 05482, USA
Tel: (802) 985-8498, Fax: (802) 985-1233
24 Rooms, Double: $150–$450*
2 Cottages: $255–$370* daily
*Breakfast not included: $15
Open: mid-May to mid-Oct, Credit cards: all major

Stowe is one of Vermont's most renowned ski and mountain resorts yet its history goes back long before skiing became popular. The Green Mountain Inn, the first inn in town and listed in the National Register of Historic Places, is part of that early history. The core of the inn still retains a feeling of days of old, and when you walk through the door you become part of the history and its memory. Enter into the lobby and receive a warm Vermont welcome then wander into the library and salon, intimately sized rooms warmed by a crackling fire. The large dining room is the setting for the hot and cold breakfast buffet and afternoon refreshments. Downstairs you find a popular, cozy bar and grill, The Whip, where you can enjoy a variety of good-value meals. As you climb the stairs from the entry you enjoy a constantly changing panorama of Vermont in the numerous original watercolors by Walton Bodgett, which run the length of the stairwell. In the main house, bedrooms vary dramatically in size, but all enjoy good lighting, wonderful baths, very comfortable beds, and decorative details, such as stenciling. Additional rooms are found in the Mill House, the Mansfield House and the Sanborn House, both built and decorated in a traditional style with very luxurious rooms offering all the modern amenities. *Directions:* Route 100 turns to Main St. as it travels through the heart of old Stowe. The Green Mountain Inn is on Main St.

GREEN MOUNTAIN INN
Owner: The Gameroff Family
Innkeeper: Patti Clark
18 Main Street
Stowe, VT 05672, USA
Tel: (802) 253-7301, Fax: (802) 253-5096
Toll Free: (800) 253-7302
106 Rooms, Double: $159–$799*
5 Townhouses
*Breakfast not included: $6.95–$9.95
Open: all year, Credit cards: all major

Amy created Stone Hill Inn, often called the best accommodation in Stowe, with the aim of offering guests the perfect blend of romance, ambiance, and privacy. Set above the road to the ski mountain, this inn attracts not only skiers, but also more particularly, guests who want a romantic getaway. Off the entry is a games room, a large room with a gas fireplace, sofas, game tables, and a guest pantry where hors d'oeuvres are served. Each of the nine guestrooms, all with identical amenities, opens onto the central garden and uses handsome, regal materials for bedcovers and drapes. I was disappointed in the furniture, which provides the guest with just a pair of armchairs and a covered circular table. A two-sided fireplace is open both to a side wall in the bedroom and the luxurious bath (two sinks, large Jacuzzi tub, separate shower). The most dramatic room and my favorite is the long, narrow breakfast room, which stretches out into the yard and is surrounded on all sides by a full expanse of windows. The tariff seems a bit high, but Stone Hill Inn affords a small, intimate-size inn in a lovely location with privacy and luxury to match. *Directions:* Traveling I-89, take exit 10 for Route 100 north. Go 11 miles to Stowe and at the blinking light go left on Route 108. Drive 3 miles, turn right on Houston Farm Road, then take the first driveway on the left.

STONE HILL INN
Innkeeper: Amy Jordan
89 Houston Farm Road
Stowe, VT 05672, USA
Tel: (802) 253-6282, Fax: (802) 253-7415
9 Rooms, Double: $325–$425
Minimum Stay Required: Weekends, Holidays, Fall Foliage
Closed: Apr & mid-Nov, Credit cards: all major
Select Registry

The Inn at the Round Barn Farm, sitting in 245 lovely acres of mountains, meadows and ponds, promises romance, relaxation, and an escape from reality. On the day of my visit the first welcoming touch I encountered was a tureen of hot soup for returning skiers in the small but cozy library. The dining room, where you savor Anne Marie's wonderful breakfasts, has windows on both sides looking out to the surrounding hills and tables set in various sizes. The guestrooms are all very different from one another in their decor but all have private bathrooms, original pine floors, rich wallpapers, and plush robes. I stayed in the Abbott Room, a suite with a king four-poster with a TempurPedic mattress, a TV hidden in an armoire, a living room with a gas fireplace, an oversized two-person corner whirlpool tub, and separate bathroom steam shower and two-person vanity. Hand-hewn beams and plenty of windows complete the scene. An unusual amenity here is the 60-foot lap pool, which extends into a greenhouse filled with flowering plants. The inn has its own groomed, marked snowshoe center and downhill skiing is just minutes away. The inn's Round Barn hosts weddings, conferences, concerts, an opera festival and art exhibits. *Directions:* Take I-89 south to exit 10, then Route 100 south for 14 miles. (From I-89 north take exit 9 onto Route 100B south for 14 miles.) Turn onto Bridge Street, through the covered bridge, and bear right at the fork. The inn is 1 mile further on the left.

❄ ☕ ⚟ 💳 ☎ 🍽 @ W P 🚭 ≈ ⚲ 🎋 🚶 🐎 ⛷ ⚘ 🍸

INN AT THE ROUND BARN FARM
Innkeepers: Anne Marie DeFreest & Tim Piper
1661 East Warren Road
Waitsfield, VT 05673, USA
Tel & Fax: (802) 496-2276
12 Rooms, Double: $165–$315
Minimum Stay Required: Weekends & Holidays
Restaurant: dinner Fri nights in winter
Closed: last 2 weeks of Apr; last week of Nov
Credit cards: all major
Select Registry

Throw away the books on decorating—start thinking outside the box and book into one of the Pitcher Inn's fabulously decorated and themed rooms, whether it's The School Room, The Trout Room, The Lodge, The Hayloft, or The Ski Room. I suppose that the most spectacular has to be The Lodge with its massive four-poster bed with eagles sitting on top of the headboard and Egyptian, Greek, and Masonic-lodge influences. Its starry ceiling overhead with the constellations in place for Christmastime is just plain wonderful. Add a bathroom with marble slab walls, a steam room, a deep soaking Jacuzzi, and you are in heaven. The Ski Room uses relics from ski areas—old bamboo poles, skis, ticket windows, a bedspread made from ski jackets. Your entrance to the room is a stone walkway set into the carpet. The inn's common rooms have plush furniture which you just sink into. The downstairs lounge with its stone fireplace and Adirondack style—is our kind of place. The dining room serves magnificent food in a bright and elegant room whose tables are set with crisp white linens and sparkling silver and glasses. The handcrafted Windsor chairs make for a refined elegance. *Directions:* I-89, I-91, I-93, and I-95 will all bring you to the vicinity of the inn. From I-89 north take Route 100 south to Warren where you find the Pitcher Inn on Main Street in the center of the village.

PITCHER INN
Innkeeper: Ari Sadri
275 Main Street
P.O. Box 347
Warren, VT 05674, USA
Tel: (802) 496-6350, Fax: (802) 496-6354
Toll Free: (888) 867-4824
9 Rooms, Double: $425–$650, 2 Suites: $800
Restaurant: closed Tue
Open: all year, Credit cards: all major
Relais & Châteaux

The Deerhill Inn sits perched high on a hill with breathtaking views of the Haystack and Mount Snow ski areas. The cozy downstairs sitting room is shared by non-resident guests coming for dinner but there is an upstairs living room that's reserved for inn guests. Decorating here is done with flair with each room enjoying its own distinct style. Waverly Fabrics chose one of Deerhill's bedrooms as the Room of the Year. The inn has ten guestrooms, three suites, a restaurant, beautiful gardens and a swimming pool. All bedrooms have private baths and most have access to a balcony or private deck. Seven rooms feature fireplaces, and whirlpool tubs. The Garden Suite has two rooms a sitting room with fireplace and a whirlpool tub tucked into a romantic alcove. On the third floor, the White Pine Suite, features handsome white-washed pine paneling and a fireplace. The Orchid room has a queen canopied bed with mosquito netting; boasts a loft and is decorated with an Oriental theme. The restaurant presents imaginative modern American cuisine featuring seasonally fresh local ingredients in a charming dining room with a fireplace, hand-painted murals, and spectacular views. *Directions:* From I-91 take exit 2 to Route 9 west, driving 20 miles to Route 100 where you go north. Drive 6 miles to Valley View Road and go up the hill for 200 yards.

DEERHILL INN
Innkeepers: Michael Allen & Stan Gresens
Valley View Road
P.O. Box 136
West Dover, VT 05356, USA
Tel: (802) 464-3100, Fax: (802) 464-5474
Toll Free: (800) 993-3379
10 Rooms, Double: $145–$250, 3 Suites: $240–$325
Minimum Stay Required: 2 nights most weekends
Open: all year, Credit cards: all major
Select Registry

The Inn at Sawmill Farm is imbued with old New England style and decor. You feel the warmth of this property as you climb the stairs to the reception area and the adjoining common room with its charming timbered ceilings, barn-board walls, and that ever-present New England fireplace. The bedrooms are swathed in floral fabrics and you're likely to find that the decor in your room is coordinated with a single pattern and color. Rooms are large and have all the amenities that you expect in a first-class inn. A new suite by the trout pond has a large living room, bedroom, windows overlooking the pond, and a wraparound deck. There's a world-class restaurant on the premises with a 15,000-bottle wine cellar. A very sophisticated menu offers five-course dinners with ingredients all prepared in very individual styles. With a great selection of cold and warm appetizers, dinner at this inn is a real pleasure. Breakfast time is no less grand, with a hot entree to give you a good start to the day's activities. Be sure to spend some time in the old tavern in the barn where the real charm of this New England inn is everywhere around you. The inn is located in the heart of Southern Vermont with more activities than you could dream of, every sport imaginable, and with more antique shops than you can visit. *Directions:* Leave I-91 at Vermont exit 2. Take Route 9 west to Route 100 north about 6 miles to the village of West Dover—the inn is on the left after the church.

INN AT SAWMILL FARM
Innkeeper: Brill Williams
Route 100 & Crosstown Road
P.O. Box 367
West Dover, VT 05356, USA
Tel: (802) 464-8131, Fax: (802) 464-1130
Toll Free: (800) 493-1133
10 Rooms, Double: $325–$465*, 4 Suites: $425–$525*
*Includes breakfast & dinner
Closed: end-Mar to end-May, Credit cards: all major
Select Registry

The Windham Hill Inn sits on 160 acres at the end of a country road on a rise with views all around. Inside the inn, there are lovingly decorated living rooms to make you feel instantly as if you've just returned to see an old friend. Fireplaces and comfortable chairs beckon and windows give magnificent views of ancient apple trees, gardens, and lawns. There are 21 guestrooms, most with fireplaces, several with large soaking tubs. I stayed in the White Barn in a first-floor room with a pot-bellied stove sitting in the corner, two luxuriously overstuffed chairs, and a sliding door to its own private deck. The bed was king size, and the bath had a two-person whirlpool tub and a shower with two showerheads—a wonderful extravagance that made me linger just a few moments longer. The inn has an excellent dining room and the chef prepared a memorable dinner while I was there. The wine list is award winning and extensive. Tea is served from 2 to 5:30 pm, and a cheese board served at 5:30 every day. The innkeepers are caring and want to be sure that your every moment will create a memory. The inn has an excellent conference/event center. *Directions:* Take I-91 north to Brattleboro, exit 2, to Route 30 and drive 21½ miles northwest to West Townshend. Turn right onto Windham Hill Road, drive 1-3/10 miles, and follow the sign to the inn.

WINDHAM HILL INN
Innkeeper: Katja Matthews
311 Lawrence Drive
West Townshend, VT 05359, USA
Tel: (802) 874-4080, Fax: (802) 874-4702
Toll Free: (800) 944-4080
21 Rooms, Double: $215–$465
Restaurant: dinner by reservation
Closed: early Apr, Credit cards: all major
Select Registry

This National Historic Register inn has thirteen rooms in three buildings—the Markham House dating to 1848, the Coleman House (1830), and a charming country barn—all nestled on 6 acres of woods, lawn, and gardens on the banks of the West River. Within walking distance are the quaint village of Weston's village green, the famous Vermont Country Store, art galleries, the Playhouse, museums, antique shops, and more. The inn's common rooms are welcoming and comfortably furnished and there's a pub that just waits for your presence. The dining room offers dinners that will tantalize all your senses. I was able to see two guestrooms: the Waite had a king cherry-wood bed, a pot-bellied gas stove, a TV, a whirlpool bath from which you could peek into the bedroom, and a steam shower. Flowered wallpaper completed the decor. In the Parkhurst there was also a king bed, wingback chairs in front of the fireplace, TV, and a whirlpool bath. There are two suites in the carriage house. Since taking over as innkeepers, Bob and Linda have incorporated their love of flowers into the property improvements. They have built an orchid greenhouse to house their collection, which is displayed throughout the inn, while a gazebo offers a romantic spot for summer and fall dining. *Directions:* Take I-91 north to Route 103 west through Chester to Londonderry. Turn right on Route 100 to Weston and to the inn on the left.

❄ 🍵 ⛷ ☕ CREDIT ☎ 🛗 🍷 @ W P 🍴 🌸 🏊 🎣 ⛷ 🚶 👫 🏇 🎿 🚣

INN AT WESTON
Innkeepers: Bob & Linda Aldrich
Route 100
Weston, VT 05161, USA
Tel: (802) 824-6789, Fax: (802) 824-3073
13 Rooms, Double: $225–$335
Closed: 2 weeks in Nov & Apr, Credit cards: all major

Set on a hillside surrounded by ancient pines, the Juniper Hill Inn is a handsome estate overlooking historic Windsor. You enter into the Great Hall, an enormous, very attractive room with soft-yellow walls—gorgeous against honey oak walls and flooring—where guests enjoy beverages and snacks in the afternoons. Off the hall is the pretty dining room with walls painted a deep burgundy and tables dressed with white linen set in front of the fireplace, where a full breakfast and four-course dinners (reservations only) are served. To the other side of the Great Hall is the sitting room, a more intimate salon with the only television available for guests. I fell in love with the library, a cozy room with a gas fireplace, lots of books, and a game table. Two very private guestrooms are found upstairs from the library: room 21, once occupied by Teddy Roosevelt, enjoys a handsome four-poster bed and a wood-burning Franklin stove, while room 20, pretty in a red wallpaper, offers a claw-foot tub and private porch. Of the other guestrooms number 2 is one of the most dramatic with its handsome four-poster bed, pretty flowered paper, fireplace, claw-foot tub, and balcony. The inn makes a great base for exploring the lovely Upper Connecticut River Valley and is also popular for weddings. *Directions:* From I-91 take exit 9 and travel south on Rte 5 for 2½ miles to Juniper Hill Road. Turn right and travel ½ mile up the hill (left at the fork) to the inn.

❄ ☕ 🎿 💳 🏨 @ W P ⍾ ≈ 🐾 🚶 🐎 🎿

JUNIPER HILL INN
Owner: Ari Nikki
Innkeeper: Robert Dean
153 Pembroke Road
Windsor, VT 05809, USA
Tel: (802) 674-5273, Fax: (802) 674-2041
Toll Free: (800) 359-2541
16 Rooms, Double: $135–$285
Minimum Stay Required
Open: all year, Credit cards: all major
Select Registry

As Route 4 takes a gentle bend and angles into the heart of downtown Woodstock, you see the Charleston House, a Greek Revival townhouse with a handsome brick and shuttered façade. From the side entrance you pass into the elegant dining room where guests enjoy a candlelit country breakfast. Continue on into the front living room where guests often settle in front of the fire. The only guestroom on the first floor, The Antique Store, is a cozy room with a high four-poster queen bed covered by pretty quilts. Climb the stairs from the living room to four more of the original guestrooms. A lovely front corner room, Pomfret Hills, is decorated in a pretty, soft-green floral and has a handsome four-poster bed and lots of windows. One of the smallest rooms, Hillary Underwood (named for the original owner) is simple in decor and its bathroom, although private, is located across the hallway. Gables, tucked under the eaves, enjoys a claw-foot tub and Good Friends, the only twin-bedded room, is decorated in blues. In an addition behind the main building are four luxurious guestrooms. Here we were able to see only one of the two ground-floor suites, Mount Peg, a handsome, spacious room with a dramatic four-poster bed, fireplace, and Jacuzzi tub in the bathroom. *Directions:* Take Route 4 into Woodstock and the Charleston House is on the east side, just across from the junction of Route 12 as it turns north.

CHARLESTON HOUSE
Innkeepers: Dieter (Dixi) & Willa Nohl
21 Pleasant Street
Woodstock, VT 05091, USA
Tel: (802) 457-3843, Fax: (802) 459-3154
Toll Free: (888) 475-3800
9 Rooms, Double: $135–$290
Open: all year, Credit cards: all major

Woodstock, Vermont is one of those New England towns designed with such charm and quaintness that you would think that one mastermind had created it. It's one of those places that has to be on your tour of New England. The Jackson House, just outside town, is a great place for a stopover. With its yellow exterior it beckons you inside where you'll find great examples of late-Victorian architecture with floors of cherry and maple setting off the fine furniture, walls, and moldings. Its traditionally decorated guestrooms include six one-room luxury suites with fireplaces, thermal massage tubs, and views of the gardens. Period antiques are used throughout most of the inn, adding to your enjoyment. I loved the third-floor Francesca room, decorated in muted tones of taupe, with its deck overlooking the landscaped grounds. The Mary Todd Lincoln room is much more Victorian in feel, with a high-back Victorian bed of the Lincoln period, a marble-topped table, tufted-velvet chair, and an exquisite Casablanca ceiling fan of bronze, copper, rosewood, and French-cut crystal. The inn has a very fine dining room and celebrated chef, which have garnered much praise. *Directions:* From Boston take I-93 to I-89, leaving at Route 4 west. Leave at exit 1 in Vermont for Woodstock. The inn is on the far side of the town on the right.

❄ ☕ 🛷 💳 @ W P 🍴 🚭 🛋 ♿ 🚶 👫 🏇 🎿 ⛷ 💃

JACKSON HOUSE INN & RESTAURANT
Innkeepers: Jennifer & Bernie English
114-3 Senior Lane
Woodstock, VT 05091, USA
Tel: (802) 457-2065, Toll Free: (800) 448-1890
15 Rooms, Double: $170–$430
Minimum Stay Required: Weekends, Holidays, Fall Foliage
Closed: 3 weeks in Apr, Credit cards: AX, MC, VS

Index

KAREN BROWN wrote her first travel guide in 1976. Her personalized travel series has grown to 17 titles, which Karen and her small staff work diligently to keep updated. Karen, her husband, Rick, parents to Alexandra and Richard, live in a small town on the coast south of San Francisco.

JACK BULLARD did much of the initial research for Karen Brown's guides to New England and the Mid-Atlantic. A native New Englander, with family ties to the Eastern Shore of Maryland, Jack still considers the East Coast to be home even though his years of management consulting took him all over the world. Eventually he found his true love in the world of hospitality and created the Inn at Occidental in the Sonoma wine country north of San Francisco. His life now in Center City Philadelphia provides him the opportunity to enjoy all the arts while continuing to consult in design, decor and antiques.

JANN POLLARD, The artist of the cover painting has studied art since childhood, and is well known for her outstanding impressionistic-style watercolors. Jann's works are in private and corporate collections internationally and she has become a popular workshop teacher in the States, Mexico and Europe. Jann's website is: *www.jannpollard.com.* Fine art giclée prints of her paintings are available at *www.karenbrown.com.*

VANESSA KALE, the talented artist who produced the illustrations for this guide, is a native of Bellingham, Washington. Vanessa spent her high school years in Sonoma California. After graduating in Art from U.C. Davis, Vanessa moved to southern California where she lives with her husband, Simon and son, Nigel. She works as a project manager for an architectural rendering company, and also as a freelance artist. *www.vanessakale.com.*

Notes

Karen Brown's World of Travel

A FREE KAREN BROWN WEBSITE MEMBERSHIP
IS INCLUDED WITH THE PURCHASE OF THIS GUIDE

$20 Value – Equal to the cover price of this book!

In appreciation for purchasing our guide, we offer a free membership that includes:

- The ability to custom plan and build unlimited itineraries
- 15% discount on all purchases made in the Karen Brown website store
- One free downloadable Karen Brown Itinerary from over 100 choices
- Karen Brown's World of Travel Newsletter—includes special offers & updates

Membership valid through December 31, 2010

To take advantage of this free offer go to the Karen Brown website shown below and create a login profile so we can recognize you as a Preferred Customer; then you can utilize the unrestricted trip planning and take advantage of the 15% store discount. Once you set up an account you will receive by email a coupon code to order the free itinerary.

Go to *www.karenbrown.com/preferred.php* to create your profile!

Karen Brown's
2010 Readers' Choice Awards

Most Romantic
The Wauwinet
Nantucket Island, Massachusetts

Warmest Welcome
Devonfield Inn
Lee, Massachusetts

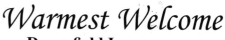

Greatest Value
Bufflehead Cove
Kennebunkport, Maine

Splendid Splurge
Lodge at Moosehead Lake
Greenville, Maine

Be sure to vote for next year's winners by visiting
www.karenbrown.com